NORBURY LIBRARY
020 7884 5215

W/D

Please return or renew this book
by the last date printed above.
Renew via phone or online
www.croydon.gov.uk/libraries

D1380542

3 8015 02611 237 9

Kamikaze

Kamikaze

Japan's Last Bid for Victory

Adrian Stewart

Pen & Sword
AVIATION

First published in Great Britain in 2020 by
Pen & Sword Aviation
An imprint of
Pen & Sword Books Ltd
Yorkshire – Philadelphia

Copyright © Adrian Stewart 2020

ISBN 978 1 52674 803 4

A CIP catalogue record for this book is
available from the British Library.

Printed and bound in the UK by TJ International Ltd, Padstow, Cornwall.

Pen & Sword Books Limited incorporates the imprints of Atlas, Archaeology, Aviation,
Discovery, Family History, Fiction, History, Maritime, Military, Military Classics,
Politics, Select, Transport, True Crime, Air World, Frontline Publishing, Leo Cooper,
Remember When, Seaforth Publishing, The Praetorian Press, Wharncliffe Local
History, Wharncliffe Transport, Wharncliffe True Crime and White Owl.

For a complete list of Pen & Sword titles please contact

PEN & SWORD BOOKS LIMITED
47 Church Street, Barnsley, South Yorkshire, S70 2AS, England
E-mail: enquiries@pen-and-sword.co.uk
Website: www.pen-and-sword.co.uk

Or

PEN AND SWORD BOOKS
1950 Lawrence Rd, Havertown, PA 19083, USA
E-mail: Uspen-and-sword@casematepublishers.com
Website: www.penandswordbooks.com

Contents

Acknowledgements

This book is dedicated to all those who helped.

There were so many, but I must mention in particular:

'Jim' Ozawa, who when we regularly refought the Pacific War together, many years ago now, first introduced and explained to me the actions and motives of the Kamikaze organizers and pilots.

David Mattiske, Maya Sieber and Simon Thayer, who between them recently revived my interest in this subject.

My agents Johnson & Alcock Limited, especially my helpful and encouraging liaison officer Ed Wilson.

My knowledgeable and industrious editor Pamela Covey.

The Birmingham & Midland Institute & Library, the Taylor Library and the US Navy Department of Information who assisted with the photographs.

Brigadier Henry Wilson and the staff of my publishers Pen & Sword Books Limited, especially Jon Wilkinson who sorted out the jacket, Dominic Allen who sorted out the plates, 'SJ' who sorted out the maps and the ever-patient Matt Jones and Laura Hirst who sorted out everything else.

I'm very lucky and I'm very grateful.

Chapter 1

'Death is Lighter than a Feather'

Lieutenant Mimori Suzuki was considered by his comrades to be rather unusual for an officer of the Imperial Japanese Naval Air Force. Not only was he regarded as an 'artistic type', but although Suzuki is one of the most common Japanese surnames, his looks seemed more European than Oriental and were often the subject of unkind banter. He was a good pilot, though, and when on 7 December 1941, he took off from aircraft carrier *Akagi* to participate in the assault on the United States Pacific Fleet in Pearl Harbor, he was doubtless ready to do his duty to the best of his ability.

Suzuki was at the controls of an Aichi D3A dive-bomber or, as it was known to the Allies, a Val, since in order to avoid the difficulties caused by Japan's complicated system of aircraft classification, it was customary to give each one an arbitrary code-name, the bombers having those of ladies, the fighters those of men. Suzuki and the rest of his squadron would direct their attack on vessels to the north-west of Ford Island, the side opposite to the one boasting the famous 'Battleship Row'. His personal target would be the seaplane tender *Curtiss*.

Although *Curtiss* was a naval auxiliary rather than a warship, she and her crew were full of fight and had already been in action before the Vals appeared. The Japanese had sent five midget submarines to join in the attack on Pearl Harbor; most unwisely since they not only did no damage but were sighted early and so could and perhaps should have given the Americans warning of what was to follow. One of them did, however, penetrate the harbour and at about 0835, was sighted by *Curtiss*. It launched a torpedo that missed; *Curtiss* retaliated by putting a shell through its conning tower. Then destroyer *Monaghan* that, unlike *Curtiss*, was already under way, charged in, dodged another torpedo, rammed the midget and finally destroyed it with depth-charges while the area resounded with cheering.

So the ships to the north-west of Ford Island were very ready for a fight when the dive-bombers appeared. They shot down at least five of these between them, *Curtiss* certainly claiming one. This was the aircraft piloted by Lieutenant Mimori Suzuki: it did not pull out of its dive but, at about 0910, it crashed into the starboard crane used by *Curtiss* to raise and lower her seaplanes. Fires were started, but although later struck by a bomb and near-missed by several others, *Curtiss* survived without serious damage. It seems likely that Suzuki had been killed or disabled before the Val struck *Curtiss* but it is possible that he flew it into her deliberately.

There is no doubt at all about another action taken this same day by Lieutenant Fusata Iida from aircraft carrier *Soryu*. A quiet, capable and very determined officer, Iida was a great believer in physical fitness and an ardent admirer of baseball, a sport that the Japanese had acquired from their future enemies, though they had found their own names for players and officials such as pitchers and umpires. He flew a Mitsubishi A6M fighter that the Allies, in accordance with the principle mentioned earlier, officially code-named the Zeke. In practice it was rarely so-called. Another Japanese designation for this aircraft was the Navy Type 00 or Zero-Sen.[1] Japan's enemies followed this example and the A6M was almost invariably called the Zero or, by RAF pilots, the Navy Nought.

During the Pearl Harbor raid, the Zeros concentrated on making strafing runs on vehicles, groups of men and especially aerodromes where the American aircraft, lined up together in the centre of the field as a precaution against sabotage, made ideal targets. In all 188 of these were destroyed, with 159 more damaged. The Zeros, it was reported, 'swooped unbelievably low' in their attacks. In the process they came under fire from machine guns, rifles and even pistols, but whereas fifteen Vals – and five Nakajima Kate torpedo-bombers – were lost, only nine Zero pilots did not return to their carriers.

One who did not was Lieutenant Fusata Iida. His fighter was fatally damaged during a strafing attack but was seen to climb away, still under control. Then it turned back and dived, clearly quite intentionally, straight at and into an aircraft hangar, effectively demolishing it and the machines it contained. The very first day of the Pacific War had seen one, possibly two, Japanese airmen make what would later be called a 'suicide dive'.

It has been suggested that they had also been the first Kamikaze pilots. In fact, their actions, though repeated on several occasions during the next two years and ten months, were fundamentally different from the Kamikaze missions as we shall see. Nonetheless they are worth recording because the motives behind them help to explain the Kamikaze creed and themselves arose from beliefs embedded in the Japanese character by events in their country's history.

For much of that history, the Japanese lived under what is usually called a 'feudal' system, the essence of which is the holding of land in return for services rendered. From the middle of the twelfth century AD when rival military clans, paying only titular obedience to the Emperor, disputed the rule of the country, this usually meant services in time of war. These became steadily more important as all central control progressively broke down and the land was convulsed by internal conflicts. By the mid-fifteenth century AD, Japan had for all practical purposes split up into a number of independent states, controlled by warlords whose constant struggles with each other would lead to the years from 1467 to 1615 becoming known as the Sengoku Period: the Era of the Country at War.

Though undoubtedly fearless and resolute, the Daimyō, as these warrior chieftains were called, were – almost without exception – cunning, ruthless, treacherous and unscrupulous. Friendships were declared and immediately denied. Alliances were formed and quickly discarded. Treaties were made and promptly broken. Like the equally self-serving noblemen at the time of England's Wars of the Roses, the Daimyō thought nothing of deserting or changing sides, even at the height of a battle.

It may therefore seem surprising that out of Japan's savage civil wars there arose a code of knightly conduct, later to be known as Bushidō: the Way of the Warrior. This, though, was intended to give moral guidance not to the Daimyō, much as they needed this, but as the name indicates, to their followers, particularly to the samurai who fought on horseback, often came from very ancient families and formed an elite class above that of the more numerous ashigaru or foot-soldiers. Bushidō stressed duties rather than rights and above all the samurai's duty to fight loyally for his lord.

This duty had to be performed regardless of the samurai's personal wishes and regardless of the danger of losing his own life. One samurai hero whose story was known to every Japanese was Kusunoki Masashige,[2] a supporter of Emperor Go-Daigo – Daigo II as we would call him – who was attempting to assert the authority of the Imperial house over that of a series of military dictators. On 5 July 1336, when the Emperor's capital Kyoto was threatened by much larger enemy forces, Kusunoki advised allowing these to enter the city where they could later be counterattacked from all sides. Go-Daigo, however, regarding such a retreat as a sign of weakness, ordered Kusunoki to engage them in battle. Though he was certain that defeat was inevitable and would mean his own death, Kusunoki complied and when his worst fears proved correct, lamented only that he did not have seven lives to sacrifice for his Emperor and his cause.

Kusunoki's example of a loyalty that combined total obedience with a magnificent if somewhat horrifying contempt for death would later be summed up by the oft-repeated proverb 'Death is lighter than a feather, while duty is weightier than a mountain.' It was an attitude made more acceptable for the Japanese because their Shinto religion held that the souls of the dead continue to be closely associated with the living as well as with each other. In the case of a warrior who fell in battle, his fate would wipe out all his faults and his spirit would immediately be summoned to the sacred Yasukuni Shrine to consort in eternal friendship with the souls of those who had similarly died in action.

Since death held few terrors and every samurai was eager to match the often legendary deeds of his predecessors, he was prepared to take extraordinary risks and there was intense competition to be the first to scale the walls of an enemy fortress or to cross a defended river. So heedless of danger were Japanese warriors throughout their country's often blood-soaked history, that it would later be said that they had a death wish and fought in order to die.

It was not true, of course: the Japanese warrior fought in order to achieve the triumph of his master and his cause. Nonetheless, there was an element of truth in this concept. European or American soldiers might take part in operations that were termed 'suicidal' afterwards or even at the time, but there seems little doubt that each one believed that luck or skill or a combination of both would somehow ensure that he personally survived, even though others might perish. A samurai, on the contrary, went into action fully accepting the possibility of his own death but consoled by the knowledge that a heroic end would ensure that his name and fame would endure. 'Death or glory' was never a Japanese warrior's motto. It was rather 'Death or victory'; glory might well be his in either case.

Indeed, despite all its fondness for dramatically heroic deeds, the warrior's code recognized the practical value on occasions of less noble activities. As we have seen, that pillar of samurai virtues Kusunoki Masashige could advocate a retreat if this seemed the best course. It was always acceptable for isolated detachments or besieged fortresses to be abandoned if they could thereby tie down part of an enemy's strength at a crucial moment. Even defeat was not of itself dishonourable if it was mitigated by acts of physical or moral courage.

An outstanding example of this attitude is provided by a famous figure from the Era of the Country at War. Tokugawa Ieyasu was in fact the man who brought this period to an end and ensured the unity of Japan, in the process rising from the leadership of a small subsidiary clan to become Shōgun or supreme military head of the entire country; a position subsequently held by members of his family for more than 250 years. His career is marked by brilliant victories, often over very heavy adverse odds, but the action for which he has been given the greatest credit is one in which he suffered defeat.

This was the Battle of Mikatagahara fought on 25 October 1572. Attacked by foes of three times their own strength and with an allied contingent withdrawing at the first assault, Ieyasu's troops were thrown back in disorder and compelled to seek refuge in Hamamatsu Castle. On reaching this, however, Ieyasu ordered the gates to be left open, while huge braziers were lit and a massive drum beaten to guide his men to safety. His cool, calculating courage had its reward. Fearing a trap, the enemy made no attack on the castle and subsequently withdrew.

By contrast, the one act for which no samurai could ever be forgiven was surrender, as this was an obvious and dreadful breach of his duty to fight loyally to the bitter end. A warrior who surrendered disgraced not only himself but his family and his clan. He would survive only as an object of ridicule and contempt, a shameful creature unworthy of being considered a human being. No wonder, therefore, that a samurai who was unafraid of death would dread the thought of being taken prisoner.

It was an attitude incomprehensible to Europeans or Americans, for whom the capture of a soldier, while not a matter of pride, was understandable and acceptable. If a unit surrendered when surrounded by superior numbers, this would be held a sensible and humane act. For a Japanese force similarly trapped, surrender was not an option. It had only three choices: it could fight its way through the enemy lines and escape; it could hurl itself upon its foes to inflict as many casualties on them as was possible before being wiped out; or it could commit mass suicide.

That this third choice was frequently made was because the Japanese considered it not only an honourable way of avoiding capture, but an act of expiation that would erase any stain left by failure or defeat. For people of other countries and other cultures, however, it has understandably aroused horror and amazement and has reinforced beliefs that the Japanese were inhumanly callous and wanted to die.

It must be conceded that the ritual aspects of suicides by Japanese cannot help but appear disgusting. They were usually carried out by the act of seppuku which means abdomen-slitting or, as it was less frequently because more vulgarly known, hara-kiri or belly-cutting. It should be said, however, that the agony of this was usually mercifully brief because a chosen friend or servant of the suicider would then strike off his head with a sword.

Equally, there was sometimes what can only be described as a hideous orgy of suicides. On 5 July 1333, for instance, Kamakura, the capital of the then military dictators the Hōjō Regents was captured, whereupon the last Hōjō, Takatoki, committed suicide and his example was followed by members of his family and, we are assured, some 800 of his retainers. Again, though, it should be related that this happened only after desperate attempts had been made to defend the city, including a 'last-ditch' stand by samurai ladies wielding long spears with curved blades called naginatas. The aim of the Japanese warrior was victory, not death, which he met only while trying to achieve success or when success had become impossible.

These then were the conventions imposed on the samurai by the code of Bushidō. They had arisen out of Japan's seemingly endless civil wars, but they continued to be respected during the following centuries of peace under the Tokugawa Shōguns and would attain a wider relevance after the end of the Shōgunate and restoration of rule by the Imperial house in

1868. This event, symbolized by the Emperor leaving Kyoto to reside in the Shōguns' capital of Edo – now renamed Tokyo or Eastern Capital – was followed by the end of feudalism, the surrender of the Daimyōs' fiefs to the monarch and the abolition of the samurai as a privileged military class.

To replace the samurai, the new rulers of Japan began to build up a modern army and shortly afterwards a modern navy as well. Though many former samurai joined these, they were formed from every class of the population, the manpower for them being ensured by the introduction of conscription. In 1877, samurai resentment exploded in an armed rebellion, directed not against the Emperor but his 'evil advisers'. It was crushed by the new conscript army, the soldiers of which proved that Japanese from every class, once properly trained and disciplined, could fight just as bravely and effectively as the old military order.

While the samurai disappeared, however, their Bushidō code did not. Instead it was extended to become the guide for members of Japan's army and navy and in due course their respective air arms.[3] Its principles were accepted with pride by the new armed services, whose men burned with eagerness to emulate 'the renowned bravery' of the samurai heroes, the exploits of whom were well-known and much admired. Now, though, the loyalty that was the cornerstone of Bushidō was not given to any territorial lord but to Japan and the country's living symbol, her semi-divine Emperor.

So all the beliefs and attitudes described earlier were relevant to and would be repeated by the Japanese fighting men when their country came into the Second World War on the side of Germany and Italy. Their bravery was remarkable, but was so taken for granted by their superiors that while official citations were given to divisions or smaller units that had distinguished themselves in action, it was rare for any individual to be so honoured. At the conclusion of probably Japan's greatest military triumph, the conquest of Malaya and Singapore on 15 February 1942, Lieutenant General Tomoyuki Yamashita, commanding Japan's Twenty-Fifth Army, awarded citations to just one officer and two NCOs, all of them posthumously.

Of course members of all the armed services of all the combatants in the Second World War showed examples of conspicuous gallantry every bit as admirable as anything displayed by the Japanese. They did not, however, possess the Japanese hatred of surrender and indifference to death.

It might well be argued that this makes their courage all the greater, but there is no doubt that the Japanese attitude did give their leaders a valuable advantage. A British commander might order a position held 'to the last man and the last round' but he would not expect this to be taken literally. A Japanese commander would probably have considered that there was no need to give such an order in the first place.

That the Japanese really did prefer death to capture was not at first appreciated and they in turn never made any allowance for the fact that their enemies had a totally different outlook and code. As a result, they regarded their prisoners with contempt and subjected them to vile treatment that earned for their country a hatred that was entirely understandable and has never completely disappeared.

This willingness to fight to the death rather than capitulate fitted in well with Japan's aims in the Second World War. It had never been intended by Japan's leaders that they should conquer America, a task for which, it was accepted, their resources were utterly inadequate. Instead their strategy would be to seize a vast extent of territory that would provide them with the raw materials, chiefly oil, rubber and tin, which their country badly needed. When this had been done – as it duly was – then their conquests would be defended with such determination that their enemies would be persuaded to accept a compromise peace and leave them with at least some of their gains in preference to fighting a costly war of apparently limitless duration.

By the autumn of 1943, however, the Americans had built up a massive fleet of aircraft carriers with which they could pursue a strategy termed 'island leapfrogging'. This consisted of penetrating immense distances to seize key islands, usually those with airfields, and ignoring all the rest which were left to 'wither on the vine'. By these means, the Americans thwarted the Japanese intention of compelling them to fight for every scrap of land throughout the Pacific. All that the Japanese could do was resist as long as possible and when that became hopeless, follow the samurai tradition of doing as much damage as they could before being wiped out.

This they certainly did on Attu in the Aleutian Islands when this was invaded by the Americans in May 1943. Faced by 11,000 US soldiers, supported by air attacks and naval gunfire, the 2,600-strong Japanese garrison resisted for over a fortnight until its numbers had been reduced to about 1,000. These were now out of food and their supplies of ammunition were so low that many were reduced to fighting with knives or bayonets.

Any Western force would have felt entirely justified in surrendering, but this was unthinkable to the defenders of Attu. In the early hours of 29 May, they made what the Americans called a 'banzai charge'[4] for the sole purpose of killing and being killed. Bursting into the American positions, they slew soldiers in their sleeping bags and, horrible to relate, massacred the patients in a field hospital. When their attack was finally held, most of those Japanese who had not been killed already committed suicide. Only twenty-eight men, all wounded, were captured alive.

If any optimists had thought that this might be a 'one-off' event, they were fully disillusioned when the great Central Pacific drive began in November 1943. Its first objectives were Tarawa and Makin in the Gilbert Islands. The capture of the former was entrusted to the 2nd Marine Division of well over 18,000 men. This greatly outnumbered the defending combat troops who have been variously estimated at from 3,000 to 4,500, the bulk of whom were naval infantrymen, the equivalent of Marines in other countries, under Rear Admiral Shibasaki. It took four days and 3,000 American casualties, a third of them fatal, before the last defenders of Tarawa put up their hands: one officer, sixteen men, all badly wounded. The 300 Japanese combat troops who made up the garrison of Makin also resisted for four days, against odds of twenty-three to one. Just a single Japanese infantryman was taken prisoner.

Japanese reluctance to surrender was demonstrated even more horribly when the Americans invaded Saipan in the Mariana Islands on 15 June 1944. Again estimates of Japanese strength vary widely, but it seems that Lieutenant General Yoshitsugu Saito had as many as 32,000 troops to defend the island, including some 6,700 sailors under Vice Admiral Chuichi Nagumo, once commander of the task force that had attacked Pearl Harbor. Many of his soldiers, however, were virtually unarmed as a result of US submarine attacks on Japanese reinforcement convoys. Yet from Saito downwards, most of them believed in the ethics of Bushidō and were prepared to die if need be.

Against them the Americans directed the 27th Infantry Division and the 2nd and 4th Marine Divisions, over 127,500 men in all, once more with strong naval and air support. A series of attacks by Japanese soldiers, screaming war cries and headed by officers brandishing their beautiful but utterly obsolete swords, failed to 'destroy the enemy at the beachhead' as Saito had ordered, and his men settled down to their usual stubborn resistance. This lasted until 6 July, by which time the bulk of the remaining defenders had been driven into the northern end of the island and their cause was clearly lost.

For Lieutenant General Saito there was only one action that his men could take. He urged them to 'utilize this opportunity to exalt true Japanese manhood' by striking a final blow at their enemies. He concentrated more than 3,000 of them, as is related by Major Frank Hough in *The Island War*, for one tremendous 'banzai charge'. Since he was elderly and far from well, he would not take part in this himself but would instead demonstrate the unimportance of death. After a last ceremonial meal, he committed seppuku. The Americans later recovered his body and buried it with full military honours. Vice Admiral Nagumo died by his own hand at about the same time. His body was never found.

Next day, the 'banzai charge' was duly delivered, the first attackers being followed by men covered with bandages or walking with the aid of crutches. 'The sick and wounded from the hospitals,' explains Major Hough, 'had come forth to die', and of course to kill as many Americans as they could before they died. The attack smashed two infantry battalions and overran two batteries of Marine artillery before it was halted and the attackers wiped out. The Americans suffered more than 400 fatalities.

On the day following, the Americans pushed on to the cliffs marking the northern end of Saipan and the beaches below them. 'Here,' says Hough, 'was enacted the crowning horror of the whole campaign.' Saipan had been a Japanese possession since the First World War and although the Americans had rounded up numbers of civilians during the first few days after their landings, it seems that these were local inhabitants. The Japanese civilians had retreated with the surviving soldiers and, like them, were trapped in the north of the island.

It soon became clear that they shared their countrymen's reluctance to surrender. Parents shot, stabbed or strangled their children. Then they hurled themselves off the cliffs or waded out into the sea to drown. A group of about fifteen women and children knelt before a soldier who shot each of them neatly through the head, then blew himself to pieces with a hand grenade. Another group of three young women carefully combed and arranged their hair, then hand in hand, they calmly stepped over a precipice. The base of the cliffs was heaped with corpses and for days afterwards floating bodies drifted past the US warships. 'Men hardened in one of the bloodiest campaigns of the Pacific,' reports Hough, 'turned away from the sight, sick at heart and physically ill.'

So ended the struggle for Saipan, officially at least. The US casualty list was more than 3,400 dead or missing and more than 13,000 wounded. No one will ever know the exact Japanese losses, but the Americans buried almost 24,000 Japanese soldiers and held about 1,800 prisoners, by far the most in any campaign to date, though it should be noted that much the larger proportion of these were Koreans.[5] Even after Saipan was formally declared secure, numerous Japanese held out in its hills and caves. Some were still doggedly refusing to surrender when the Second World War itself came to an end.

From the evidence given of the Japanese temperament and the Japanese traditions, it can be seen that the actions of Lieutenants Suzuki and Iida at Pearl Harbor were, in Japanese eyes, natural and reasonable. So great was the Japanese fear of capture that no pilot ever carried a parachute when on missions into enemy air space. Nor did any pilot think of landing a damaged machine in enemy or enemy-controlled territory; this might give him a chance of survival but would result in his being taken prisoner, the worst fate he could imagine.

Therefore when their aircraft were damaged so badly that they were unable to return to their carriers, neither Suzuki nor Iida had any chance of surviving. It was only sensible in that case that they should sell their lives dearly by inflicting as much harm on their enemies as they could by the manner of their deaths.

Their gesture would be repeated many times by other Japanese pilots in similar circumstances. The first such came as quickly as 10 December 1941 when the Japanese Naval Air Force attacked British battleship *Prince of Wales* and battle-cruiser *Repulse* with Mitsubishi Nells and the more modern Mitsubishi Bettys, both land-based twin-engined warplanes capable of carrying either bombs or torpedoes. The two capital ships were sunk at the ridiculously low cost of two Bettys and one Nell shot down, plus one Betty that crashed on landing and was 'written off', though its crew were unhurt. The Nell that was lost had just released its torpedo when it was fatally hit by AA fire from the *Prince of Wales*, then attempted to ram the battleship but crashed into the sea close to her starboard side.

An attack by seven Betty bombers on the US aircraft carrier *Enterprise* on 1 February 1942 was much less successful. Every one of the attackers was shot down by flak or by fighters of her Combat Air Patrol (CAP), while only slight damage was done to the *Enterprise* and that because a crippled aircraft made a suicide dive. Luckily, it did no more than strike her flight deck a glancing blow before plunging into the sea.

Inevitably, perhaps, the ferocious Guadalcanal campaign provided other illustrations of this peculiarly Japanese method of attack. On 8 August 1942, the day after the original American assault, twenty torpedo-carrying Bettys attacked the US transports and their escorting warships. They scored only one hit on destroyer *Jervis*; she was forced to retire from the area and was sunk next day by another air attack. In return, American fighters downed five Bettys and AA fire thirteen more.

Yet in the middle of this destruction, the Japanese airmen gave another example of their relentless resolve. A pair of Bettys, both already in flames – although in many ways an excellent aircraft, the Betty did tend to catch fire far too easily – attempted to ram their targets. One of them was torn to pieces by AA fire but the other crashed into transport *George F. Elliott* with a thunderous explosion. Blazing petrol poured over her deck, it seems that part of her crew may have abandoned her prematurely and she eventually went to the bottom together with most of her valuable supplies. She was the first but certainly not the last vessel to be destroyed by suicide attack.

She was certainly not the most important vessel either. On 26 October 1942, in the Battle of Santa Cruz, the fourth of six major naval actions that were fought out during the Guadalcanal campaign, suicide attacks played a part in the sinking of an American aircraft carrier, the USS *Hornet*.

Hornet and her fellow 'flat-top' *Enterprise* were engaged in combat with a superior Japanese force containing three large fleet carriers and one light carrier. When the first wave of warplanes from these arrived at 0910, *Enterprise* had taken refuge under a convenient rain-squall, so it was against *Hornet* that fifteen Val dive-bombers and eighteen Kate torpedo-bombers directed a splendidly coordinated assault. The Combat Air Patrol was not well handled and made few interceptions, and although the carrier and her escorting vessels put up a tremendous AA fire that ultimately downed twelve Vals and at least six Kates, *Hornet* had already received one bomb-hit on the starboard side of her flight deck aft and two near misses by other bombs, when the most spectacular incident of the raid occurred.

Leading the Vals' attack was a very experienced and capable officer, Lieutenant Commander Mamoru Seki, who had led strikes on US carriers earlier in the campaign. His aircraft was fatally hit by AA fire and the men on *Hornet* watched in horrified fascination as it deliberately hurtled down towards them trailing a long column of flame like the tail of a comet. Though his Val was hit several more times, Seki smashed through *Hornet*'s superstructure on into and through her flight deck where two of his three bombs exploded, starting a furious fire.

As smoke and steam shrouded the stricken carrier, the other Japanese pilots closed in upon her. In ten dreadful minutes, two torpedoes ripped into her starboard side, causing major flooding, and three more bombs hit her, one exploding on the flight deck but the others boring deep into her hull. Finally, a Kate that had already dropped its torpedo was set ablaze but its pilot still rushed on, flying so low over the water that many on *Hornet* lost sight of their attacker until this dashed itself into the carrier's bow close to the forward elevator. Burning from bow to stern, with 111 of her crew dead and 108 wounded, *Hornet* slowed to a halt. Later raids would inflict additional damage and *Hornet*, by then abandoned, was eventually finished off by torpedoes from Japanese destroyers. It was not just the two suicide attacks that sank the carrier, but all those who saw them affirmed that these were the most terrifying part of their ordeal.

They were not the only suicide attacks in this battle. At about 1015, *Enterprise* and her escorting warships became the target of nineteen Vals. Again catching the Combat Air Patrol by surprise, these scored two hits and one very near miss on *Enterprise*, putting her forward elevator out of action, though at the cost of fifteen of their own number. Happily, through over-eagerness, the Vals had not waited to coordinate their assault with that of their torpedo-planes. When eleven dark-green Kates appeared soon afterwards, the Americans were ready for them and they were annihilated by the Wildcat fighters of the CAP. Lieutenant Stanley 'Swede' Vejtasa alone downed six of them and killed Commander Shigeharu Murata who had led the torpedo-bombers at Pearl Harbor.

One of Vejtasa's victims did not go down immediately, however, and its pilot, clearly resolved to strike a final blow, devised a new type of suicide attack. Somewhat oddly, he chose destroyer *Smith* as his target – perhaps she was the only ship he felt his crippled aircraft could reach – and rather than drop his torpedo, he made certain of a hit by flying with it into *Smith*'s forecastle, which disappeared in a mass of flames. Lieutenant Commander Hunter Wood responded by the unusual but effective course of putting his ship's bow close behind battleship *South Dakota*. Her foaming wake helped *Smith*'s damage control parties to master the fires, but the destroyer lost twenty-eight men dead and another twenty-three wounded.

There would be similar suicide attacks later, though they did little damage. On 19 June 1944 in the Battle of the Philippine Sea, for instance, a Japanese pilot imitated the strike on *Smith* by flying his Nakajima Jill – successor to the Kate – into the US battleship *Indiana* while still carrying its torpedo. His sacrifice was wasted, however, for he struck her armoured belt on the waterline, the torpedo did not explode and she suffered only a few damaged plates. On the evening of 13 October 1944, a low-flying Betty did launch its torpedo – ineffectually – at US aircraft carrier *Franklin* and was then set on fire. Thereupon, the pilot deliberately crashed into the carrier's flight deck, slid across it and went into the sea. *Franklin* received only minor injuries but lost one man killed and ten wounded.

All the attempts described were unplanned and spontaneous, taken in the heat of battle by individual pilots whose aircraft were fatally damaged and frequently in flames. Since they had no parachutes, they were doomed in any event and they may have looked on their actions as the only way they could carry out their missions. Their attitudes therefore were not totally different from those of European or American pilots who also often took astonishing risks in order to achieve their objectives, though in their case it seems that they never gave up all hope of survival.

They were also prepared to hazard their lives for the sake of others: for example, bomber pilots would remain at the controls of crippled or burning aircraft so that their crews, though probably not themselves, would have a chance to escape by parachute. They would thus have been able to view with understanding and no doubt approval occasions when Japanese pilots sacrificed themselves for the greater good; actions for which again precedents could be found in the code and the achievements of the samurai.

Thus in June 1575, the castle of Nagashino was closely besieged and had enough food left for only a few more days. On the 22nd, Torii Suneemon quietly left the fortress at midnight, slipped through the enemy lines and ran 25 miles to give warning of Nagashino's danger. A relief force was quickly prepared and in the meantime Torii hurried back to give Nagashino's defenders the good news. Unhappily, the besiegers were not to be caught napping a second time and Torii was overcome and captured; a disgrace which he would gloriously redeem.

Promised his life and a large reward if he would inform his friends that no help could come and they would be wise to surrender, Torii pretended to agree. Since his captors were understandably suspicious, he was tied to a wooden cross that was set up in front of the castle and surrounded by a number of spearmen. When the defenders had gathered on the ramparts, Torii shouted: 'Before three days are out you will be relieved. Stand fast!' This was, of course, his last act but the siege was lifted and one enemy samurai, Ochiai Michihisa, was so impressed by Torii's bravery that he adopted a representation of Torii on the cross as his own banner.

A modern illustration of such cool courage was shown on 8 May 1942 during the Battle of the Coral Sea by Warrant Officer Kenzo Kanno, a Kate pilot from the Japanese carrier *Shokaku*. His was one of several reconnaissance machines sent to locate an American carrier force. This he did shortly before 0830 and thereafter he remained over the American vessels, reporting their movements, for as long as he dared before finally breaking away, already very low on fuel, to return to his own ship. On the way, however, he sighted a formation of Japanese warplanes making for the US force. This, he felt, was not heading in quite the correct direction and moreover was proceeding through an area of very bad visibility.

So Kanno, though he must have realized the inevitable consequence of his decision, turned his aircraft to fly alongside that of Lieutenant Commander Takahashi, leader of the Japanese striking force. Only when he had guided this to within sight of the American fleet – it was then about 1030 – did Kanno turn back once more towards *Shokaku*. By now he had no chance of reaching her and he and his two crew members could have had no hope of surviving. Perhaps therefore it was merciful that he should have encountered a flight of Dauntlesses, normally used as dive-bombers but in this case doubling as interceptors; four of them would later claim sole credit for the Kate's destruction.

A more dramatic but equally sublime example of selfless courage was given on 19 June 1944 during the Battle of the Philippine Sea. While the Japanese airmen were making unsuccessful attacks on American warships, the carriers from which they had come were also being attacked, far more effectively, by American submarines. One of these sank Kanno's old ship – and a previous member of the carrier division that had raided Pearl Harbor – the *Shokaku*. Another directed her torpedoes at Japan's latest and largest 'flat-top', the *Taiho*.

As the deadly weapons streaked towards their target, Warrant Officer Sakio Komatsu was just taking off from *Taiho*'s flight deck in his Zero. Suddenly he noticed a torpedo about to strike his ship. Without hesitation, he dashed his fighter onto it; torpedo, aircraft and pilot all vanishing in a mighty detonation. Sadly his sacrifice proved in vain. Another torpedo did find its mark; this cracked a tank containing aviation fuel and some hours later the fumes from it were ignited and two colossal explosions sent *Taiho* to the bottom.

When Warrant Officer Komatsu made his noble if unavailing attempt to save his ship, he was, like Kanno and the pilots who had carried out suicide attacks on enemy warships, responding instinctively to a particular situation. His action was not planned or organized, still less ordered. Yet just over a fortnight later, the Japanese would embark on a mission that was unavailing, unplanned, atrociously organized, but ordered, and it would cast dark shadows forward into the future.

During the Saipan campaign, the American carriers not only supported their ground troops and fought off the main Japanese naval strength in the Battle of the Philippine Sea, but 'worked over' enemy bases from which Saipan's defenders could be given assistance. One such was the tiny island of Iwo Jima from which Betty bombers and Jill torpedo-planes had made night attacks on the US fleet. The losses they suffered either in these or when caught on the ground by American strikes at Iwo Jima were so great, however, that by 4 July 1944, all the island's Bettys and all except eight of its Jills had been destroyed.

Losses among Iwo Jima's fighters were also depressingly high, even though they were not used to escort the bombers but remained strictly on the defensive. After some early casualties, a reinforcement of thirty Zeros under Commander Tadashi Nakajima – of whom more later – was transferred from Yokosuka just south of Tokyo to join the fifty remaining on the island. Unfortunately the ability of their pilots was not high in most cases and when they arrived – on 20 June – Nakajima did not dare to bring them in at the small landing strip to which they had been allocated. Instead they all came down on Iwo Jima's main airfield and then taxied for over a mile up a steep, winding road to their new base, much to the amazement and amusement of watching ground troops.

One at least of the new arrivals was very experienced. Warrant Officer Saburō Sakai had become Japan's leading fighter 'ace' by August 1942. Then still a petty officer, he was credited with sixty 'kills' and although the Japanese include in such totals shared victories and what in other air forces would be termed 'probables', he was undoubtedly a very fine pilot. This was proved even on 7 August, on which date in combat over Guadalcanal he was struck by machine-gun fire from a Dauntless and terribly wounded in the head. Despite being permanently blinded in his right eye, he somehow managed to get his battered Zero back to his base, landed safely and promptly collapsed from loss of blood.

On recovering, Sakai desperately wanted to return to the fight but understandably was not considered fit for this. Therefore, as he tells us in his memoirs – interestingly entitled *Samurai* – he was condemned to 'long and wearying months of training student pilots'. He was so engaged at Yokosuka in June 1944, when the call came to send reinforcements to Iwo Jima. Commander Nakajima, under whom Sakai had served previously, requested him to be one of these and the request was joyfully accepted.

Though obviously handicapped by his reduced field of vision, Sakai showed he had lost few of his flying skills when, on 24 June, all Iwo Jima's eighty Zeros were ordered off to oppose a raid by some fifty US Hellcat fighters sent to shoot up Japanese aircraft on the ground. He believed he downed two Hellcats and when cornered by fifteen others, he quite certainly out-flew and out-manoeuvred them until, low on fuel and ammunition, they gave up and returned to their carriers. An exhausted Sakai then landed and his ground crew, who had watched with admiration, found to their astonishment that there was not a single bullet hole in his Zero.

There was no cause for any other satisfaction, however. The Americans had had only slight losses but forty Zeros, half the defending force, failed to return. That was only the start of their continuous attrition. Another raid in early July again cost them half their number. Still another cost them more than half of those that remained. There were now just nine Zeros left on Iwo Jima.

On 4 July, the air officer commanding, Captain Kanzo Miura, reached a dramatic decision. He had already determined, contrary to the advice of most of his staff, that he would throw all his surviving aircraft, Zeros and Jills alike, into an attack in broad daylight on the American carriers. Commander Nakajima, who was ordered not to participate, warned the airmen that they would be 'flying to almost certain death' but no doubt each one secretly felt that he at least would come through. There was thus no warning of what was to come when Miura, mounted on a crate, addressed the pilots chosen for the mission.

Miura's instructions were never formally recorded, his speech seems to have been a rambling one, and it is respectfully suggested that Sakai may not have remembered it with quite the word-for-word accuracy indicated by his account in *Samurai*. There can be no doubt, though, of the main import of the speech. The Jills were not to drop their torpedoes but to crash with their torpedoes still aboard into enemy carriers. The Zeros were to make suicide dives likewise. 'You have your orders,' Miura concluded. Saburō Sakai experienced 'a cold, sinking feeling of revulsion'.

It would appear that Miura had not previously mentioned his intentions to his staff officers and they had been decided on impulse in a desperate desire to inflict some damage on his enemies. Certainly he cannot have thought out the implications of his orders, which were frankly contradictory. He insisted that all eight Jills and nine Zeros should remain in a tight formation, but he also urged that each man should sink an enemy carrier, so they would have to split up if they were to engage such widely separated targets. He expected the Zeros to sink enemy warships, but none of them had been equipped with bombs which at this stage of the war the Zero could be adapted to carry, so in reality they could not hope to inflict meaningful damage. He instructed the fighter pilots not to engage enemy aircraft until the target was reached, but then they could not protect the torpedo-planes if the formation was intercepted.

Intercepted it was. American radar guided a swarm of Hellcats to it when still some 60 miles from its objective. The Zeros, as Miura had wished, made no attempt to break their tight formation. They were therefore unable to help the Jills, two of which were hit immediately; their torpedoes exploded, blowing them to pieces. 'You can follow orders just so far,' reflected Sakai grimly, and he and his two wingmen, Petty Officers Shirai and Shiga, did engage the Hellcats. Sadly, all the other Zeros followed their orders and Sakai saw two of them and five more Jills shot down in flames before he and his wingmen shook off the Hellcats by plunging into a violent rainstorm. Then, still unable to find the US warships, all three returned to Iwo Jima. Another very experienced pilot, Warrant Officer Muto, did the same, as did the one remaining Jill, having jettisoned its torpedo.

Sakai reports that Muto was ashamed he had failed to carry out the orders given, but his own reaction was anger at the stupidity of those orders. Since Captain Miura later died in action, we will never know what he felt, but perhaps he realized his folly, for he listened politely to his pilots' reports, then merely thanked them briefly. Nor did he report this affair to his superiors. Next day, American warships shelled Iwo Jima, shattering the remaining Japanese aircraft and demolishing virtually every building on the island. It seemed certain that it would now be invaded, but the Americans neglected their opportunity – an error that would later cost them dearly – and the surviving Japanese naval airmen were evacuated. Muto was killed later but Sakai survived the war, having become first an ensign, then a sub-lieutenant, the first NCO pilot so promoted other than posthumously and having received the rare honour of an individual citation.

'Sent out on a fool's mission' was Sakai's curt summary of this first formal suicide operation under orders. A little over three months later, there would be plenty of others. These, though, would be elaborately planned and carefully organized and a Japanese word hitherto unknown to most Europeans and Americans would become terrifyingly familiar.

Notes

1. This referred to the last two numbers of the year when the A6M had gone into production, counting from 660 BC, the legendary date for the foundation of Japan by the first Emperor, Jimmu Tennō. The year in question was 1940 AD or 2600 by Japanese reckoning.
2. His name is given in the Japanese fashion with the surname preceding the personal one. It has been the practice of Western historians to follow this style when dealing with figures from before Japan's modern era, considered as starting with the restoration of Imperial rule in 1868. Thereafter, however, since a man's family was then much less important, names are usually presented in the Western style with the surname last. Though somewhat contradictory and confusing, both these precedents have been followed here in order that names of the earlier Japanese individuals may be recognized by those familiar with them.
3. Unlike Great Britain, Japan did not have a separate independent air force.
4. 'Banzai' literally means 'ten thousand years', implying 'May our Emperor live for ten thousand years.' It became the Japanese war-cry.
5. Korea at this time was part of the Japanese Empire.

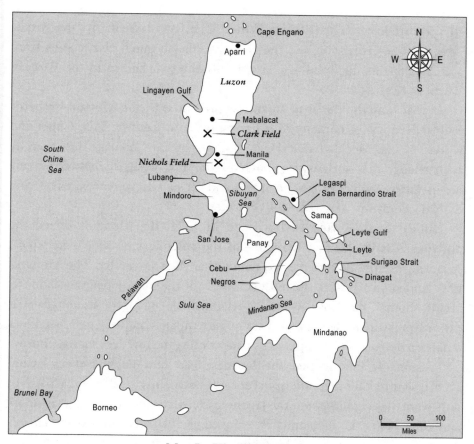

Map I – The Philippines.

Chapter 2

Desperate Measures

Kamikaze. The Divine Wind. The Wind Sent by the Gods. The expression and the concept, like so much else, comes from Japan's medieval age, specifically the year known in the Western World as 1281 AD.

At that time the threat to Japan was presented by the Mongol Emperor Kublai Khan. Not content with having overrun Central Asia, China and Korea, he had decided that Japan should pay him homage and thereby acknowledge that she was a tributary state. The Japanese, always fiercely independent, would have none of this and six successive embassies bearing Kublai's demands were scornfully rejected.

Kublai then resorted to force and in 1274, the Mongols seized the outlying islands of Tsushima and Iki, the defenders of which, in typical Japanese fashion, died to the last man rather than surrender. The Mongols next landed on Kyushu, the most southerly of the main Japanese islands. It seems, though, that this was more a reconnaissance in force and a means of putting pressure on Japan than a serious attempt at conquest, and faced by a stubborn defence and hampered by bad weather, the invaders soon withdrew.

Presumably hoping that the Japanese had now learned their lesson, Kublai sent further delegations to repeat his demands in 1275 and 1279. Not only were these ignored, but the Japanese executed the luckless ambassadors and their staffs. Understandably enraged, Kublai determined on Japan's destruction. With the aid of his Chinese and Korean subjects, he prepared a vast armada, supposedly of several thousand vessels though probably really of only several hundred, and in late June 1281, these carried his Mongol warriors, estimated by some at 150,000 and by the most conservative at 100,000, to another invasion of Kyushu.

For fifty-three days of unrelenting struggle, the Mongols slowly but steadily expanded their beachhead, with their superior numbers, superior experience and in some ways more modern weapons gradually overcoming desperate Japanese resistance. By mid–August, Japan's doom appeared certain. Then the elements intervened. The summer months in Japan are notorious for their storms and on 15 August, a typhoon of unprecedented size and ferocity swept over Kyushu.

Astonishingly, the Mongols had not considered the possibility of bad weather and their fleet was literally blown away. Many vessels went down in the open seas, others ran ashore on the mainland and yet others, crippled and harried by Japanese light craft, were wrecked on Kyushu. The Mongol troops in the bridgehead, cut off from supplies and reinforcements, were slaughtered. The Japanese took no prisoners: after all, the Mongols had taken none at Tsushima or Iki. In all, Kublai Khan lost at least 60,000 men and the Mongol threat was lifted forever. Well aware that they owed their salvation to the typhoon, which they believed had been sent by their gods to protect them, the Japanese named this the Kamikaze, meaning the Divine Wind.

In the autumn of 1944, Japan was again under threat, if not of destruction at least of catastrophic defeat. June had seen the fall of Saipan and defeat in the Battle of the Philippine Sea that had cost the Japanese three carriers: *Shokaku* and *Taiho*, as mentioned earlier, to submarines; *Hiyo* to strikes by aircraft from the US carriers. Far worse, all the Japanese air groups had been almost annihilated. Since a carrier is useless without aircraft and their crews, until these were replaced the Japanese could make no effective use of those that remained. Despite frantic efforts, it became clear that this problem could not be rectified before the Americans made their next and still more threatening move.

There had been considerable doubts among America's military and naval leaders as to the target for this. Many believed it should be Formosa (modern-day Taiwan), but at a conference held in Honolulu on 26 and 27 July 1944, General Douglas MacArthur, whose South-West Pacific Area forces had been steadily capturing Japanese bases in New Guinea, insisted it should be the Philippines. After much discussion, he won over President Franklin Roosevelt and also Admiral Chester Nimitz, Commander-in-Chief of the Pacific Ocean Areas; in other words the whole of that ocean except for the part under MacArthur.

Originally, the Americans intended to begin the reconquest of the Philippines in mid-November with an assault on Mindanao, the most southerly and second-largest of the main islands, but evidence of Japanese weaknesses led to a dramatic change of plan. The final decision was that the initial landing should take place as early as 20 October and should be on Leyte in the east of the Central Philippines.

This was a brilliant move. Leyte is a natural gateway to the Philippines and its capture would divide the Japanese forces into two main groups which could be overcome separately, thereby virtually ensuring their defeat. This in turn would result in the supply lines between Japan and the vital raw materials in Malaya and the Dutch East Indies – already weakened by US submarines – being severed completely and her final defeat becoming almost certain. No wonder that General MacArthur called the Leyte operation 'the crucial battle in the war in the Pacific'. No wonder, either, that the Sixth US Army of Lieutenant General Walter Krueger, which duly went ashore in Leyte Gulf on the north-east of that island on 20 October, was supported by not one but two massive American fleets. The Seventh Fleet of Vice Admiral Thomas Kinkaid carried the soldiers into Leyte Gulf and thereafter assisted the landing beaches. Kinkaid, who had given loyal service to MacArthur since November 1943, controlled 738 ships, including 6 battleships and 18 escort carriers, specifically designed to support convoys or amphibious operations.

Further protection was provided by the Third Fleet of Admiral William Halsey. Unlike Kinkaid, Halsey was responsible to Nimitz, not MacArthur, but that his duty to guard MacArthur's soldiers and sailors was 'essential and paramount' was made clear to him both by the general and by Nimitz. Under Halsey came Task Force 38: Third Fleet's carriers. This was controlled by Vice Admiral Marc Mitscher but unhappily Halsey, who had returned to sea-duty after a long spell behind a desk and was 'spoiling for a fight', tended to issue orders directly to the commanders of Task Force 38's four Task Groups, ignoring the much more experienced Mitscher who, as Professor Samuel Eliot Morison, the US Navy's Official Historian reports,[1] became 'little better than a passenger in his beloved Fast Carrier Forces Pacific Fleet'.

On 22 October, Halsey detached one Task Group for rest and reprovisioning. It was perhaps regrettable that this was the strongest of the four, containing 3 fleet and 2 light carriers, but even without it, Halsey still controlled 5 large and 6 light carriers, escorted by 6 battleships, 2 heavy cruisers, 7 light cruisers and 44 destroyers. The number of aircraft on the carriers varied but on average each of the fleet carriers had 42 Hellcat fighters, 30 Helldiver bombers and 18 Avenger torpedo-planes, and each light carrier had 22 Hellcats and 9 Avengers. These resources were more than enough to enable Third Fleet to cope with any force that the Japanese could send against it. Not that many thought this would prove necessary: American Intelligence insisted until the last moment that the Imperial Navy would not dare to intervene as the odds against it were too high.

Japanese Intelligence was much better informed. As early as 7 October, it correctly warned that Third Fleet would shortly launch carrier strikes against Formosa, Okinawa and the Philippines as a prelude to the invasion of the last-named which would take place at Leyte in the last ten days of October. This information was promptly conveyed to the then commander-in-chief of Japan's Combined Fleet, Admiral Soemu Toyoda.

A fine strategist and a determined, aggressive opponent, Toyoda was well aware of the threat posed by the Leyte landings. Already a mounting loss of tankers, which had been made the priority target for American submarines, had necessitated the division of his fleet. His carriers and supporting vessels remained in Japanese waters, receiving new equipment and training their replacement air crews. The majority of his heavy gunnery units, however, had had to be based at Lingga Roads near Singapore in order to be close to their fuel supplies.

Should the Philippines fall, as Toyoda explained after the war, 'the shipping lane to the south would be completely cut off.' If his warships then stayed in Japanese waters they could not operate because of their shortage of fuel. If they remained in the south they could not fight because they could not be supplied with ammunition. He therefore decided to commit his entire fleet in an attempt to smash the Leyte landings – and hence the American reconquest of the Philippines – since 'There would be no sense in saving the fleet at the expense of the loss of the Philippines.'

Toyoda's plan was called 'Sho-Go'. It was daring but frankly desperate and this fact and the circumstances in which it was drawn up have prompted some to regard it as a kind of naval 'banzai charge' in which the Imperial Navy would go down fighting. Yet 'Sho-Go' translates to English as 'Operation VICTORY' and whether this title was chosen optimistically or defiantly, victory was what the Japanese sought and very nearly attained.

As was mentioned earlier, the Japanese found it impossible to provide trained replacements for their lost naval airmen in time to oppose the Leyte landings. Moreover, when Third Fleet began its predicted pre-liminary assault on Formosa on 12 October, Toyoda transferred some 150 warplanes from carriers to land bases. As the pilots of these were probably incapable of operating from their mother-ships in any case, this made little difference to the real strength of the Japanese carrier force but their poor performance in combat emphasized to Toyoda that his carriers would be of little assistance in gaining the victory he so desperately needed.

Toyoda could, though, bring against the Americans a formidable gunfire strength in the warships at Lingga Roads, officially known as the 'First Striking Force'. The Sho Plan aimed to get this into Leyte Gulf where it could destroy the American beachhead and the transports, supply ships and supporting warships of Seventh Fleet. On 18 October, it sailed for Brunei Bay in Borneo, where its ships were refuelled, and at 0800 on the 22nd, the bulk of these, under the command of Vice Admiral Takeo Kurita, set out again for the Philippines.

Kurita's group, that for the sake of convenience may be called the Central Force, contained the super-battleships *Yamato* and *Musashi*, the largest battleships ever built and the biggest warships to fight in the Second World War. They had a standard displacement of 64,000 tons and were over 72,000 tons when fully laden. They carried the largest naval guns in existence: nine of 18.1in calibre, set in three triple turrets, two forward and one aft, having a range of 22.5 miles, far greater than that of the 16-inchers that were the heaviest possessed by any American battleship.

Supporting these monsters were the 16in-gunned *Nagato*, the 14in-gunned *Kongo* and *Haruna*, 10 heavy cruisers, 2 light cruisers and 15 destroyers. Their mission was to advance along the coast of Palawan, the most westerly of the Philippine islands; then swing east across the Sibuyan Sea and through the San Bernardino Strait between Luzon, the largest of the Philippine islands, and Samar, the island immediately north of Leyte; and finally turn south, sail east of Samar and attack Leyte Gulf from the north.

At 1500 on 22 October, Vice Admiral Shoji Nishimura left Brunei with the remainder of First Striking Force: battleships *Yamashiro* and *Fusō*, heavy cruiser *Mogami* and four destroyers. Nishimura's task was to move south of Palawan, proceed eastward across the Sulu Sea, turn sharply north between Leyte and the small island of Dinagat and attack Leyte Gulf from the south.

Nishimura's squadron would become known as the Van of the Southern Force. The Rear of the Southern Force was provided by the Second Striking Force of Vice Admiral Kiyohide Shima. Its two heavy cruisers, one light cruiser and four destroyers left their base at Okinawa on 18 October and by the 22nd were steaming south past the west coast of Luzon to enter the Sulu Sea from the north. Shima then followed Nishimura at some 40 miles distance, intending to come to his aid once battle had been joined.

It should be noted that we are assured by C. Vann Woodward in *The Battle for Leyte Gulf*,[2] that if only half of Kurita's ships, let alone all or most of the Central and Southern Forces had reached the Gulf, the Japanese would have gained a spectacular victory. The majority of the American transports had left by 25 October, the date when the Japanese planned to enter the Gulf, but there was a considerable shortage of supplies and Woodward declares that it would still have 'created an extremely critical situation' if the transports that remained there had been destroyed.

Nor were transports the only American vessels that Kurita would have encountered. The Americans had captured the airfields at Tacloban and Dulag on 22 October, but these had been flooded by torrential rain and not until the end of October could they be used effectively. Halsey's fast carriers were 'unable to provide extended support for Leyte' as he admitted in a signal to MacArthur on 26 October and the nearest American air base was 500 miles away. In these circumstances, Seventh Fleet's remaining sixteen escort carriers – two had left to collect replacement aircraft – were essential for the safety of the beachhead, and they lay right in Kurita's path. Had they been sunk on 25 October, the troops ashore would have been deprived of any meaningful air cover.

In the Gulf itself, Kurita could also have destroyed the amphibious force command ships containing the staffs of Vice Admiral Kinkaid, Rear Admiral Barbey controlling the northern landing forces and Vice Admiral Wilkinson in charge of the southern landing forces. Then Kurita could have turned his guns on the beaches which were piled high with food, ammunition and other equipment, all within easy range, as were the temporary headquarters of the army commanders, including that of MacArthur. 'The effect,' Woodward believes, 'would have been a disaster of incalculable proportions.'

Moreover, it would almost certainly have been followed by a greater disaster. 'General MacArthur's Army,' declares Professor Morison, 'would have been cut off like that of Athens at Syracuse in 413 BC. Third Fleet alone could not have maintained its communications.' Deprived of food, ammunition, supplies, air support and probably its leaders, Sixth Army would have been at the mercy of Leyte's defenders who could be reinforced by fresh troops from the other Philippine islands. It seems that the Japanese army suddenly realized this, because two other groups of ships also headed for Leyte, though not for Leyte Gulf. Containing in all one heavy and one light cruiser, four destroyers and four transports, these had the task of carrying men and equipment to Ormoc Bay on Leyte's west coast.

Had these catastrophes occurred, they would have dealt a severe blow to American morale and a worse one to the morale of the people of the Philippines. They would have sparked furious criticism from those who had wanted to attack Formosa instead. They would have given the Japanese vital time in which to train new airmen for their carriers. By showing the Americans that the reconquest of the Philippines would be terribly costly if not impossible, the Japanese might even hope for a compromise peace in which they would be allowed to retain or at least be granted special privileges in some of their gains in the 'colonial territories' in the south, of which the Americans did not approve, in return for a surrender of the Philippines, America's own colony.

All these fair prospects, however, depended on Kurita being able to get at Seventh Fleet and the invasion bridgehead, and his path to these was blocked by Halsey's mighty Third Fleet. The means chosen to remove this obstacle provided the most remarkable feature of the Sho Plan, one that could only have been proposed by the Japanese but did follow an example from earlier in the war.

On 24 August 1942, in the Battle of the Eastern Solomons the then C-in-C of the Imperial Navy, Admiral Isoroku Yamamoto, had ordered light carrier

Ryujo to attract the attention of two US carriers, allowing two large Japanese carriers to take the Americans by surprise. *Ryujo* had a fine previous record but Yamamoto was fully prepared for her to be sunk. His plan achieved a measure of success. *Ryujo* was sunk but Val dive-bombers scored three hits on the *Enterprise*, putting her out of action for two crucial months.[3]

Admiral Toyoda had not forgotten this precedent and had for some time considered using a particular pair of his warships in a similar role: the battleship-carriers *Hyūga* and *Ise*. These had originally mounted twelve 14in guns but at the end of 1943, their four guns aft were removed and replaced with a flight deck, intended to carry twenty-two seaplanes. These would be launched by catapult, land in the sea after making their attacks and be hoisted aboard by cranes. Unfortunately, neither the aircraft nor pilots trained to fly them were ever provided, so the vessels remained in reality merely battleships with a reduced armament.

By the time of the Leyte landings, as mentioned earlier, the shortage of carrier-based aircraft and capable carrier-based air crew meant that the once formidable Japanese 'flat-tops' could be of little value in a straightforward assault on the Americans. Toyoda therefore decided to add some of them to *Hyūga* and *Ise* as decoys, leaving five others, including Japan's three latest fleet carriers, in home waters waiting for the success of the Sho Plan to give them time to receive the machines and trained pilots they needed. The ones Toyoda was willing to sacrifice were the large *Zuikaku* and the light carriers *Zuihō*, *Chiyoda* and *Chitose*.

So on the evening of 20 October, these four, accompanied by *Hyūga*, *Ise*, three light cruisers and ten destroyers, together to be known as the Northern Force, left Japan to head south-westward towards the Philippines. Their course would bring them up against the US Third Fleet and there was no way that they could have posed a threat to this, even had the carriers possessed their full complement of warplanes, which was far from the case.

In fact, the Northern Force had only 116 aircraft, about a third of their pilots were so inexperienced that they were flown off to shore bases, and most of the remainder were incapable of landing back on the mother-ship after making an attack. The force also lacked modern strike aircraft. Indeed one reason why Toyoda had regarded the light carriers as expendable was that neither *Chiyoda* nor *Chitose* could operate Jill torpedo-bombers, of which the Northern Force had twenty-five, while none of the three could carry its seven new Yokosuka Judy dive-bombers which needed a longer take-off run than they could provide.

None of these factors, however, affected the Sho Plan. It was not the Northern Force's task to engage American warships and any damage it did inflict would be in the nature of a bonus. It was instructed to 'manoeuvre east of Luzon to lure the enemy northward'. The enemy, of course, was Third Fleet. If this could be enticed away from the San Bernardino Strait, Kurita would have a clear run to Leyte Gulf. By the time Third Fleet returned, he would have completed his work of destruction and could retire through the Surigao Strait which would by then have been penetrated by Nishimura and Shima.

In command of the Northern Force was Vice Admiral Jisaburō Ozawa, an impressive figure, unusually tall for a Japanese, who enjoyed the reputation of having the ablest strategic brain in the Japanese high command. An early advocate of the value of aircraft carriers, he had achieved great success in the first months of the war and even in defeat at the Battle of the Philippine Sea, he had shown a sublime personal courage in desperate circumstances and an ability that earned from Professor Morison the compliment that he was 'a worthy antagonist'.

Ozawa was in no doubt as to what would happen to his Northern Force if his diversionary move succeeded. 'I expected complete destruction of my fleet,' he declared after the war, 'but if Kurita's mission was carried out, that was all I wished.' Coolly and unselfishly, he did everything possible to perform his difficult, appallingly dangerous and potentially fatal task. In the early hours of 24 October, his Northern Force arrived off the north-eastern point of Luzon which a sixteenth-century Spanish navigator had prophetically named Engaño: Cape Deception.

Japan's carrier-based aircraft could be of little direct help to their surface warships and it seemed questionable whether her land-based naval air units could be either. When Halsey had made his preliminary attacks on Formosa and the Philippines, he had inflicted heavy casualties on these, both in the air and on their landing-grounds, and their inexperienced crews, despite ludicrously inflated claims, had caused only minor losses in return.

On 20 October, Vice Admiral Teraoka, commanding Japan's First Air Fleet, had at most 100 warplanes available and that only after the hasty repair of damaged machines. On the 22nd, however, Vice Admiral Shigeru Fukudome, whose Second Air Fleet was based in Formosa, sent every aircraft he had to the Philippines, bringing the Imperial Navy's strength in the islands to between 300 and 400, though not all were operational. About 180 reinforcements later arrived from Japan and Vice Admiral Ozawa flew in some 40 more, including most of his valuable Jills, from his carriers. Japan's Army Air Force, hitherto unwilling to co-operate in naval matters, contributed some 200 further aircraft from Lieutenant General Tominaga's Fourth Air Army, plus 80 reinforcements that arrived on 24 October.

It might have been thought that at least air protection for Kurita could have been provided, but in practice only a token handful of fighters did so. Later marks of the once-dominant Zero had already proved to be outclassed by the new American Hellcats and Fukudome believed they would be best employed escorting Japanese bombers and torpedo-planes in mass attacks against the US carriers, thereby preventing these from launching strikes at Kurita and so 'opening the way' for their heavy gunnery units.

Unfortunately, the Battle of the Philippine Sea had seen even massed aerial attacks thwarted and shattered, not only by the growing ability of the Hellcat pilots but by the American invention of a new AA shell. This had what was called a 'proximity-armed fuse': a miniature radar set in its nose that reflected signals back from an attacking aircraft. When the interval between the outward and return signals became very short, this meant that the shell was close to its target. It then detonated automatically without the need to score a direct hit.

Naturally the Japanese sought ways of rectifying this situation. Several solutions were proposed but none proved feasible. Perhaps therefore it was inevitable that several officers should conclude, like Captain Miura, that only by making suicide dives could their pilots injure enemy warships and, unlike Captain Miura, should be prepared to make their opinions clear to their superiors. Some of them will appear later; for the moment mention need only be made of those who proved to be particularly influential.

Captain Eiichiro Jyo had had an outstanding career which included being an aide-de-camp of the Emperor and a naval attaché in Washington.

In June 1944, he had commanded light carrier *Chiyoda* in the Battle of the Philippine Sea and in a report of his experiences, he flatly stated: 'No longer can we hope to sink the numerically superior enemy aircraft carriers through ordinary attack methods. I urge the immediate organization of special attack units to carry out crash-dive tactics, and I ask to be placed in command of them.'

Rear Admiral Masafumi Arima, who commanded First Air Fleet's 26th Air Flotilla in Luzon, is not recorded as making similar dramatic pleas for suicide operations and was apparently soft-spoken and tactful, yet his officers who liked and respected him were well aware that he did favour these. Nor was he prepared just to urge others to employ them; he was determined to carry out a suicide mission of his own.

On 15 October 1944, Arima ordered out two waves of his aircraft against Third Fleet carriers that had been striking at Luzon's airfields. The first of these was intercepted by the Combat Air Patrol and only three Judys got through to attack the carrier *Franklin*. Her AA gunners shot down all of these, but not before one had released its bomb which struck *Franklin*'s flight deck just before the Judy crashed into the sea about 100ft away; it caused only slight damage but killed three sailors and injured twelve others. As the aircraft of Arima's second wave made ready for take-off, Arima himself arrived at Nichols Field, wearing flight gear and no insignia of rank. This was especially noticeable since he was normally meticulous about wearing full uniform, but it was his way of avoiding a violation of the regulation that flag officers were not to fly combat missions.

Arima had in fact decided to lead this attack in person and his dismayed staff officers who knew his views and his character realized that it was his intention to ram an enemy carrier. They tried hard to change his mind but in vain; he boarded the leading Judy and was the first to take off. He was not to carry out his plan, however, for once again the CAP intercepted the raiders long before they came within range of their targets and those not driven away were shot down, including that of Rear Admiral Arima.

Nonetheless, when the Imperial Navy learned that *Franklin* had been damaged, it was believed that this must have been caused by her having been struck by Arima's suicide dive; an assumption that in itself shows the lack of confidence now generally felt in the effectiveness of orthodox aerial assaults. News of Arima's imaginary success spread throughout the air units in the Philippines, to be hailed as a demonstration of Japanese spirit and proof of the right way to inflict damage on the enemy. Arima was said to have 'lit the fuse of the ardent wishes of his men' and his example confirmed the opinions of a more senior officer who arrived at Nichols Field two days later.

Vice Admiral Takijirō Ōnishi had been an early and enthusiastic believer in the importance of naval aviation. He was himself a good pilot who had led numerous sorties when in command of Japan's Second Combined Air Group in her war with China. He had been an admirer of Admiral Yamamoto and, as a rear admiral and chief staff officer of the Eleventh Air Fleet, he was one of those with whom Yamamoto consulted regarding the planning of the Pearl Harbor strike. On the outbreak of the Pacific War, he was chief staff officer to Admiral Tsukahara, leader of the Navy Land-Based Air Force and earned a considerable reputation by his conduct of early operations in the Philippines and Indonesia. Brave, determined, energetic and resourceful, he won the respect and loyalty of the officers who served under him.

Yet as even his admirers admitted, Ōnishi 'was not altogether popular throughout the Navy'. He was very outspoken, unmoved by and intolerant of criticism and a harsh, rigid disciplinarian who required his orders to be carried out to the letter, though in fairness he was similarly meticulous in obeying any orders he received. Many considered him wilful, arrogant, overbearing and difficult to please, while for his part he could be contemptuous and disdainful; he did not suffer fools gladly and placed in that category most of those who disagreed with him. As a result, he never received the affectionate trust accorded to, for instance, his fellow aviation enthusiasts Yamamoto and Ozawa.

After his service in the early campaigns of the Pacific War, Ōnishi reluctantly accepted a post in the Aviation Department of the Ministry of Munitions in Tokyo, where he was in charge of aircraft production. In this role, he observed Japan's falling rate of production and the inadequate performances of many of those types that were produced. He undoubtedly considered the possibility of suicide attacks and had listened to the arguments and proposals of that fervent supporter of these, Captain Eiichiro Jyo, though he did not at first accept them.

Yet when Ōnishi reached the Philippines on 17 October 1944, he had decided that such attacks were necessary, although originally it seems, only while the Sho Plan was carried out. He officially relieved Vice Admiral Teraoka as head of Japan's First Air Fleet on the 20th, but in practice he began to take charge from the moment his aircraft landed at Nichols Field. In the late afternoon of 19 October, he appeared at Mabalacat airfield in Central Luzon and summoned a meeting of his subordinates. Of these, the most important were Captain Rikihei Inoguchi, First Air Fleet's senior staff officer, and Commander Asaichi Tamai, senior staff officer of 201st Air Group, the main tactical naval air unit in the Philippines and effectively its leader as the Group Commander, Captain Yamamoto, had been injured in an air crash and was now in hospital.

It is reported that Ōnishi appeared grim and tired and his face was heavily lined. That he had every reason for gravity quickly became apparent. He reminded his listeners that 'the fate of the Empire depends upon the outcome of the SHO Operation' and the task of First Air Fleet was to see that the Americans did not prevent Kurita reaching Leyte Gulf. This meant that it had to neutralize the US aircraft carriers for at least a week. 'In my opinion,' he concluded, 'there is only one way of assuring that our meagre strength will be effective to a maximum degree. That is to organize suicide attack units.'

Ōnishi did not order that such units should be formed. He stated his beliefs and waited for his officers, particularly Inoguchi and Tamai, to express their own. Both had previously heard suggestions of this kind but Tamai had doubted whether such tactics were desirable, while Inoguchi had called them 'outrageous' and 'inhuman'. Now though, both, like Ōnishi before them, changed their minds. They declared that they shared his opinions and he could leave it to them to organize his suicide attack squadron. Tamai then approached the pilots of his 201st Air Group to see if they were willing to join such a squadron – there was no question of their being ordered to do so – and all of them volunteered their services without hesitation. The motive behind all these actions was later summarized by

Admiral Toyoda as 'If the surface units are taking such desperate measures, we too must take similar desperate measures.'

Inoguchi and Tamai then discussed who should be asked to command the new unit. They agreed that Lieutenant Yukio Seki, a former pilot of carrier-based bombers who had recently come to Luzon from Formosa, had the necessary combination of leadership skills and flying ability. He was summoned and the situation explained to him. He thought for some time, and his decision could not have been an easy one for he had a young wife and a widowed mother to consider, but eventually he declared firmly that he positively insisted on accepting the post.

By early October, the organization of the new attack squadron had been completed and Inoguchi suggested it be named the Kamikaze Corps, hoping this would be a good omen and its pilots would sweep away the American fleets as the original Divine Wind had swept away that of the Mongols. It consisted at first of only twenty-six Zeros, of which half would be fitted with 550lb bombs. These would be the ones to crash-dive onto American warships, a task for which the fast and highly manoeuvrable Zero was ideally suited; it would soon be joined in this role by the speedy Judy dive-bomber. The other half of the Kamikaze Unit's Zeros would escort the suiciders to the target and then return to base to report the results of the strikes and the effectiveness of the tactics employed. Significantly, the most experienced pilots were given the escort role.

Vice Admiral Ōnishi divided his force into four sections, the titles of which he had already decided: Yamato, Shikishima, Asahi and Yamazakura, the first two being old poetic names for Japan and the last two referring to symbols for her, the rising sun and the wild cherry blossom respectively. Encouraged by the readiness and enthusiasm with which his ideas had been accepted, Ōnishi was already looking to expand his attack corps and on 20 October, he sent the four bomb-carrying Zeros of the Yamato section to Cebu, the island immediately west of Leyte, intending that these would provide the basis of a suicide force there. They were guarded by four more Zeros, three of the pilots being quite unaware of the nature of the formation they were escorting, while the fourth was flown by a trusted staff officer whose job it was to form the new Kamikaze Unit envisaged.

This was none other than Commander Tadashi Nakajima who had been contemptuous of Captain Miura's orders for the use of suicide dives by the naval airmen on Iwo Jima but, like so many others, had now had a change of heart. In his case, there were two excellent reasons for this: the suicide strikes were now being properly prepared and organized, and while Miura had instructed his men in effect to commit suicide, the Kamikaze Corps would only send out volunteers.

So strongly did Nakajima feel on this point that when he addressed the airmen at the naval air base just north of Cebu City to explain his mission and call for volunteers, he stated that this was not expected of everyone. Those who had family responsibilities or other special reasons for reluctance were specifically urged not to volunteer. Each man ready to go on suicide missions was to write his name on a piece of paper and place it in an envelope to be given to Nakajima at 2100, and he alone would ever know their identities. In fact, when Nakajima opened the envelope, he found that the only pilots who had not volunteered were a couple in hospital. By 21 October, a new twenty-strong Kamikaze squadron was ready for action on Cebu.

Also on 21 October occurred an incident that has aroused both interest and controversy. In the British Official History, *The War at Sea*, Captain S.W. Roskill reports that the Australian heavy cruiser *Australia* 'was hit by a Kamikaze suicide bomber' and remarks that it 'was the first suicide attack on any Allied ship'. This, though, was clearly not the case. There seems little doubt that the hit was intentional but, as we have seen, there had been several previous 'impulse' strikes of this kind.

Alternatively, Roskill may be suggesting that this was the first attack carried out by the newly-formed Kamikaze Corps. This, however, is denied by Professor Morison and surviving Kamikaze organizers like Inoguchi and Nakajima. Moreover, at this date the only aircraft used by the Corps, whether on Luzon or Cebu, were Zeros, whereas in the Official History *Royal Australian Navy 1942–1945*, G. Hermon Gill confirms that watchers on both *Australia* and heavy cruiser HMAS *Shropshire*[4] lying only a short distance away, all identified the attacker as a Val dive-bomber, though it could have been an Army Air Force Mitsubishi Sonia light bomber which had a distinctive fixed undercarriage like the Val.

Further light is cast by *Shropshire*'s Captain Godfrey Nichols, who is thus quoted in the Australian Official History:

> During the dawn stand-to a low-flying aircraft approached from the land between *Australia* and *Shropshire*. It was taken under fire and retired to the westward. Observers in *Shropshire* report that the aircraft was hit and touched the water but recovered. It then turned east again and although under heavy fire, passed up the port side of *Australia* and crashed into the foremast at 0605. There was a large explosion and an intense fire in the Air Defence position and bridge.

A similar account is given in *Fire Across the Pacific* by David Mattiske, who was then serving on *Shropshire*:

> The attacking Jap made his first run at *Shropshire*; our starboard side 4-inch guns were extremely quick and alert, getting away accurate fire which caused him to veer off. When well past us he turned and came back again at us low and fast, and once again the starboard guns got in a burst under his belly which threw him away from *Shropshire* heading for *Australia*, which was also sending up a volume of fire. Unfortunately, he got through *Australia*'s barrage and crashed into her foremast, knocking it over at an angle; exploding around the superstructure and Compass Platform he caused frightful damage and fire.

It seems clear therefore that this pilot did not set out with the intention of making a suicide dive and it was another 'impulse' attack: when damaged by AA fire, the pilot had decided to sell his life dearly. *Australia*, then, was not the first victim of an 'official' suicide strike. Of course, official or unofficial, the effect of an aircraft crashing into a ship is much the same and *Australia* lost twenty of her crew dead, including Captain Deschaneux, with seventy-four others wounded, of whom ten died later, mainly from the effect of burns. It was a grim overture to what would become history's largest naval engagement.

The Battle of Leyte Gulf began on 23 October 1944 and was fought out all round and over the Philippine islands until the 26th. It contained dramatic incidents, controversial decisions, astonishing changes of fortune and, on both sides, steadfast resolution and unselfish courage, and it is regretted that space prevents more than a summary of those parts of it that do not affect the Kamikaze Corps.

It began in the Palawan Passage, to the west of the island of that name between it and a series of dangerous reefs and shoals. Here Kurita's Central Force was spotted by US submarines *Darter* and *Dace*. Torpedoes from the former sank heavy cruiser *Atago*, Kurita's flagship, and so damaged heavy cruiser *Takao* that she had to return to Brunei escorted by a couple of destroyers. *Dace* sank heavy cruiser *Maya*. The subs' success was marred when *Darter*, trying to get in another attack on *Takao*, ran aground to become a total loss, but all her crew were rescued by *Dace*.

Next day, 24 October, saw the ruin of Japan's land-based naval air strength. Vice Admiral Fukudome sent three major raids against Third Fleet, but his warplanes could locate only one of the three Task Groups remaining with Halsey and all organized attacks on this were broken up, mainly by Third Fleet's Hellcats, with horrifying losses. Commander David McCampbell, leader of Air Group 15 from *Essex*, who had destroyed seven enemy aircraft during the Battle of the Philippine Sea and would become the US navy's highest-scoring pilot with a total of thirty-five 'kills', made the record score of nine on this occasion, an achievement later recognized by the award of a Congressional Medal of Honor.

Only after all concerted attacks had been defeated did a single skilful Judy pilot, who had been lurking under cloud cover awaiting his opportunity, show what could be done. Timing his attack perfectly, he put a 550lb bomb into light carrier *Princeton* before being shot down by an American fighter. Attempts by other vessels to aid *Princeton* resulted only in several of them suffering injuries and eventually she had to be sunk by her own escorts. Minor raids later by Fukudome's airmen did no damage. Japanese fears that their land-based naval aircraft would not get many hits by orthodox attacks had been fully justified.

This also proved the case with Japan's carrier-based warplanes. Vice Admiral Ozawa launched 40 Zero fighters, 21 Zero fighter-bombers, 8 Jill torpedo-planes and 7 Judy dive-bombers against Third Fleet, though in view of his pilots' inexperience this was more to draw attention away from Kurita than in expectation of inflicting damage. Third Fleet's Hellcats intercepted and dispersed the raiders and only the Judys broke through to the US carriers, the anti-aircraft fire of which claimed three of them. The others plunged down with such determination that the Americans later believed – wrongly – that they had been suicide attackers, but their courage was ill-rewarded. A near-miss was scored on fleet carrier *Essex*, another on fleet carrier *Lexington* and two on light carrier *Langley* but none caused serious harm. Just one Judy returned to Ozawa.

It was precisely this situation that the Kamikaze Corps had been created to rectify, but for many days it conspicuously failed to do so. As early as 21 October, its airmen set out to engage US carriers but were unable to locate any. Towering cumulonimbus thunderclouds prevailed throughout the Philippines, bringing rain, wind and poor visibility that proved too great a handicap to pilots whose aircraft had no radar to assist them. Nor was the weather their only enemy. On the afternoon of the 21st, word reached the Kamikaze units in Cebu that a carrier force had been sighted and five Zeros that had been hidden and camouflaged some distance from the runway were brought out and made ready: three armed with bombs; the others to act as escorts. The pilots were in the command post receiving their instructions when American aircraft swept down on the airfield, reducing all the Zeros to flaming wrecks.

Commander Nakajima, with commendable resolution, hastily had three more Zeros prepared and sent off in the direction from which the attackers had come. They left at 1625, led by Lieutenant (Junior Grade) – sub-lieutenant in the Royal Navy – Yoshiyasu Kuno. He had flown one of the Zeros that had escorted the Yamato section to Cebu without knowing the nature of this formation. On discovering it was a suicide attack unit, he had not only volunteered to join it but had gone to Nakajima, whom he knew personally, to insist that his application be accepted.

Kuno was an experienced pilot who was well aware of the problems caused by bad weather and Nakajima has revealed that Kuno had told him that if he (Kuno) could not locate any carriers he would go on to Leyte Gulf where there were 'sure to be many targets'. His little flight did encounter bad weather and did fail to find any carriers, so two of its aircraft returned to Cebu, but not Lieutenant Kuno. He made for Leyte Gulf but was presumably intercepted by Seventh Fleet fighters. He was never seen again.[5]

Throughout 21, 22, 23 and 24 October, Kamikaze flights from Luzon and Cebu left in search of the elusive US 'flat-tops', only to be forced to return by rain or shortage of fuel or both. Ardent volunteers like Lieutenant Seki were inconsolable, apologizing almost in tears for the lack of results. Their superiors must have been frantic with worry, wondering if the founding of the Kamikaze Corps had been a waste of time and effort.

To complete their misery, on 24 October aircraft from those Third Fleet carriers that the Kamikazes had been intended to destroy had no difficulty in locating all the Japanese surface forces and delivered a whole series of strikes throughout the day, especially against Kurita's Central Force. The super-battleship *Musashi*, struck by at least thirteen torpedoes and as many bombs, finally sank at 1935. A torpedo–hit forced heavy cruiser *Myōkō* to return to Brunei and she was followed by a pair of destroyers that had rescued survivors from *Musashi*. Nonetheless, Kurita still commanded four battleships, six heavy cruisers, two light cruisers and eleven destroyers and now mistakes by Admiral Halsey all but justified the name chosen for Toyoda's Operation VICTORY.

For a start, Third Fleet's airmen, like those of all countries in similar circumstances, had greatly overestimated the damage they had caused. Halsey, however, accepted their reports at face value and concluded that Central Force had been reduced to a bunch of cripples, 'tremendously reduced in fire power and life', and even if they did manage to 'plod through' the San Bernardino Strait, they would not be 'a serious menace to Seventh Fleet'.

Halsey was, in fact, no longer interested in Central Force. Nor was he interested in the Southern Forces which he left to Seventh Fleet, although he never warned Kinkaid of this. Ozawa's Northern Force had also been located and its strength badly exaggerated by Halsey's scouts. Taking their word for this, Halsey concluded that here was his most dangerous foe and without leaving a single ship to watch the San Bernardino Strait, he set off after it with his whole Third Fleet. Night–flying reconnaissance aircraft had been sent out by light carrier *Independence* and these now reported that

Kurita still had with him four battleships including one of the *Yamato* class – *Yamato* herself of course – and they were 'plodding' forward at 20 knots. Halsey simply ignored them. Protests from Rear Admiral Gerald Bogan, commanding the Task Group containing *Independence*, and Vice Admiral Willis Lee, Halsey's battleship commander, were ignored as well.

Japan's decoy tactic had succeeded beyond the wildest hopes of Toyoda or Ozawa. To cap it all, when Halsey signalled his intentions, he did not say he was going north 'at full strength' or 'with all my forces' or something similar, but 'with three groups'. This seemed to indicate that there was a fourth group that was not going north. Halsey had earlier announced that he proposed to form a new Task Force 34 of four battleships and supporting vessels to deal with Kurita if he came through the San Bernardino Strait. Nimitz, Mitscher and most crucially Kinkaid all thought that this was the fourth group and it was remaining on guard at San Bernardino.

Thus Seventh Fleet was not only left wide open to attack, but was totally unaware of its danger. The only good point about this was that Kinkaid, believing his northern flank was secure, felt able to give his subordinate Rear Admiral Jesse Oldendorf 6 battleships, 4 heavy cruisers including HMAS *Shropshire*, 4 light cruisers and 28 destroyers including HMAS *Arunta* to block the Surigao Strait against the Japanese Southern Forces.

During the night of 24/25 October, Oldendorf ambushed the Van of the Southern Force, killed Vice Admiral Nishimura and sank battleships *Yamashiro* and *Fusō* and three destroyers. Only heavy cruiser *Mogami* and destroyer *Shigure* got away and the former was so damaged as not to be under proper control. When Vice Admiral Shima appeared on the scene, *Mogami* collided with his flagship, heavy cruiser *Nachi*, and shortly afterwards Shima wisely retired. Later air attacks finally brought the diehard *Mogami* to a halt – she was finished off by a Japanese torpedo – and sank *Abukuma*, the light cruiser with Shima's formation.

Early on 25 October, the destruction of another Japanese force began. Halsey had at last given tactical command to Mitscher who, in a series of brilliantly organized strikes, sank light carrier *Chitose* and destroyer *Akitsuki*, left light carrier *Chiyoda* dead in the water and seriously damaged several other vessels including the large carrier *Zuikaku*. At the same time, however, there came an urgent signal from Kinkaid, made not in code but in plain English, appealing for assistance because Kurita's battleships were engaging his escort carriers and threatening to penetrate to the Leyte Gulf beachhead.

Had Halsey responded immediately, he would probably have been able to destroy Kurita's warships, but he ignored a series of calls from Kinkaid, only to have his own chief, Nimitz, demand to know what had happened to Task Force 34. After brooding over this – for about an hour! – he finally sent Lee's battleships and Bogan's Task Group southward, but too late to intervene.

Astonishingly, Halsey's mistakes were rectified, albeit at heavy cost, not by his powerful Third Fleet but by Seventh Fleet's slow, vulnerable escort carriers that had never been intended to fight enemy battle fleets. On the morning of 25 October, these were stationed to the east of the Philippines in three groups known from their voice radio call-signs as 'Taffy 3', '2' and '1' reading from north to south. The first two each contained six escort carriers, 'Taffy 1' only four, and all had the support of three destroyers and four of the smaller, slower destroyer escorts designed only for anti-submarine duties.

Taffy 3, commanded by Rear Admiral Clifton Albert Frederick Sprague, as the most northerly of the groups – it lay east of central Samar and north-east of Leyte Gulf – was the one on which Kurita fell. It was hopelessly outnumbered and its pilots were untrained and largely unequipped for the action that developed. Yet resolute, unselfish courage was not a solely Japanese trait. Sprague's escort vessels and aircraft hurled themselves at their formidable foes, backed up by the aircraft of Rear Admiral Felix Stump's Taffy 2, which also received Taffy 3's machines when they needed more fuel and ammunition. The air attacks in particular did considerable damage and heavy cruisers *Chōkai*, *Chikuma* and *Suzuya* were all crippled and sank later.

Inevitably, though, the weight of Kurita's gunfire took its toll. Escort carrier *Gambier Bay*, destroyers *Hoel* and *Johnston* and destroyer escort *Samuel B. Roberts* were sunk and three other escort carriers damaged. By 0925, it seemed certain that Taffy 3 must be annihilated, Taffy 2 was coming under fire as well, and Kurita was only 45 miles away from the Leyte Gulf beachhead. Then suddenly at Kurita's command his entire Central Force reversed course, and this was only a prelude to its full retirement.

Abandoning the whole purpose of the Sho Plan, Kurita slipped back through the San Bernardino Strait and out of the Philippines altogether, losing light cruiser *Noshiro* and two destroyers in the process. Sprague's escort carriers had repulsed the most powerful Japanese surface fleet ever to engage an American formation.

After the war, Kurita gave many complicated, confused and contradictory reasons for his action, but perhaps Sir Winston Churchill in *The Second World War* gives the best explanation:

> It may well be that Kurita's mind had become confused by the pressure of events. He had been under constant attack for three days, he had suffered heavy losses, and his flagship had been sunk soon after starting from Borneo. Those who have endured a similar ordeal may judge him.

It is sad to note that while Kurita's Central Force was heading for safety, Ozawa's Northern Force, which had ensured that the San Bernardino Strait remained open as an escape route, was still suffering. Mitscher's airmen sank *Zuikaku* and light carrier *Zuihō*. Torpedoes from an American submarine sank light cruiser *Tama*. A cruiser-destroyer force sent in advance by Mitscher to deal with stragglers sank destroyer *Hatsutsuki* and finished off light carrier *Chiyoda* that went down in a mass of flames. With her perished Captain Eiichiro Jyo whose advice had done much to encourage Vice Admiral Ōnishi to form the Kamikaze Corps. Yet remarkably, Ozawa, who had transferred his flag to light cruiser *Ōyodo* when *Zuikaku* had first been crippled, brought back to Japan twelve of his nineteen ships, including two picket destroyers sent home earlier.

Clearly then, Japan's Northern Force had not been sent on a suicide mission. On 25 October, however, the Americans at last encountered a unit that emphatically had. At 0740, while Rear Admiral Clifton Sprague's Taffy 3 was being harried by Kurita, the four escort carriers of Taffy 1 – *Santee*, *Suwanee*, *Sangamon*, *Petrof Bay* – commanded by another Sprague (but no relation), Rear Admiral Thomas, saw four Zero fighter-bombers shoot out of the low clouds above them. They were Kamikazes from Cebu, accompanied by two other Zeros as escorts, and they were about to unleash their pent-up fury on the United States navy. Without hesitation, three of them hurtled towards their targets.

Surprise was complete. Escort carrier *Santee* did not fire a single shot in her own defence before the first Zero, strafing as it came, crashed into her flight deck and burst through this into her hangar. Its bomb exploded as it hit, blowing a hole 30ft long by 15ft wide in the flight deck and starting fires that were spread by fuel from the Zero's tanks and those of some of *Santee*'s own aircraft. The flames threatened eight 1,000lb bombs, and had they exploded *Santee* would have been lost. Miraculously they did not – it has been suggested they had not been fused – and heroic efforts by damage control parties managed to bring the fires under control after eleven anxious minutes. Nonetheless, sixteen dead men and twenty-seven wounded gave grim evidence of the perils of a Kamikaze attack.

Recovering from their shock, Taffy 1's AA gunners opened up on the other enemy aircraft. One circled menacingly round *Suwanee*, then dived on *Sangamon* under fire from both escort carriers. At the last moment, a 5in shell from *Suwanee* hit the Zero and flung it to one side. It came down just off *Sangamon*'s port side, but as it hit the water its bomb went off, shrapnel causing some damage and killing one luckless seaman on *Sangamon*'s forecastle. The third Zero, also struck by AA fire, near-missed *Petrof Bay*, this time without causing any damage.

All eyes were now on the fourth Zero as it circled above, waiting for a good opportunity. No one saw the periscope of a Japanese submarine that an evil chance had sent to this precise spot. A torpedo hit *Santee*'s starboard side amidships, but caused surprisingly little damage and no casualties. It did, though, distract attention from the Zero which was now also being threatened by a Hellcat. Dodging this, the Kamikaze went for *Suwanee* and although hit by AA fire and trailing smoke, it struck her flight deck about 40ft forward of the after elevator, tearing a 10ft hole through which its engine and other parts burst to the hangar deck; its bomb exploded between flight deck and hangar deck, blowing a 25ft hole in the latter. Fires were started, the after elevator was jammed and *Suwanee*'s steering was temporarily put out of action.

Once again, though, the damage control parties proved their worth. A special mention must go to William Brooks, chief ship's fitter, who opened the valves controlling the water curtain and sprinkler system in the hangar and thereby saved the aircraft there from catching fire; an action he would repeat on 26 October in even grimmer conditions. The after elevator remained inoperable but *Suwanee*, like *Santee*, stayed in formation and was able to resume air operations within a couple of hours.

So far, not so good for the Americans, but worse was soon to follow. At 0725, Kamikazes of the Shikishima unit had taken off from Mabalacat airfield, Luzon. This was a very well-organized strike force. The five bomb-carrying Zeros were led by the commanding officer (flying) of the Corps, Lieutenant Yukio Seki, and the three escorting fighters by Chief Warrant Officer Hiroyoshi Nishizawa, the Imperial Navy's most successful 'ace', credited with eighty-seven 'kills'. The formation approached at a very low level, avoiding the Combat Air Patrol and detection by American radar. At 1049, the five attackers climbed steeply, then hurled themselves at their targets: four of the remaining five escort carriers in Clifton Sprague's Taffy 3.

Sprague's AA gunners met them with a furious crossfire. Two of them, trying to get at Sprague's flagship *Fanshaw Bay*, were shot down in flames at a safe distance. One went for *Kitkun Bay*, firing as it came, just missed her bridge at which it had apparently aimed, crashed into the port side of her flight deck and bounced off it into the sea; its bomb exploded when it hit, causing damage and starting fires. The remaining pair attacked *White Plains*. Both were damaged by 40mm machine-gun fire and one, trailing smoke, swung away towards *St Lo*. The other charged at *White Plains* from astern, but was hit several more times; it rolled over, narrowly missing the flight deck, and exploded in the air, injuring eleven men and peppering the ship with splinters and the gruesome remains of the pilot.

Meanwhile, the Zero that had turned its attention to *St Lo* was bursting through its victim's protective barrage. Flown according to Nishizawa's later report by Lieutenant Seki, it smashed through the flight deck into the hangar, where it exploded, hurling debris and blazing fuel over the flight deck and setting off bombs and torpedoes stored in the hangar. A ghastly chain of destruction followed: a small explosion that sent up clouds of smoke; then a bigger one that split open part of the flight deck; then a really huge one that blew the forward elevator high into the air, to fall back on the flight deck upside down.

St Lo was clearly doomed. At 1100, Captain McKenna ordered her engines stopped and her crew to 'Abandon ship'. This was carried out successfully, despite raging fires and further massive explosions, one of which apparently tore out part of *St Lo*'s hull since a list to port changed to a sharper list to starboard, while others flung parts of the flight deck and entire aircraft hundreds of feet into the air. At 1125, *St Lo*, which had earlier defied the giant guns of *Yamato*, sank by the stern. The escorting Zeros retired, not to Luzon but to the nearer Kamikaze base at Cebu, where they reported the first but far from last sinking by the Kamikaze Corps.

In the meantime, another Japanese formation, this time of fifteen Judys, destined to become second only to Zeros as the Kamikazes' favourite suicide attackers, had appeared above Taffy 3. The CAP intercepted it and downed most of the raiders, only five of which got through. One dived on *Kitkun Bay* but AA fire shot off both its wings; it went into the sea just short of its target, shrapnel causing minor damage. The other four attacked the only escort carrier in Taffy 3 not previously made a Kamikaze target. This was *Kalinin Bay*, the crew of which may well have felt they deserved a break as in the fight with Kurita she had been struck by one 14in and thirteen 8in shells. Her AA gunners set all four of her attackers on fire and two came down at a safe distance, but a third crashed into the port side of her flight deck and the last crashed into the after part of her superstructure. Yet *Kalinin Bay* remained in formation and her fires were quenched in less than five minutes. By now, her damage control parties must have felt capable of coping with anything.

There would be one more Kamikaze strike in the Battle of Leyte Gulf. At about noon on 26 October, a flight of six Zeros was detected by Taffy 1's radar. The CAP intercepted and brought down three of them, but apparently these were the escorting fighters, not the suicide attackers. The three Zero fighter-bombers dodged the interceptors but one of a pair that attempted to hit *Petrof Bay* was shot down by an Avenger returning from an anti-submarine patrol and the other was torn apart by the escort carrier's AA fire. Both crashed astern of her.

That left just one Kamikaze, but one was enough and although damaged, it plunged into *Suwanee*, right on top of an Avenger that had just landed and was standing on the forward elevator. The elevator was wrecked, the three-man crew of the Avenger were killed, as of course was the Japanese pilot, and two more Avengers and seven fighters on the flight deck also went up in flames; blazing petrol poured over the AA gun positions and over the sailors manning them. Luckily, despite being wounded and temporarily knocked unconscious, Chief Ship's Fitter William Brooks was again able to turn on the sprinkler system and prevent the machines in the hangar from catching alight.

Suwanee's fires burned for several hours and she later also suffered an 'orthodox' bomb hit forward, but her determined crew finally extinguished the flames. Even so, her misfortunes on this and the previous day had cost her 143 officers and men killed or missing and 102 injured, some of whom died later. Among those lost was Lieutenant Premo who was badly burned when getting help for some injured officers and men, including Captain Johnson, trapped on the bridge; they were duly rescued but Premo died a few hours later. Another even more poignant sacrifice is described by Professor Morison, quoting *Suwanee*'s executive officer – the equivalent of a Royal Navy first lieutenant – Commander Van Mater:

> After several calls to have medical supplies brought to the forecastle for those seriously injured were unproductive of results, an enlisted man informed Chief Aviation Electrician's Mate C.N. Barr that he would try to get through the flames to get medical supplies because he could no longer stand the sufferings of the wounded. Despite Barr's efforts to stop him, the man climbed to the 20mm mounts just forward of the flight deck. A second later a torpedo-bomber directly in his path exploded and the man was seen holding on the starboard side of the flight deck with one leg blown off. A moment later he fell into the water and was not seen again. Every effort to ascertain his name has proved unavailing.

This was the last suicide attack in the Battle of Leyte Gulf. After days of frustration and disappointed hopes, the Kamikazes had finally participated: brilliantly, dramatically, effectively, and far too late.

Notes

1. In his *History of United States Naval Operations in World War II*, Volume XII, *Leyte June 1944–January 1945*.
2. Mr Vann Woodward was a University Professor of History before and after the war. During it he was an Intelligence Officer in the Office of the Chief of Naval Operations.
3. Leading the attacking Vals was Lieutenant Commander Mamoru Seki, the officer who later made a suicide dive into US aircraft carrier *Hornet*.
4. In the early months of the Pacific War, the Australians lost a number of warships, culminating in that of heavy cruiser *Canberra* on 9 August 1942 in the Battle of Savo Island in the Guadalcanal campaign. At the personal suggestion of Churchill, Britain presented *Shropshire*, a similar 8in-gunned cruiser, to the Royal Australian Navy, with which she gave distinguished service for the remainder of the conflict.
5. It may be that accounts of this episode later reached the Allies and prompted the suggestion that the hit on *Australia* was caused by a Kamikaze attack. However, not only was this made by a bomber, not a Zero, it occurred at 0605, whereas Kuno did not even take off until 1625.

Chapter 3

'A Splendid Opportunity to Die'

The Sho Plan had failed. The Battle of Leyte Gulf had been lost. Even on a simple count of warships sunk, the Imperial Navy had suffered a crushing defeat. The far larger American fleets had been deprived of 6 ships: 1 light carrier, 2 escort carriers, 2 destroyers and 1 destroyer escort, totalling almost 37,000 tons. The Japanese mourned the loss of fleet carrier *Zuikaku*, light carriers *Zuihō*, *Chiyoda* and *Chitose*, battleships *Musashi*, *Yamashiro* and *Fusō*, heavy cruisers *Atago*, *Maya*, *Chōkai*, *Chikuma*, *Suzuya* and *Mogami*, light cruisers *Abukuma*, *Tama*, *Noshiro* and *Kinu* and nine destroyers: twenty-six in all, of almost 306,000 tonnage.[1]

Yet the defeat went far beyond just the vessels sunk. It is true that the bulk of Kurita's battleships had escaped and, as a 'fleet in being', would present a threat to MacArthur and Kinkaid during their later operations in the Philippines. In reality, though, the destruction of so many supporting vessels meant that the surviving battleships could not be adequately defended. The battle, Admiral Nimitz confirms, 'had finally wiped out the Japanese fleet as an effective fighting force.'

This was only too apparent to the Japanese. Vice Admiral Ozawa would later report that after Leyte Gulf, Japanese 'surface forces became strictly auxiliary'. *Hyūga* and *Ise*, for example, the tough battleship-carriers, had defied the aerial might of Third Fleet and escaped with trivial damage during the battle, but were afterwards employed only in carrying loads of petrol from Singapore to the Japanese homeland. Most of Japan's remaining major warships were not used even on such secondary duties; they remained helplessly in harbour until eventually destroyed by the relentless American air attacks.

In addition, as Admiral Mitsumasa Yonai, the Japanese Navy Minister at the time of the battle, would admit after the war, 'our defeat at Leyte was tantamount to the loss of the Philippines.' This was just what the Sho Plan had been designed to prevent and when the gamble did not come off, Japan was faced with all those adverse consequences to which reference has already been made. Recognition of this prompted Yonai and most of Japan's leading naval officers to join her civilian ministers and the Emperor's advisers in urging that the war be brought to an end as soon as possible.

With certain important exceptions. As was mentioned earlier, most of those who formed the Kamikaze Corps had believed that this would exist only during the limited period when the Sho Plan was being followed. Whether Vice Admiral Ōnishi shared this view is questionable, but if he did, the failure of the plan changed his aims. Captain Inoguchi, pointing out to him that the Americans' victory had in effect secured their bridgehead on Leyte, queried: 'Should not the crash-dive tactics be stopped?' Ōnishi did not agree; he replied curtly and decisively: 'I honestly think that it is better for all concerned to continue the suicide operations.'

Some later accounts have portrayed Ōnishi's decision in impossibly lofty terms, claiming that the organizers of the Kamikaze missions 'fought for an ideal. Their road towards that ideal was "Bushidō", but the goal was "world peace".' To this, one can only echo the comment of Stan Smith in *The Battle of Leyte Gulf*: 'If a noble ideal such as "world peace" was their goal, Japan was taking the long way around.'

Indeed, Ōnishi personally made it quite clear that his goal was a Japanese victory; that this would presumably be followed by peace was coincidental. Moreover, now that Japan's navy had been neutralized and her air forces were in a very bad way, he felt that only by continuing and greatly expanding Kamikaze attacks could a Japanese victory be achieved. When informing Inoguchi of his decision, he gave his reasons as follows:

These young men with their limited training, outdated equipment, and numerical inferiority are doomed even by conventional fighting methods. It is important to a commander, as it is to his men, that death is not in vain. I believe therefore that a broad perspective indicates the wisdom of crash-diving tactics. To think otherwise would be taking a narrow view of the situation.

In fact many leading Japanese did take the 'narrow view', not least the Japanese Emperor. When the Chief of Naval Staff, Admiral Koshiro Oikawa, reported the Kamikaze successes of 25 October, tactfully making no mention of the losses suffered by the navy and the navy air force, Hirohito[2] did not approve. While praising the pilots for doing 'a magnificent job', he asked point- blank: 'Was it necessary to go to this extreme?'

Vice Admiral Ōnishi was very upset to learn of his Emperor's reaction, rightly considering it a criticism of his tactics. As a supposedly loyal servant of his sovereign, one might have expected him to reconsider. In practice, however, senior naval officers – and to an even greater extent, senior army officers – took notice of the Emperor's wishes only if they shared his views, which they rarely did. Their attitude is neatly summed up by Professor Richard Storry in *A History of Modern Japan*: 'They were loyal to their conception of what the emperor ought to be. To the emperor as he was they were grossly disloyal – and a few of the more sophisticated among them were well aware of this fact.' Ōnishi urged his followers to make every effort to assuage the Emperor's obvious concern, but this was to be done not by ending the Kamikaze strikes but by increasing their number and effectiveness.

Prince Takamatsu, younger brother of the Emperor and official head of the Military Affairs Bureau, was hostile towards not just Ōnishi's ideas but Ōnishi personally, believing that his outlook was dangerously mistaken and his abilities were greatly overrated. His opinions were strongly supported by his progressive wife Princess Kikuko, who incidentally was a granddaughter of the last Tokugawa Shōgun, and by officers with whom he came into contact. Many senior naval figures also strongly opposed the use of suicide attacks; among them may be mentioned Admiral Yanoi, Admiral Oikawa, Vice Admiral Ryunosuki Kusaka, Toyoda's chief staff officer, and Rear Admiral Sadatoshi Tomioka, the Naval General Staff's most brilliant and respected director of plans.

Ōnishi, though, simply ignored the views of those who disagreed with him. He did more: by forceful arguments and sheer weight of personality, he won over Admiral Toyoda and Vice Admiral Fukudome, both of whom had had reservations about the wisdom and morality of Kamikaze attacks. Fukudome indeed, while finally convinced that such operations were necessary and would be effective, remained uneasy about the damage they would do to his pilots' morale, but his doubts were soon removed by those same pilots.

As was mentioned earlier, reinforcements of aircraft and airmen soon reached the Philippines from Japan. Among these was the Twelfth Air Fleet and its men had already learned of the exploits of the Kamikazes and been uplifted by them. On arrival at Clark Field north of Manila on 26 October, they immediately asked to be incorporated into the Kamikaze Corps. Fukudome granted their wishes but still intended to use the pilots of his own Second Air Fleet just in conventional operations. They, however, were so desperately keen to participate in what were tactfully called 'special attacks' that on 27 October, 701st Air Group alone formed four new Kamikaze units.

After that, the Kamikaze movement became unstoppable. First, Second and Twelfth Air Fleets all joined forces to become the Combined Land-Based Air Fleet under Fukudome's command. Ōnishi became chief of staff and Captain Inoguchi remained responsible for conducting the Kamikaze missions. These soon became so numerous that they greatly outnumbered and largely replaced conventional air strikes.

Ōnishi had realized his first aim. Thanks to the spirit of his pilots, he could now hope, says Major General J.F.C. Fuller in *The Second World War 1939–1945*, 'to make good deficiency in technical superiority by an excess of valour unequalled in the history of war.' Major Frank Hough expresses Ōnishi's achievement more severely in *The Island War*: 'Kamikaze in its essence was simply large-scale organization of what had always been Japan's greatest military asset: the willingness of her men to die.'

Yet it must be repeated that the aim of Ōnishi and those who agreed with him was to win the war or at least obtain a favourable compromise peace. No doubt Ōnishi was pleased that his pilots were willing to die, but this made him all the more determined to see that they died effectively by inflicting the maximum damage on their enemies. Consequently he was much concerned with the training and the tactics of his Kamikazes.

During 1944, the training of any pilot was strictly limited by Japan's perennial shortage of petrol. Accidents ran literally into hundreds and those who survived were thrown into action with a minimum of flying hours behind them. In this respect Kamikaze training had an advantage in that it was, for instance, not necessary to teach these pilots skill in aerial combat or give them lengthy sessions of gunnery practice because it was their duty to avoid enemy fighters if at all possible, and if it was not, then to leave the fighting to their escorts. The first Kamikaze pilots had been very capable airmen, but the later ones normally had only limited flying ability and even less flying experience.

Indeed, the period of additional training for a Kamikaze pilot often lasted only seven days, in which the greatest emphasis was placed on take-offs and formation flying. Rapid take-offs were important because of the dangers of American air strikes when the Japanese aircraft were most vulnerable: on the runway or while getting into formation immediately afterwards. In addition, pilots who had not previously flown a Zero fitted with a bomb had to become accustomed to its different handling characteristics when it was. A close formation was also essential so that the escorting fighters could give proper protection to the attack aircraft and so that pilots with limited navigational training could be guided to their target by a more experienced leader.

Or, for that matter, could be guided back to base if their target could not be located. Some Americans believed that the aircraft the Kamikazes used for actual attacks were provided with only enough petrol for a one-way trip. In reality, the leaders of the special attack force never considered this as it would have meant the loss of men without anything to show for it. It seems likely, however, that some were still lost needlessly because they could not find their way home. We learn of one pilot from Clark Field, Luzon who failed to locate the enemy, lost contact with his flight in bad weather and finally landed – safely – in a field about 100 miles from his base.

For the last three days of their training, the Kamikaze pilots varied the monotony of take-offs and formation flying – though these still continued even now – by practising diving on a ground target while carrying a bomb. This they did with an enthusiasm that those watching frequently found terrifying. It is surprising that it did not terrify the pilots as well. In *Morning Glory: A History of the Imperial Japanese Navy*, Stephen Howarth relates the experiences of Ensign Yoshiki Shigihara, a Kamikaze trainee who was saved from death by the ending of the war:

> The young man would fly to 5,000 feet and go into a dive of 30° at 250 knots. At 2,500 feet he steepened the dive to 45°; and at 1,500 feet he steepened it again to 60° – still at 250 knots – and at less

than 200 feet he pulled through. That is, he pulled through if he had judged the height and speed absolutely accurately: there was a fraction of a second between life and an explosive, useless death on the ground, and three of Shigihara's colleagues killed themselves accidentally.

Undoubtedly it was fear of such mishaps that restricted the amount of attack practice given by the Kamikaze trainers. They expected their pupils to be killed, but this was only acceptable if they could wreck Allied warships in the process. The training did, however, include many lectures and discussions about the best ways in which this might be achieved.

The first question that had to be decided by the Kamikaze planners was how targets were to be approached. Japanese Intelligence had learned that US radar was least effective at very high and very low altitudes and the Kamikaze pilots were therefore directed to come in at one or other of these. Low-level attackers, flying close to the surface of the sea, were most likely to achieve complete surprise and were difficult for the Combat Air Patrol to sight or oppose. High-level raiders operated at between 20,000 and 23,000ft, at which altitude the aircraft had to be supplied with oxygen equipment and the aircrews trained in its use. They were easier to detect but they could be engaged by the defending fighters only after these had made a long climb to get at them, and they were out of range of the American AA guns with their lethal proximity-fused shells.

Whichever course of action was adopted, the pilots, having reached their objective, would quickly learn that it was no easy matter to hit a fast-moving warship swerving wildly in rapid evasive action. They would therefore have to decide how best to make their actual attacks. If they came in at low level, they could pretend to be delivering a torpedo strike; then at the last minute rise to between 300 and 500ft and make a shallow dive onto their target. Or they could climb earlier and more steeply to between 1,500 and 2,000ft before starting their dive. This was generally considered more likely to inflict serious damage, but it needed skilful airmanship and was not practised on the training course because the risk of accidents was very high.

In a high-level approach, the Kamikaze pilots also had two possible methods of attack. They could wait until they were directly above an enemy warship in its radar's 'blind spot', then come down vertically. A successful hit thus achieved could result in tremendous damage, but the aircraft's speed was such that it was easy for inexpert pilots to lose control or be unable to counter their target's alterations of course. Average pilots were therefore told to approach in a shallow dive of about 20°, preferably out of the sun, until they were at a height of 5,000ft, after which their angle of dive should increase steadily as described earlier. They did practise this type of attack in their training, so it was reasonable to assume it would ensure a high percentage of hits.

Since the Kamikaze pilots could remain in control of their machines up to the moment of impact, they were able to strike more accurately than any bomb or torpedo and there was much debate as to the best point on an enemy warship at which to aim. Carriers were still the priority targets. Some favoured hitting the funnel or the bridge, but the Kamikaze planners rightly urged that if possible their pilots should strike one of the carrier's elevators; this would give them the best chance of breaking through into the hangar and should at the very least reduce the target's operational effectiveness.

If there were no carriers present or the Kamikazes could not get at them as a result, for instance, of being damaged by fighters or AA fire, they were instructed in the best ways of harming alternative victims. In the case of battleships or cruisers, they were told to hit the bridge, thereby knocking out the vessel's control centre. By contrast, it was felt that destroyers, smaller warships and transports should be struck amidships; then the blow had a good chance of proving fatal, perhaps causing the target to break in half.

That so much thought went into the most effective ways of injuring their foes shows that the Kamikaze missions were not intended merely to cause 'senseless destruction and suffering' as Professor Morison has stated, still less that they were a reckless waste of lives as other American (and some Japanese) writers have maintained. They were sent out with the express objective of changing the course of the war and they came close to achieving that aim.

Certainly the Allied leaders did not regard the Kamikaze attacks as senseless. President Roosevelt was deeply concerned about them, believing that their use would prolong the war and in the meantime they were constantly killing forty or fifty American sailors for the loss of each Japanese pilot. He said as much to Lord Halifax, Britain's Ambassador to the United States, who passed on the information to Churchill, adding that Roosevelt was 'not looking too good'.

Churchill was equally worried by the threats posed by these new tactics and bombarded his naval advisers with queries as to how they could be mastered, together with fanciful and totally impracticable suggestions of his own. Most British and American naval officers entertained similar anxieties. Admiral Sir Bruce Fraser, Commander-in-Chief of the British Pacific Fleet – of whom and of which more will be heard in due course – called the Kamikaze raids 'the most dangerous form of attack so far developed.' Even American Admiral Raymond Ames Spruance, victor of the Battles of Midway Island and the Philippine Sea and the epitome of cool, calm decision, admitted privately that he 'fretted and worried' about the dangers the Kamikazes presented. Perhaps the most telling testament to their effect is that the existence of the Kamikazes was not revealed to the general public until 12 April 1945, nearly six months after their first assaults.

Post-war reports confirm that the Kamikaze attacks were far from senseless. *The United States Strategic Bombing Survey (Pacific War)* which came out in 1946, for instance, while clearly regarding the entire concept as somewhat disgusting, describes it as 'macabre, effective, supremely practical under the circumstances' and admits that the losses it inflicted 'were serious and caused great concern'.

Nonetheless, accepting as we must that the Kamikaze missions were effective, practical and, after their defeat at Leyte Gulf, the only real way the Japanese could strike at Allied warships and landing forces, most Europeans and Americans still look with horror at Ōnishi and the other leading Kamikaze commanders. Allied military and naval officers in the Second World War, while realizing that their men must suffer casualties, did their best to reduce these to a minimum. The Kamikaze leaders planned operations where it was desired and intended that their men would be killed. Yet if their position is fully analysed, there are good reasons why they should not be condemned too harshly.

In the first place, the formation and early rapid expansion of the Kamikaze Corps did not come about because it was desired by Japan's military and civilian rulers. As we have seen, many of these, even if recognizing its value, were unalterably opposed to the whole idea. Others only came to accept it with hesitation and resistance. Even when Ōnishi first formally proposed the organized use of suicide attacks, he did not order them but waited for the approval and confirmation of his officers. 'You can't order such a thing,' Captain Inoguchi declared after the war was over.

Instead the Kamikaze Corps was created and developed because the pilots who made up its personnel passionately desired this. The men of Twelfth Air Fleet who formed Kamikaze units without any prompting from their superiors and those of Second Air Fleet who formed them contrary to the intentions of their superiors give vivid examples of this desire. They did not wait even for a call for volunteers; they acted entirely on their own initiative.

During the early days of the Kamikaze Corps, there was in fact a quite remarkable absence of any form of pressure from above. It is true that Lieutenant Seki was specifically asked if he would undertake the leadership of the Corps but he was perfectly entitled to decline, had a good excuse for declining since his previous experience had been on bombers, not Zeros, and was given time to consider the matter. The men under him had already volunteered for Kamikaze duties before Seki was appointed. It will also be recalled that when Commander Nakajima formed the Kamikaze unit in Cebu, he was so far from putting pressure on his pilots that he specifically stated that he did not want them all to volunteer and conducted what was in effect a 'secret ballot' to ensure there would be no 'peer pressure' either.

Equally, Vice Admiral Ōnishi certainly did put pressure on Vice Admiral Fukudome, an officer of equal rank, strongly urging that Second Air Fleet should accept the principle of special attacks. He did not, however, adopt a similar attitude towards his subordinates. One such was Lieutenant Commander Tadashi Minobe, leader of a force of Nakajima Irvings – twin-engined, two-seater night-fighters – in the Philippines. Minobe's men were noted for their aggressive determination and there were instances of their ramming American bombers when out of ammunition. These attacks, though, were spontaneous, not ordered, and since the night-fighters' crewmen were equipped with parachutes, they could hope to and did save their own lives after achieving their unorthodox victories.

Minobe, indeed, was one of those who strongly opposed suicide attacks and openly made his opinions clear to everyone, including his superiors. His stance must have been very unwelcome to Ōnishi who had reason to believe that if Minobe's airmen were given the choice, the majority at least would volunteer to join the Kamikaze Corps. It is possible that Ōnishi 'pulled strings', for Minobe was eventually sent back to Japan where he commanded a fighter group with distinction for the rest of the war. It is certain that while Minobe was under his control, Ōnishi never took any steps or gave any orders that might result in Minobe's night-fighters taking part in suicide missions.

In fact, during the early days of the Kamikaze Corps, its leaders found much less difficulty in recruiting men to fly special attacks than they did in persuading men not to do so. It has been mentioned that the most experienced airmen were intended only to be escorts for the actual attackers. Saburō Sakai states bluntly that 'As a fighter pilot I was never inclined to approve the suicide missions.' No doubt there were others who, 'as fighter pilots', shared these views, but many of the finest did not and were far from pleased that they were not allowed to go on a 'one-way' flight.

Sakai's old friend and former comrade-in-arms Chief Warrant Officer Nishizawa certainly held a different opinion. As we have seen, he commanded the escort for Lieutenant Seki's flight that destroyed escort carrier *St Lo* on 25 October, and thereafter he and his two wingmen landed in Cebu. Here Nishizawa, inspired by Seki's action, went to Commander Nakajima under whom he, like Sakai, had served in the past, and volunteered to take part in a Kamikaze attack planned for the following day. Nakajima refused, later telling Sakai: 'I wouldn't let him go. A pilot of such brilliance was of more value to his country behind the controls of a fighter plane than diving into a carrier, as he begged to be permitted to do.'

Nishizawa, bitterly disappointed, agreed to hand over his Zero fighter and those of his wingmen to the Cebu Kamikaze unit. Sakai tells us that Nishizawa's own aircraft was armed with a 550lb bomb and, flown by Chief Petty Officer Katsumata, took part in the attack on Rear Admiral Thomas Sprague's 'Taffy 1' on 26 October, though whether it was the one that badly damaged escort carrier *Suwanee* as Sakai relates cannot be confirmed with certainty. On the same day, Nishizawa and his wingmen were evacuated in an old unarmed transport aircraft to Luzon where they could be provided with new Zeros. The transport was intercepted by Hellcats and everyone on board was killed.

On the following day, 27 October, another distinguished Japanese 'ace' arrived in Cebu. Lieutenant Naoshi Kanno was eventually credited with twenty-five 'kills', including a B-24 Liberator bomber that he rammed from behind, wrecking its rudder and causing it to crash, after which he successfully landed his own damaged aircraft. He had joined the 201st Air Group in the Philippines in late August 1944, but in October he temporarily returned to Japan to arrange the transfer of Zero reinforcements to Luzon. He was still away from the Philippines when the Kamikaze Corps was formed. Had he been present, he would have been offered the post of commanding officer (flying) instead of Seki. There is no doubt that he would have accepted, for he later expressed profound regret that he had been deprived of this high honour.

As it was, Kanno was entrusted with leading a flight of seventeen Zeros to the advanced Kamikaze base in Cebu on 27 November. On the way there the Zeros were intercepted by sixteen Hellcats but they drove these away, claimed to have shot down a dozen of them and lost only one man. On arrival, and thereafter in both Cebu and Luzon, we are told that Kanno 'pressed eagerly and insistently, formally and informally, to join a suicide unit.' His applications, however, were as persistently refused for the same reason as Nishizawa's had been: he was too valuable to lose. He was eventually transferred to the 343rd Air Group defending the Japanese homeland and was killed in action on 1 August 1945.

It should also be recorded to the credit of the Kamikaze organizers that while they would not permit men like Nishizawa and Kanno to join the Kamikaze Corps, they were quite prepared to allow their own relatives to do so. Captain Inoguchi had already lost his brother Rear Admiral Toshihira Inoguchi, who had been the skipper of battleship *Musashi* and had gone down with her during the Battle of Leyte Gulf. He now learned that his brother's son Lieutenant (junior grade) Satoshi Inoguchi was 'anxious to fly a Kamikaze mission'. Captain Inoguchi spoke to his nephew but did not attempt to dissuade him.

Vice Admiral Ōnishi had no children of his own, but his family was very close to that of a former classmate at the Naval Academy, Vice Admiral Takeo

Tada, Chief of the Naval Affairs Bureau and later Deputy Navy Minister. Ōnishi was particularly close to his friend's son Lieutenant (junior grade) Keita Tada, to whom he was an 'honorary uncle' and who addressed him by this title. The young man joined the Kamikaze Corps and visited Ōnishi to bid him farewell. After he had left, we learn that Ōnishi 'stood silently looking into the darkness for a long time.' He too had not tried to change the decision his 'nephew' had made.

Fate would decree that neither of these young airmen would realize their ambition of ramming an American warship. American fighters or American anti-aircraft guns shot down both of them before they could get at their targets, Inoguchi on 3 November and Tada on the 19th. This, though, in no way alters their unselfish determination or the steadfast devotion to duty of Vice Admiral Ōnishi and his chief staff officer.

Had their elders attempted to prevent their joining the Kamikaze Corps, there is no doubt that Inoguchi and Tada would have been extremely annoyed. Captain Inoguchi and other leading staff officers of the Corps survived the war and in later accounts or replies to American interrogators, they made it clear that they felt no shame or pangs of conscience for the decisions they had taken or the orders they had issued. On the contrary, they were surprised that anyone could ever have thought this. They pointed out that the only time their decisions were queried was when they rejected a volunteer because he was considered more useful in other duties, like Nishizawa and Kanno, or for family reasons such as his being an only son; and the only time their orders were resented was when they forbade a man to take part in a particular Kamikaze operation, for example on the grounds of inexperience.

Commander Nakajima, like Captain Inoguchi, survived the war and has given detailed accounts of how he was harried by airmen demanding that they be sent on suicide missions as soon as possible, or pleading that they be the ones chosen for an operation where numbers were restricted by a shortage of aircraft. Those who were not selected would shout 'Unfair! Unfair!' or complain that their chosen colleagues were getting 'special favours'. On one occasion when some thirty pilots but only five Zeros were available, Nakajima silenced protestors by telling them not to be 'so selfish'. When the Zeros took off, each of the pilots shouted to him: 'Thank you very much Commander!' or 'Thank you for choosing me!'

Of course it can be argued that Inoguchi, Nakajima and other officers making similar statements would naturally wish to emphasize that no pressure was put on the men to whom they gave their orders. Yet the assertions of the organizers are corroborated in every respect by the last letters that the pilots sent home. For instance, Nakajima, describing how he had had to instruct a young officer to stand down from a night operation because he was untrained for this, states that both he and the man's replacement Chief Petty Officer Shioda 'felt sorry' for him. In his last letter, Cadet Jun Nomoto, reporting how a fellow cadet had been dropped from the list of those assigned to take part in a suicide attack, declares: 'Cannot help feeling sorry for him.'[3] With the aid of the pilots' letters, supported by the statements of the organizers and remembering always the influences of Japan's medieval history, it may be permissible to try to explain the Kamikazes' motives and attitudes. Of course the pilots were individuals whose attitudes varied and whose motives were often mixed. Certain points, however, appear to be beyond dispute.

All Kamikaze pilots, without exception, were devoted patriots. Their outlook is summed up by Ensign Heiichi Okabe who declares: 'We shall serve the nation gladly in its present painful struggle. We shall plunge into enemy ships cherishing the conviction that Japan has been and will be a place where only lovely homes, brave women and beautiful friendships are allowed to exist.'

Japan was now threatened by the remorseless American advance and the Kamikazes were united in their desire to defend her and turn the tide of war. With Japan they frequently coupled their Emperor, sometimes to the confusion of Western observers. Thus Lieutenant Seki records that he will ram an aircraft carrier 'to repay the Imperial Benevolence'. Ensign Susumu Kaijitsu expresses his desire 'to reciprocate the grace which His Imperial Majesty has bestowed upon us.' 'I shall be a shield for His Majesty,' says Chief Petty Officer Isao Matsuo, 'and die cleanly along with my squadron leader and other friends. I wish that I could be born seven times, each time to smite the enemy.' 'We must give our lives to the Emperor and country,' Captain Inoguchi explains to his interrogator, 'that is our inborn feeling.'

Inoguchi was talking to an American and therefore felt it necessary to refer to both 'Emperor and country'. Among Japanese this duality would not have been needed, for Emperor and country were virtually synonymous. Far more than other heads of state, the Japanese ruler symbolized the unity of his people, while the longevity of the Imperial Family 'unbroken through ages eternal' represented Japan's uniqueness as a nation.

Again we can turn to a letter by a Kamikaze pilot for a summary and confirmation of this attitude. Ensign Teruo Yamaguchi was not impressed by the 'deceits' of 'our wily politicians' and had found service life 'certainly not comfortable', yet he proclaims unhesitatingly:

> The Japanese way of life is indeed beautiful, and I am proud of it, as I am of Japanese history and mythology which reflect the purity of our ancestors and their belief in the past – whether or not those beliefs are true. That way of life is the product of all the best things which our ancestors have handed down to us. And the living embodiment of all wonderful things out of our past is the Imperial Family which too, is the crystallization of the splendour and beauty of Japan and its people. It is an honour to be able to give my life in defence of these beautiful and lofty things.

It is not unfair to point out that there might be ways other than suicide attacks in which Japan and her Emperor could be defended. As we have seen, these operations did not meet with the approval of men as aggressive and determined as Minobe or as capable and courageous as Sakai. For that matter they did not win the approval of the Emperor or the Imperial Family. Even Lieutenant Seki had doubts as to whether an experienced pilot like himself might perhaps have been of more value as a trainer, though he was not the 'reluctant hero' that some have suggested; Inoguchi states unequivocally that Seki did not just agree to become the Kamikazes' commanding officer (flying), but said: 'You absolutely must let me do it.'

Vice Admiral Ōnishi and those who shared his views, however, were totally sincere in their belief that Japan could be saved only by suicide attacks. That their outlook was not unreasonable is shown by its having been accepted by ardent young men from important families who were products of the Naval Academy or had had a high standard of education: 70 per cent of those whose letters have been or will be quoted were university graduates.

Acceptance of the Kamikaze creed meant for these men a willingness to die, and no doubt there were many reasons why they reached that state of mind. Despite the inevitable hatred of the enemy that war always engenders, the men of the Imperial Navy could always respect and admire valiant foes. At the beginning of the war, a Japanese naval aircraft dropped a wreath of flowers over the seas where *Prince of Wales* and *Repulse* had gone down. As late as the Battle of Leyte Gulf, survivors of US destroyer *Johnston* on rafts or swimming nearby saw the captain of the Japanese destroyer that had sunk her standing at the salute in instinctive recognition of her gallantry. Nonetheless, his uncle's account makes it reasonably clear that Lieutenant Inoguchi joined the Kamikaze Corps because it gave him the best chance of squaring accounts for his father, and presumably others will have had similar thoughts.

Then there were pilots who felt that they would not be useful for much longer and that a Kamikaze attack would be the best way in which they could harm the enemy while they were still capable of doing so. Commander Nakajima quotes the case of Lieutenant Yuzo Nakano who suffered from tuberculosis and had only just come out of hospital. He had no idea if and when he would have a relapse that would render him unfit for service. He therefore requested that he be sent on a suicide mission as soon as possible, and his wish was granted.

A variation on this theme is revealed by Saburō Sakai concerning his fellow 'ace' Nishizawa, who it will be recalled had wanted to make a Kamikaze strike but had been considered too valuable to lose. Commander Nakajima, who took the decision, quickly regretted it. He later told Sakai that Nishizawa 'was convinced that he would die soon', that he 'had a premonition. He felt he would live no longer than a few days.' Nishizawa was right. As related earlier, he died in an unarmed transport aircraft the very next day.

Another motive was definitely rooted in Japan's feudal past. Her obviously perilous position could suggest that her fighting men had been inadequate in the performance of their duty. It had always been traditional for a warrior to atone for failure by suicide. So now some pilots probably felt morally obliged to die, thereby removing any stain of disgrace. What better way of making good their error than by taking their own lives and simultaneously bringing benefit to their threatened country? It would appear that Ensign Okabe had this motive. He certainly believed that Japan had little prospect of winning the war and it would probably be better for her people if she did not, because they would then be 'tempered through real ordeals which will serve to strengthen.' Yet at the same time he was willing to fly on a suicide mission, writing: 'The training and practice have been rigorous, but it is worthwhile if we can die beautifully and for a cause.'

Most Kamikaze pilots, however, did consider, like their leaders, that Japan could still win the war and their attacks were the means by which she would do so. Commander Nakajima states that his men had a 'firm conviction' that they would 'help defeat the enemy'. As usual the pilots' letters home provide confirmation, although it seems that they took Japan's triumph so much for granted that they mention it only briefly in passing. Thus Ensign Ichizo Hayashi remarks that: 'Morale is high as we hear of the glorious successes achieved by our comrades who have gone before.' Later he adds: 'From all reports it is clear that we have blunted the actions of the enemy. Victory will be with us.' Ensign Kaijitsu expresses his belief still more simply: 'I am confident that my comrades will lead our divine Japan to victory.'

In these circumstances, just as it had been the duty of the samurai to do battle for their lord, sacrificing their own lives without question if the need arose, so the Kamikaze volunteers instinctively felt it was their duty to do battle for their country and their Emperor and the need to sacrifice their lives in this great cause had already arisen. 'If the pilots had entertained a hope of survival,' declares Captain Inoguchi, 'their determination and singleness of purpose would have weakened. This would lessen their chance of success in hitting the target, and they would but die in vain.' The Kamikaze sorties, reports Commander Nakajima, 'were a routine matter. There were no theatrics or hysterics. It was all in line of duty.'

Yet it is one thing to state coldly that attacks of this nature were likely to prove most profitable, but quite another to expect men to carry them out in the certain knowledge that whatever they achieved, their own lives would be forfeited. Inoguchi acknowledges that the desire to live is the strongest one of all, and a fear of death is instinctive and natural. The Kamikaze pilots, though, displayed a strength of mind that enabled them to overcome any fear. No wonder then that those not of Japanese blood have found this astonishing.

Ensign Shigihara described to Stephen Howarth the way the Kamikazes mastered their feelings:

> Each day a list would be posted bearing the names of those who were to fly their last, their only mission. Each day, as men consulted the list, fear would flutter in their stomachs; and, with every man whose name came up, Shigihara saw an identical reaction. The chosen man would stiffen, turn pale and walk away in silence; then a short time later he would be seen again, laughing, joking, doing his normal work in an utterly normal manner. It was as if the moment of death was not the impact on an enemy ship, but the icy second of recognizing his own name. Thereafter, nothing seemed to matter; and there was never any thought of altering one's allotted fate. But, when the moment of impact on an enemy ship actually came, many Americans saw the pilots throw their hands over their faces to cover the last instant.

Furthermore, Shigihara joined the Kamikaze Corps late in the war – it ended in time to ensure his survival – and by then Japan's situation was still more desperate and, as we shall see, the original purely voluntary nature of the Corps had been diluted. For most of its existence, the reaction of its members on being chosen for a mission was not acceptance but exultation. This was so great that it was never quenched by postponements or abortive sorties that would sometimes result in weeks or months elapsing before a pilot finally died in action.

Any thoughts that these comments reflect only propaganda statements or excuses put forward by those who ordered suicide attacks must again be dispelled by the pilots' final letters to their families. 'I have never felt better and am now standing by, ready for action,' Ensign Kaijitsu remarks cheerfully. 'I slept well last night; didn't even dream,' comments Lieutenant (junior grade) Nobuo Ishibashi: 'Today my head is clear and I am in excellent health.' 'I am in the best of health at this last moment,' Cadet Nomoto – who dictated this letter to a friend immediately before take-off – tells his parents:

'It is a great honour to have been selected for this duty.' 'Dear Parents: please congratulate me,' says Chief Petty Officer Matsuo on his own 'last day', 'I have been given a splendid opportunity to die.'

It was perhaps easier for the Japanese to hold such views because death for them was not so terrible or so final as for Europeans or Americans. They believed that the souls of the dead remained in close contact with the living as well as with each other and there is little doubt that this was a comfort to the Kamikazes as to other Japanese. 'Though my body departs,' Kaijitsu tells his family, 'I will return home in spirit and remain with you forever.' 'I shall return in spirit,' Matsuo assures his parents, 'and look forward to your visit at the Yasukuni Shrine.'

The Yasukuni Shrine, it will be recalled, was where the souls of warriors who fell in battle congregated; all warriors, not just Kamikazes who had no special privileges in death. Nonetheless, the Kamikazes were very interested in the final abode of their spirits and often discussed or made jokes about it. Commander Nakajima advised his men that at the Yasukuni Shrine, 'precedence is determined entirely by time of arrival.' This prompted much banter to the effect that they would then outrank him and a suggestion that he be made mess sergeant 'was greeted with roars of approving laughter'. Sensing the mood of the occasion, Nakajima pleaded for better treatment and finally won the concession that he be the mess officer.

Commander Nakajima never did qualify for admittance to the Yasukuni Shrine. Neither did Ensign Shigihara, since to his regret and some shame he was saved from death by the close of hostilities. Like most other would-be suicide attackers similarly prevented from carrying out their missions, he would pay regular visits to the shrine to pray for 'the souls of all those who succeeded where he failed.'

One of the Kamikaze pilots quoted held very different views, however, so he deserves to be examined more closely. Ensign Ichizo Hayashi was a Christian. This faith had been viciously persecuted in Japan's feudal period and, being the religion of her enemies, was not regarded with favour during the Second World War. So although Hayashi was popular with his comrades and had impressed his superiors that he 'had the makings of a first-class pilot', he took care that the crucifix he wore was kept out of sight under his shirt. As a Christian, he had no regard for the Yasukuni Shrine and believed suicide to be a sin, for which he asked forgiveness.

Yet Hayashi was first and foremost a Japanese. He was completely determined to strike a blow against his country's enemies. He could easily have visited his mother, to whom he was very close, before his final mission, but he declined to do so, saying it was enough to have sent her his farewells in writing; presumably he feared a meeting with her might have weakened his resolution. He endured the morale-sapping ordeals of having two operations for which he had been chosen cancelled and lengthy delays before he took off for the last time. In the letter that was sent on to his mother afterwards, he declared:

> I am going to score a direct hit on an enemy ship without fail. When war results are announced you may be sure that one of the successes was scored by me. I am determined to keep calm and do a perfect job to the last, knowing that you will be watching over me and praying for my success. There will be no clouds of doubt or fear when I make the final plunge.

This was a typically Japanese attitude that is echoed by those of his fellow-countrymen who did not share his religious convictions. In the letters written when they were about to die, the Kamikazes, apart from requests to look after relatives, appear anxious only to give assurances that they will die effectively. 'I feel confident of my ability in tomorrow's action,' reports Cadet Nomoto. 'Will do my utmost to dive head-on against an enemy warship to fulfil my destiny in the defence of the homeland.' 'My greatest concern,' reflects Ensign Kaijitsu, 'is not about death, but rather of how I can be sure of sinking an enemy carrier.'

Indeed the Kamikazes' only fear was not of death but of failure. Pilots of aircraft that were grounded by some mechanical defect were inconsolable. So were the ground crews responsible for the machines in question, since like those of other air forces they were steadfast in their loyalty to and their support of the men who flew the aeroplanes they serviced. Commander Nakajima relates the story of Ensign Masahisa Uemura who desperately wanted to volunteer for Kamikaze duties but felt he 'was not a good enough flyer.' Nakajima told him not to worry: 'I'll find a chance for you.' I saw him smile then for the first time in three days, Nakajima reports. 'He bowed deeply and said, "Thank you sir. I will be waiting".'

This thirst for success undoubtedly helped the pilots, for it ensured that they remained too busy to have time for depression or gloomy reflections; they constantly attended lectures and had frequent discussions among themselves, all designed to help their attacks to cause as much harm as possible. Nakajima tells us of Ensign Tatsuya Kariyama who gladly joined ... talk of old times and shared experiences, but refused to ... explaining: 'Sorry, but I am going on a suicide attack ... to be in top condition.' When Kamikaze assaults were ... often saw pilots break off an attack and instead dive ... they had just spotted, or make more than one ... so as to be certain of inflicting serious injuries. ... assaults were made, particularly in the earlier ... the pilots had considerable confidence ... their lives

Moreover, when Kami... days of their organization's existence, the pilots ... that their studies and their training would enable them to sell ... with the maximum benefit to their country and the maximum detriment to their enemies. They were not apathetic or fatalistic, they were exultant: this was their greatest moment. Lieutenant (junior grade) Ishibashi relates: 'I think of springtime in Japan while soaring to dash against the enemy.' Chief Petty Officer Matsuo, a member of a Judy squadron, announces: 'We are sixteen warriors manning the bombers. May our deaths be as sudden and clean as the shattering of crystal.'

These then were the thoughts and motives of the men who formed the Imperial Navy's last fighting unit, who brought death and destruction to an immensely powerful foe and who, as even an opponent of the Kamikaze Corps like Saburō Sakai acknowledges, gave Japan 'tremendous new strength'.

Notes

1. Light cruiser *Kinu* and two of the destroyers had been among the vessels carrying reinforcements to Leyte. All three had been sunk by air attacks.

2. His name should be pronounced 'Hiroshto'.

3. The experiences of Captain Rikihei Inoguchi and Commander Tadashi Nakajima are contained in *The Divine Wind* of which they were co-authors together with Roger Pineau, one of those responsible for *The United States Strategic Bombing Survey (Pacific War)* and later an assistant of Professor Morison. The letters were collected over a period of four and a half years after the war by a Mr Ichiro Ohmi. Many are included in *The Divine Wind* and examples can also be found in *Divine Thunder: The Life and Death of the Kamikazes* by Bernard Millot, in *Kamikaze: Japan's Suicide Gods* by Albert Axell and Hideaki Kaze, and in *Kamikaze: To Die For The Emperor* by Peter C. Smith.

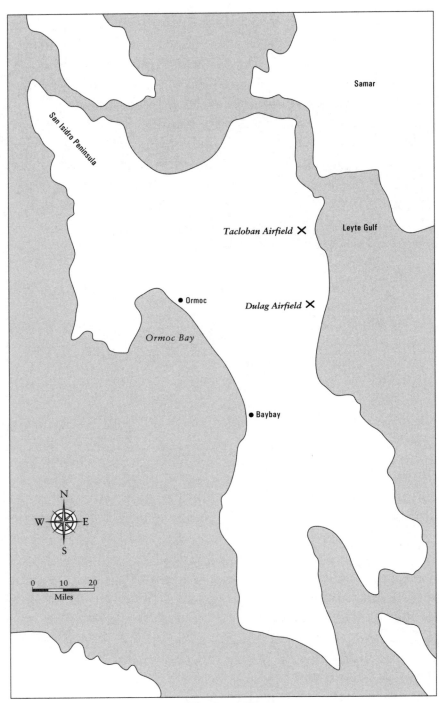

Map II – Leyte.

Chapter 4

The Fall of the Philippines

'Douglas, where do we go from here?' President Roosevelt had queried at one of the conferences preceding the American invasion of the Philippines. 'Leyte, Mr President,' replied General MacArthur, 'and then Luzon!' Victory in the Battle of Leyte Gulf had ensured that his troops were firmly established on the first of these islands, but it would be many weeks before they could move on to Luzon. While the great battle was being fought, the Japanese had put 2,000 men ashore at Ormoc Bay, and after it was over, destroyers and smaller craft continued to provide Lieutenant General Sosaku Suzuki with reinforcements of men and equipment for his dogged defence of Leyte.

They did this at heavy cost since American carrier-based aircraft continued to assault all enemy vessels sighted. At the same time, however, Third and Seventh Fleets endured an unpleasant ordeal at the hands of the Kamikazes, though not one approaching that of 25 October. On the 27th, the first day after the battle, for example, a series of suicide aircraft, chiefly from Nichols Field, Luzon, took off for Leyte Gulf but achieved no successes whatsoever.

Among the raiders was a flight of three Judys from the 701st Air Group led by Lieutenant Naoji Fukabori. On the way, he discovered that the fuse of his bomb was defective, so he landed at the airfield at Legaspi in the extreme south-east of Luzon and immediately north of the San Bernardino Strait in order to rectify the problem. It was late afternoon before he had done so and by the time he reached Leyte Gulf, the sun had set and it was too dark for him to detect any targets. He therefore flew to Cebu, where he found the aerodrome threatened by a pair of American intruders. He had to circle overhead until they left the area, but finally touched down safely. When urged not to complete his mission until other Kamikazes could accompany him, he quietly but firmly replied that his comrades had already performed their tasks and he must carry out his own early next morning.

Before retiring to sleep, Fukabori composed his 'last letter', this one addressed not to his family but to his superiors. In it he calmly and intelligently set out the lessons he thought could be learned from his experiences. He regarded the timing of a Kamikaze attack as most important, explaining that it was impossible to locate suitable targets after dark, but a raid at either dawn or dusk should take the defending fighters by surprise. In these circumstances, even elderly Val dive-bombers could be used for Kamikaze strikes; as indeed they would be, if nowhere near as often or as effectively as the Judys that had largely replaced them. He suggested a deliberate adoption of his own involuntary action of proceeding to Cebu prior to making an attack; then not only could this be timed more precisely but the attackers would have more petrol in their tanks, thus causing more damage when it was ignited on impact.

Fukabori ended his report with a plea and a promise. The former was that Kamikaze pilots should not be impatient but should choose their victim carefully and wait for a favourable moment. The latter was a declaration that 'The good faith of our pilots makes me confident that the Imperial prestige will last forever. Our pilots are young but their behaviour is brilliant.'

Next morning, Fukabori set off on his solo attack, though the Cebu unit did provide him with a four-strong fighter escort. Rather sadly, it appears that he enjoyed scant success. Japanese sources suggest that he attacked light cruiser *Denver*, but it may be that her damage was caused by a large orthodox bombing raid on this same day. In any event, the damage was only slight. Fukabori's attempt was, however, only the start of another flurry of Kamikaze missions.

The first of these came next day: 29 October. Some Allied warships seemed to be the favourite targets of Japanese airmen for no particular reason. One of these was the fleet carrier *Intrepid*. In February 1944, she had participated in highly successful US raids on the Japanese base at Truk, but had been hit and badly damaged by an enemy torpedo-bomber. At Leyte Gulf she had been the flagship of Rear Admiral Gerald Bogan and had played a distinguished role, as both Kurita and Ozawa could have testified. On this 29 October, her aircraft and those of two other carriers had made offensive sweeps over the Manila area, claiming to have destroyed seventy-one Japanese aircraft in combat and thirteen on the ground against the loss of ten Hellcats.

Nonetheless, *Intrepid* was not a lucky ship as the hit at Truk, the only one suffered by a US carrier in that operation, showed. On 29 October, she became the first fleet carrier to be struck by a Kamikaze, which had apparently followed her aircraft as they returned from their raid and thereby eluded the Combat Air Patrol. The damage was slight but *Intrepid* had ten men killed and six more wounded, and this would not be the last time that she was made the target for Ōnishi's men, whose unwelcome attentions would give her the unkind nickname of 'The Evil I'.

On 30 October, six Zeros from Cebu eluded the CAP because their height was underestimated and although they faced heavy AA fire, two of them broke through to strike fleet carrier *Franklin* and light carrier *Belleau Wood*. *Franklin* had a casualty list of fifty-six dead and fourteen wounded, and thirty-three of her aircraft were destroyed. *Belleau Wood* lost only twelve aircraft, but ninety-two of her crew were killed and fifty-four injured. Both had to return to the Americans' advanced base at Ulithi for extensive repairs. The bulk of Task Force 38 followed them for a short and well-deserved rest, leaving only Rear Admiral Bogan's three 'flat-tops' in the Leyte area.

A good part of Seventh Fleet also retired temporarily but on 1 November, those vessels that remained became the objective of a whole series of Kamikaze attacks. The organizers of the Corps had devised a new way of deceiving Allied warships: they sent off raids of both Kamikazes and orthodox bombers more or less simultaneously in the early morning. American destroyer *Killen* was hit by a bomb that caused damage and flooding but destroyer *Bush*, though subjected to eight separate conventional attacks, manoeuvred so cleverly that she escaped unharmed. She would not always be so fortunate.

Of course the Kamikazes could not be completely denied. The sharp-shooting HMAS *Shropshire* had now created a system of firing her 8in guns at the special attack aircraft which, by the way, the Australians named 'zombies'. As David Mattiske relates: 'We fired a high-explosive shell set to explode at 1,500 yards, and a shell that size, even exploding within 250ft of a Jap, was enough to throw him off course, and if we got reasonably close was enough to bring him down.' Unfortunately, he tells us, on 1 November, 'one of our early successes turned nasty.' A suicide pilot, thrown off course when heading for *Shropshire*, dived at US destroyer *Claxton* instead; he near-missed her but he came so close that his wing decapitated a luckless AA gunner and his bomb exploded as he hit the water, causing serious damage and flooding.

Claxton's attacker had been a Val dive-bomber, as Lieutenant Fukabori had suggested, but not long afterwards, another *Shropshire* success 'turned nasty' when she was attacked by a type of aircraft not previously used for suicide raids: a twin-engined Yokosuka Frances bomber. *Shropshire*'s gunners set this on fire, but it crashed into the superstructure of US destroyer *Ammen*, knocking off most of her forward funnel and half the after one, killing five men and wounding twenty-one more.

The Kamikazes attacked with Vals again on the afternoon of 1 November. One was hit by AA fire but plunged on and smashed into US destroyer *Abner Reed*, exploding a magazine and leaving her dead in the water, listing badly and covered in a huge column of smoke that rose thousands of feet into the air. Her skipper, Commander Purdy, ordered torpedoes to be jettisoned but in the confusion they were fired instead, causing battleship *Mississippi* and HMAS *Shropshire* to take hasty and happily successful avoiding action. 'Abandon ship' was then ordered and shortly afterwards *Abner Reed* rolled over and sank by the stern. Other destroyers, including *Claxton*, were so prompt and efficient in their rescue work that she lost only twenty-two men.

On 5 November, the bulk of Task Force 38 returned to the Leyte area with Vice Admiral John McCain taking over command from the understandably exhausted Mitscher. He received a warm, if not friendly welcome from the Kamikaze Corps in the form of four Zeros from Mabalacat, Luzon. These broke past the CAP and though three were downed by her anti-aircraft guns, the remaining one dashed itself into the superstructure of McCain's flagship, the carrier *Lexington*.[1] She extinguished her fires within twenty minutes and continued to conduct flight operations but 50 dead or missing and 132 wounded were added to the grim total of the casualties caused by the Imperial Navy's modern samurai.

American warships suffered no further Kamikaze attacks for almost three weeks, a fact illustrating the greatest flaw in suicide tactics. Kamikaze pilots were a wasting asset. The original batch of enthusiastic, skilful volunteers had died in action. A training school for their replacements had been set up in Formosa and small groups of capable pilots continued to volunteer for special attacks in the Japanese homeland, but until men from these sources reached the Philippines, the Kamikaze Corps would not be fully effective. It was a problem that would face the leaders of the Corps throughout its entire existence.

Not that the Americans had much respite during those three weeks. In some respects the situation became even more unpleasant. True to their samurai heritage, the Kamikaze pilots preferred to engage warships which they considered worthy opponents, but now that they were temporarily of a less high standard, their organizers began to direct them against transports and auxiliary vessels that were not so strong or so well-armed. These were, in fact, desirable targets because not only were they easier to hit but they enabled the Japanese to inflict serious losses which they hoped might make their enemies more likely to agree to a compromise peace.

Already on 3 November, the first troopship had fallen victim to the Kamikazes. The *Matthew P. Deady* had been rammed by a suicide bomber off Leyte and lost 59 dead and more than 100 injured. On 5 November, the repair ship *Achilles* was damaged by a suicide attacker, suffering heavy casualties, forty-three of them fatal. On the 12th, five transports of various types were hit, among them the *Jeremiah M. Daily* and the *Thomas Nelson*, both of which were packed with army personnel; they lost almost 150 and more than 230 men killed or wounded respectively. Attacks on 17 and 19 November saw four more cargo vessels damaged, and these would continue to become targets for the Kamikaze Corps throughout the rest of the war.

By 25 November, however, experienced reinforcements had reached the Corps from both Japan and Formosa. Some Japanese officers argued that it would be better to continue the assaults on the vulnerable transports but the Kamikaze organizers and pilots alike were eager to resume their strikes on Allied warships. On the 25th, therefore, under the command of Lieutenant Kimiyoshi Takatake, a force of more than thirty suicide attackers plus escorting fighters set out against the mighty Task Force 38.

If the Task Force's seamen had relaxed in the belief that the worst was now over, they would have been horribly disillusioned by the series of ferociously determined attacks that began soon after 1230 and lasted for just over half an hour. The Combat Air Patrol did its best to intervene; it intercepted one group of six Zeros making for carrier *Hancock*, and apparently shot down five of them since only one made its dive on her. This was blown to pieces by her AA guns and only a blazing wing fell on her flight deck, starting a small fire that was quickly extinguished.

Inevitably, though, some of the raiders broke past the CAP with unpleasant results. Carrier *Essex* became the target of a pair of Judys. She shot down one at a safe distance but the other, although hit repeatedly, continued its dive and crashed on top of two of the 20mm gun mountings that had been firing at it, demolishing them and killing or fatally wounding fifteen crewmen. Happily, the carrier was not seriously harmed.

Others fared less well. A Kamikaze who chose to attack *Intrepid* defied her fierce AA fire and crashed into and through her flight deck, which was buckled by the explosion of his bomb.

Another hit and badly damaged the flight deck of light carrier *Cabot*. A third also attacked *Cabot* and narrowly missed her, tearing a 6ft hole in her hull. Despite her injuries and the loss of thirty-six of her crew dead and sixteen others wounded, *Cabot* stayed in formation and was able to resume flight operations an hour later.

Intrepid was less fortunate. Already on fire and in trouble, she attracted the attention of another pilot who struck her at a shallow angle; his Zero disintegrated, scattering blazing fragments in all directions, but his bomb went on into the hangar where it exploded, causing further fires. *Intrepid*'s damage control parties had contained these some fifteen minutes later and she also remained in formation, but her casualties amounted to sixty-nine dead or missing and thirty-five wounded, while her injuries meant that seventy-five of her warplanes that were already airborne could not land back on her. They later flew to Tacloban airfield on Leyte and *Intrepid* retired to Ulithi for repairs.

Most of Task Force 38 also withdrew temporarily from Philippine waters, so the Kamikaze Corps redirected its efforts against Seventh Fleet. On 27 November, a flight of apparently only five suicide attackers plus four escorts took full advantage of the bad weather that had grounded the CAP. One rammed battleship *Colorado* amidships and another one near-missed her. Light cruiser *Montpelier* shot down a Kamikaze, but it bounced off the water and into her. Light cruiser *St Louis* was hit near the stern by two Kamikazes. All suffered casualties, thirty-five of them fatal, and *St Louis* in particular sustained serious damage, having her after turrets knocked out.

At sunset on the 29th, another small Kamikaze flight took similar advantage of the absence of the CAP. One pilot is reported to have given an impressive display of 'stunt flying' over battleship *Maryland*, presumably out of bravado, before plunging into her. He struck just between her two forward turrets, causing considerable damage and sixty-one casualties, thirty-one of them fatal. A pair of picket destroyers was also hit. *Saufley* suffered minor damage to her hull but *Aulick*, hit squarely amidships, had her bridge and much of her superstructure wrecked, two of her 5in guns knocked out, thirty-two men killed and sixty-four others injured.

This spate of successes gave considerable relief and encouragement to the leaders of the Kamikaze Corps, especially Vice Admiral Onishi, on whom strain and exhaustion had taken their toll. Furthermore, reports of them, often grossly exaggerated, stimulated another wave of enthusiastic volunteers. So it may seem surprising that there now occurred another lull in suicide operations. This, though, was caused not by a shortage of aircraft or of pilots as the Americans optimistically believed, but because the Japanese were conserving their strength to oppose a new American landing that their Intelligence had warned was imminent.

It had been General MacArthur's original intention to land on Mindoro Island, over 250 miles north-west of Leyte but immediately south of Luzon, on 5 December, thus providing a useful 'stepping stone' for the assault on the largest of the Philippine Islands. Lieutenant General Krueger and Vice Admiral Kinkaid had, however, persuaded him to postpone the Mindoro operation and instead use the Americans' amphibious units for action nearer to hand.

By this time, the American strength on Leyte had risen to over 183,000 and both the island's eastern and southern parts had been overrun. Yet the 35,000 Japanese defenders still held the western part of the island around the port of Ormoc and the north-western area known as the San Isidro Peninsula, and they were still resisting attacks from the south and north-east with their usual fierce determination. It was therefore decided to land in Ormoc Bay, thereby not only taking the Japanese in the rear but closing the route by which they had been receiving supplies and reinforcements. Fighter cover would be provided by P-38 Lockheed Lightnings from Tacloban airfield, Leyte.

Since heavy rains had greatly hampered American efforts to supply their forces in the south-west of Leyte, it was further decided that prior to the main Ormoc Bay operation, a transport unit of destroyers and amphibious craft would land reinforcements of men and equipment at Baybay, a small port on Leyte's west coast south of Ormoc that was already in American hands. This was duly carried out on the night of 4/5 December, but next day as the US vessels retired to Leyte Gulf, the Kamikazes reappeared. At least five were shot down by the Lightnings or the warships' guns, but destroyer *Drayton* was hit and suffered damage and casualties, a Landing Ship Medium (LSM) was hit and sunk and a second LSM was near-missed and so damaged that she had to be taken in tow.

Later that day, the transport unit again came under Kamikaze attack from a pair of Val dive-bombers. The protecting screen of Lightnings downed one of them, but the other took on destroyer *Mugford* and revealed a new Kamikaze trick. Instead of crashing into her with its bomb aboard, it first dropped its bomb – which missed – and then flew into her, causing damage that temporarily disabled her and started fires, though these were soon brought under control. This was a tactic that would be repeated on later occasions and cause some confusion, not least as to whether particular raiders had been Kamikazes or not. *Mugford* had two sailors killed and six others who subsequently died from burns.

This was not an encouraging omen for Rear Admiral Arthur Struble whose Ormoc Attack Group had been instructed to carry out the main landings on the early morning of 7 December. Fortunately the Japanese had anticipated that these would be made much further afield and consequently were taken by surprise. The Americans got ashore virtually unopposed and by 0900, just under two hours after the first troops had landed, the beachhead was declared secure.

Only then did the Japanese react, but they did so with a vengeance. Their weapon was the Kamikaze Corps and throughout the morning and early afternoon, this delivered a series of raids of such concentrated ferocity that the Lightnings were unable to intercept them all and at least one of Struble's destroyers used up its entire supply of ammunition. The tactic of releasing orthodox weapons, bombs or torpedoes, and then attempting to ram was again employed, as was a new trick of concentrating a very large number of aircraft against one particular target, thus swamping its AA gunners.

The first, strongest and fiercest onslaught commenced at 0945, and was made by twelve Frances bombers protected by four fighters. The Lightnings tried to intervene, but were held off by the escorts and could only damage two of the bombers. Three others, though, broke away and attacked USS *Ward*. She was now a destroyer transport, but before being converted to this role she had been a plain destroyer and had fired the first shots of the Pacific War when she shelled, depth-charged and sank a Japanese midget submarine attempting to penetrate Pearl Harbor.

Ward's luck had now run out. She shot down two of her attackers, but the third struck her squarely amidships and exploded, bringing her to a halt, blazing furiously. There were a few casualties, but none of them were fatal. The ship, though, was doomed. The fires were soon completely out of control; her crew reluctantly abandoned her, and she was finished off by shellfire from destroyer *O'Brien*. The *O'Brien*'s skipper, Commander William Outerbridge, must have performed this task with particular regret: as a young lieutenant his first command had been *Ward* and it was on his first patrol as her CO that he had sunk the midget.

Meanwhile, the rest of the bomber formation made a mass attack on another veteran of the Pacific War, destroyer *Mahan*. In the volume of his Official History dealing with the Leyte campaign, Professor Morison gives a breathtaking description:

> No. 1 burst into flames and splashed about 50 yards short of *Mahan*, knocked down by her machine-guns. No. 2 passed right over the ship. Nos. 3 and 4 bombers were shot down at a safe distance. No. 5 hit *Mahan* just abaft the bridge. No. 6 hit her at the waterline; and almost simultaneously No. 2, which had turned back, hit her

between waterline and forecastle deck. No. 7 contented itself with a thorough strafing, in the course of which it was splashed by the ship's gunfire. No. 8, already in flames from its conflict with the P-38s, tried to crash but splashed instead. No. 9 passed over the ship and disappeared. All this within four minutes.

Mahan, like *Ward*, was doomed. Fires raged and despite the efforts of her damage control parties could not be quenched. Again like *Ward*, *Mahan* had to be abandoned and was finished off by American gunfire. Of her crew, ten had been killed or were reported missing and thirty-two others were injured.

As mentioned earlier, the Kamikaze assaults on the Ormoc Attack Group continued well into the afternoon. The American AA gunners, sticking grimly to their posts, performed magnificently, and three destroyers and one destroyer transport were saved when Kamikazes were shot down or blown up at the last moment, but inevitably some broke through. Destroyer *Lamson* was hit and set badly on fire but survived and was towed to safety at a cost of twenty-one dead and fifty wounded. A Landing Ship Medium was hit and sunk and a Landing Ship Tank was near-missed and damaged. Also destroyer transport *Liddle* blew a Zero to pieces when it was only 30ft away, only to be rammed by another one, losing thirty-six killed or missing, including Lieutenant Commander Brogger, and twenty-two wounded.

Seventh Fleet had paid a high price for its success at Ormoc and would continue to suffer over the next few days, during which it kept the landing force supplied. The Kamikazes were as determined as ever and had come up with a different device for confusing their enemies: the employment of aircraft types not usually seen on suicide missions. On 19 December, it was Betty bombers which damaged destroyer *Hughes* and sank a transport, a Landing Craft Tank and a PT (motor torpedo) boat. On the 11th, it was Jill torpedo-planes, one of which crashed close to the starboard bow of destroyer *Reid*, starting a fire and causing severe underwater damage. Moments later, another Jill crashed into *Reid* near her stern and completed her destruction; she capsized and sank almost immediately with the loss of 103 men, 45 more being wounded.

On 12 December, the Kamikazes reverted to their favourite attack aircraft: the Zero. Destroyer *Caldwell*, which had shot down a suicider in the nick of time on the 11th, was not so fortunate on the 12th. The Kamikazes again varied their tactics. Most of the Zeros made orthodox bombing attacks on *Caldwell* and scored a hit, but one played the trick of dropping his weapon and then following it into the target. Both bomb and machine struck *Caldwell*, causing damage and fires. She survived, but with thirty-three of her men dead or missing and forty more injured.

Despite all this unpleasantness, Seventh Fleet's Ormoc operation had been worthwhile. As Lieutenant General Krueger later confirmed, it 'proved to be the decisive action' of the Leyte campaign. By Christmas Day, MacArthur could declare that organized resistance had ended and on the same day, General Yamashita directed Lieutenant General Suzuki to evacuate as many men as possible to protect other Philippine islands. That was not quite the end of the story. As Morison observes, 'Japanese unorganized resistance can be very tough.' Suzuki did not leave Leyte with his staff until March 1945 – he was killed by an American air-raid a few weeks later – and the last of his soldiers were eliminated only in early May. Samar, immediately north of Leyte, a larger island but strategically less important and so less well defended, had already been secured on 19 December.

Returning to mid-December, we find that in any case the spotlight was about to move away from Leyte. The Americans were now ready to make their bold push across the Philippines to Mindoro as a preliminary to their assault on Luzon. Rear Admiral Struble, who had conducted the Ormoc operation, was again in command and his transports and accompanying warships were given a covering force that included six of Seventh Fleet's escort carriers. All these vessels proceeded through the Surigao Strait, then sailed across the Mindanao Sea south of the Central Philippines into the Sulu Sea, where they would turn north and head up the west coasts of the islands of Negros and Panay to land at San José in the south-west corner of Mindoro.

Japanese Intelligence had again given warning of the Americans' intentions, though it was anticipated that they would invade Negros or Panay rather than Mindoro. The Kamikaze Corps was therefore ready for them. As the US vessels rounded the southern cape of Negros into the Sulu Sea shortly before 1500 on 13 December, a suicide bomber, defying heavy AA fire, crashed into the port side of Struble's flagship, light cruiser *Nashville*. It started fires, wrecked the bridge and the combat information and communications centres, killed or fatally injured 133 officers and men and wounded 190 others, including Struble and Brigadier General Dunckel, the officer in charge of the landing troops. Destroyer *Haraden* was also struck a couple of hours later. She got off comparatively lightly with fourteen dead and twenty-four wounded, but both warships had to retire to the repair facilities at Leyte Gulf.

It was another impressive illustration of the effectiveness of suicide strikes, and the Kamikazes' leaders were anxious to follow it up with a maximum effort on the 14th. Accordingly, the largest formation yet sent out in a single raid by the Kamikaze Corps and containing aircraft of types it had not previously used was hastily assembled and was sent out at 0730.

The raid was headed by two Nakajima Myrts – the Americans seem to have been running out of ladies' names – which were single-engined naval reconnaissance aircraft with a two- or three-man crew, a long range and a speed of almost 400 mph; attributes that made them ideally suited for this task. As escorts, there were not only thirteen Zeros but also twenty-three Kawanishi George fighters which, like the Myrts, had only recently entered service and had not been fully tested in combat. This was perhaps lucky for the Allies because the George had a top speed of 425 mph, was as manoeuvrable as any Zero and enjoyed the advantages of a more powerful armament, some armour plate to protect the pilot and self-sealing petrol tanks. Another significant difference from the Zero was that the George was solely land-based and could not operate from carriers; an indication of how Japan was now very much on the defensive.

To deliver the actual attacks, the Kamikaze organizers had gathered six Frances and three Judy bombers and seventeen bomb-carrying Zeros. This group could have inflicted considerable harm and the Americans were fortunate that it was never given the opportunity to do so. Bad weather, so often prevalent in the Philippines, denied the raiders any chance of finding their targets; then they encountered a strong formation of Hellcats which dispersed them. In increasingly poor visibility they were never able to reassemble; eventually they gave up and headed for a number of different and widely scattered landing-grounds. This meant that their superiors could not use them in a new mass attack next day, though at least they were individually available for later missions, with one exception.

Ensign Yonosuke Iguchi was the navigator of one of the Judys and the officer in charge of the Judy flight. He had been noted for the eagerness with which he had attended lectures and studied every aspect of suicide attacks. As it turned out, he was too eager. One lesson that had been learned was that pilots, in their excitement, quite frequently forgot to release the safety-pin of their bomb before ramming their target, with the result that it did not explode. Iguchi had obviously determined that he would not make this mistake and had already armed his weapon in preparation for his attack when it became clear that he was not going to locate the warships and transports he had been seeking.

In these circumstances, Iguchi was supposed to jettison the bomb, since it would almost certainly have exploded as the Judy landed. Unhappily, he quickly discovered that the bomb-release mechanism had jammed and would not operate. All attempts by Iguchi and his pilot, Petty Officer Takebe, to get rid of this lethal cargo failed, so Iguchi, like Lieutenant (junior grade) Kuno before him, decided to make for Leyte Gulf where he was sure he would find a suitable target. Sadly, again like Kuno, his hopes were in vain. Since his penultimate radio message confirmed that he had reached the Gulf and there were no enemy fighters in sight, he presumably fell victim to the AA gunners of the vessels in the Gulf who by now would have been very experienced and capable. His very last message was to wish long life – specifically 'ten thousand years' – to his Emperor.

On 15 December, the landings on Mindoro duly took place without opposition from the Kamikazes or from the weak Japanese land forces holding the island. Only after the US troops were safely ashore did the Kamikazes intervene, sinking two Landing Ships Tank and causing minor damage to escort carrier *Marcus Island* and a pair of destroyers. Yet the Americans still had to provide food, ammunition and equipment for their soldiers on Mindoro over a lengthy supply line that was very vulnerable to the assaults of the Kamikazes. These, moreover, were aided by a natural disaster about which their enemies kept very quiet but of which some news did reach the Japanese and must have delighted Vice Admiral Ōnishi and his supporters.

Prior to the invasion of Mindoro, Halsey's Third Fleet had made effective preliminary raids on Japanese air bases and had had every intention of renewing these to prevent any interference while Mindoro was secured. On 17 December, Third Fleet was refuelling but shortly after noon, this was discontinued as the weather was growing worse. Next morning, a small but savage typhoon, which the American meteorologists had not anticipated or discovered, fell on Third Fleet, its exceptionally high winds and mountainous seas threatening to inflict on the US navy a disaster comparable with that suffered by Kublai Khan.

This combination of events led to the loss of another US veteran. We first met destroyer *Monaghan* at Pearl Harbor where she had sunk a midget submarine. She had served throughout the Pacific War, including at the Battle of Midway Island, where she had first been part of the destroyer screen protecting *Enterprise* and later one of the vessels trying vainly to save the original *Yorktown*. She had fought in a clash at the Komandorski Islands in the North Pacific on 26 March 1943, in which an American cruiser/destroyer group had repulsed a much stronger Japanese force. Now her luck had also run out. She desperately needed refuelling and when this was postponed, her captain, still hoping to do so later, waited too long before reballasting his largely empty tanks with sea water. At the height of the typhoon, *Monaghan* capsized and sank.

She was not the only casualty. Destroyers *Hull* and *Spence* also went down, while seven other vessels, including four light carriers, were badly damaged. Halsey's carriers indeed had a very rough time: battered by winds and waves, they lost a total of 186 aircraft that either went overboard or were dashed into each other and wrecked. Close on 800 seamen perished and Third Fleet had to return temporarily to Ulithi for rest and repairs.

With Third Fleet's carriers unavailable to carry out their proposed raids on air bases in Luzon, the Kamikaze Corps was able to attack vessels off or making for Mindoro with little interference. During December and January, they did just that, often combining their raids with those of orthodox bombers so as to confuse the American AA gunners. During this period, they sank tanker *Porcupine*, two ammunition ships – both of which blew up spectacularly, killing the entire crew – two transports and two more Landing

Ships Tank. Several other vessels, including five destroyers and a destroyer escort were damaged, suffering high casualties in many cases.

By the end of December, however, the Americans were already firmly in control of Mindoro, though enemy resistance was not completely quelled for another month. They had built a new airfield at San José, from which Lightning fighters had been operating since the 24th, and two more airfields would shortly be added. These would prove invaluable in helping to provide cover for the next American advance: the long-awaited descent on the island of Luzon.

Planned for 9 January 1945, this bore a considerable resemblance to the invasion of Leyte. Under the overall command of General MacArthur, the assault would again be made by the men of Lieutenant General Krueger's Sixth Army, again carried by Vice Admiral Kinkaid's loyal Seventh Fleet. The landing would again be in the charge of the newly-promoted Vice Admiral Barbey and of Vice Admiral Wilkinson, and Seventh Fleet's supporting warships would once more be controlled by Vice Admiral Oldendorf, also newly-promoted. Admiral Halsey's Third Fleet would again be in support and on 3 January, would conduct preliminary strikes on Luzon, Formosa and Okinawa. These would inflict heavy losses on Japanese warplanes but unfortunately they did not remove the greatest threat to Seventh Fleet, which this time came not from Admiral Toyoda's battleships but from Vice Admiral Ōnishi's Kamikaze Corps.

For their part, the Japanese were well aware that the Corps was their main weapon and were very ready to use it. Their Intelligence had done more good work and correctly advised that Luzon would be invaded on 9 January. On 28 December, the Japanese even announced their knowledge in a broadcast made in plain English, presumably thinking this would dishearten the Americans and perhaps cause them to change their plans.

What the Japanese did not know was exactly where on Luzon the Americans would come ashore. Most rightly favoured Lingayen Gulf about halfway up Luzon's western coast where they had themselves landed in December 1941, but others considered it might be at Aparri in the far north of Luzon, also the scene of a Japanese landing. In either case, the Kamikazes' leaders felt they must concentrate their whole strength on Luzon. Their advanced base at Cebu had contributed to the attacks on the Mindoro invasion forces but thereafter, apart from one last (unsuccessful) mission on 28 December, all these ceased and all Kamikaze personnel retired to Luzon.[3]

On 2 January 1945, vessels from Kinkaid's Seventh Fleet left Leyte Gulf to make the initial move in what one might term the Battle of Lingayen Gulf. This first group formed part of Vice Admiral Oldendorf's Bombardment Group and contained sixty-four minesweepers, ten destroyer transports carrying demolition teams, and numerous auxiliaries such as tankers, tugs and gunboats, plus an appropriate escort that included two Australian warships, the sloop *Warrego* and the frigate *Gascoyne*.

Oldendorf's main body, which could boast the impressive total of 12 escort carriers, 6 battleships, 8 cruisers, among them HMAS *Australia* and *Shropshire*, and 41 destroyers or destroyer escorts including HMAS *Arunta* and *Warramunga*, followed on 3 January. Since it was capable of a greater speed than its vanguard, it would catch up with this on 5 January and the whole group would enter Lingayen Gulf together on the 6th. Here, as can readily be deduced from its title and composition, it would clear any mines or underwater obstacles, bombard the shore batteries for three days and thereafter provide close support for the landing forces.

These would leave Leyte Gulf in two groups on the evening of 4 January and the morning of the 5th and reach Lingayen Gulf on the 9th. It is said that they and their protecting warships, among which were five more escort carriers, formed a column over 40 miles long from front to rear. General MacArthur was present on light cruiser *Boise*. Vice Admiral Kinkaid and Lieutenant General Krueger were in the former's flagship, the amphibious force command ship *Wasatch*, that had also been the Seventh Fleet flagship at the time of the Leyte landings.

Seventh Fleet's route to the invasion beaches was the same as that followed for the Mindoro landings, save of course that it did not end at Mindoro but proceeded up the west coasts of Mindoro and Luzon. In the late afternoon of 2 January, the vanguard of the Bombardment Group was spotted – Admiral Nimitz tells us 'by a Japanese lookout in a church steeple on high ground on the north-eastern point of Mindanao' – and word soon reached Luzon. Next morning a suicide bomber rammed tanker *Cowanesque*. Amazingly, she did not catch fire and lost only two men killed, but Oldendorf's ships had a long way to go before they reached Lingayen Gulf and could expect a warm reception when they did so.

Their ordeal began on 4 January. Fighters from the escort carriers shot down a number of enemy aircraft, but in the late afternoon as the Bombardment Group was passing to the west of the island of Panay, a solitary Frances bomber appeared at about 15,000ft above it and immediately went into a steep dive. Shortly before 1730, it smashed into the centre of the flight deck of escort carrier *Ommaney Bay* and burst through this into the hangar where its bombs exploded with a roar that was heard in Oldendorf's van group, miles away out of sight beyond the horizon. A raging fire was started that quickly reached *Ommaney Bay*'s magazines. Shaken by explosions, flaming literally from end to end and covered by enormous clouds of smoke, the escort carrier was clearly doomed. 'Abandon ship' was ordered and torpedoes from an American destroyer sent her to the bottom, together with the bodies of ninety-three of her crewmen.

On 5 January, the directors of the Kamikaze Corps sacrificed one of their finest men. Lieutenant Shinichi Kanaya had repeatedly volunteered for suicide missions, but he had always been rejected because he was a brilliant and untiring trainer of Kamikaze units and it was considered that he was too valuable to lose. Now, faced with Oldendorf's massive Bombardment Group, it was felt that this could only be harmed by large numbers of suicide aircraft manned by the very best of pilots.

Large numbers of suicide aircraft were duly sent out and one group of fifteen bomb-carrying Zeros, with a couple more to act as escorts, was led by Lieutenant Kanaya. His men encountered a strong Combat Air Patrol but were able to break past this with the loss of only one of their number. The remainder, as usual, were met with heavy AA fire but continued their attacks. Other Kamikaze units made similar assaults and in the confusion that followed it is impossible to determine how much damage Kanaya's formation inflicted, but in view of his known determination and his acknowledged ability as a trainer, it was probably considerable.

Total damage inflicted was certainly considerable. In Seventh Fleet, three American warships – escort carrier *Manila Bay*, heavy cruiser *Louisville* and destroyer escort *Stafford* – were all hit and damaged, the last two very seriously; a Landing Craft Infantry was also hit. Very near misses caused lesser damage to escort carrier *Savo Island*, destroyer *Helm* – which had once engaged a midget submarine trying to enter Pearl Harbor – and seaplane tender *Orca*. In all, the US ships had almost 100 casualties.

Nor was it only American warships that suffered. Australian destroyer *Arunta* was attacked by a Zero which just missed her bridge and crashed into the sea off *Arunta*'s port side. Its bomb exploded, killing two men, wounding five more, holing the ship's hull in several places and wrecking her steering gear, causing her to steam in circles for several minutes until control was regained. Her damage, however, was quickly repaired.

Much greater harm befell HMAS *Australia*. It will be recalled that she had already been the victim of an 'impulse' suicider shortly before the Battle of Leyte Gulf, but that was quite a minor affair compared with her misfortunes in the Battle of Lingayen Gulf. If carrier *Intrepid* had been rudely called 'The Evil I', the Australians must have been tempted to employ their favourite epithet and label their heavy cruiser 'The Bloody A'.

Australia's misadventures began on the 5th, when she was attacked by half a dozen Kamikazes. A heavy AA barrage shot down one and turned away four more, one of which subsequently rammed *Manila Bay*, but the last one crashed into the port side of *Australia*'s upper deck amidships. Its bomb exploded, causing a fire. This was quickly brought under control, but three officers and twenty-two men were dead and thirty more of her crew had suffered injury.

Australia would endure further troubles on 6 January, and not only her. This was the day when the Bombardment Group entered Lingayen Gulf and the Japanese unleashed a whole series of suicide attacks during which every aircraft still serviceable was employed. The last of these raids was carried out by five Zeros that had officially been 'written off' by earlier American air-raids but had been restored to flying condition by the devoted ground crews who had worked all through the previous night to achieve this result.

Earlier we met Lieutenant Yuzo Nakano who was in poor health and desperate to go on a suicide mission in case he should have a relapse that would send him back to hospital and end his service career. Commander Nakajima, who had to choose the pilots for this last mission, decided that as

The Kamikaze creators.

ABOVE LEFT: Vice Admiral Takijirō Ōnishi, founder and leader of the Kamikaze Corps.

ABOVE RIGHT: Rear Admiral Masafumi Arima, whose deliberate suicide mission inspired Ōnishi to adopt crash-dive tactics.

BELOW LEFT: Captain Rikihei Inoguchi, Ōnishi's senior staff officer responsible for Kamikaze operations during the Philippines campaigns.

BELOW RIGHT: Commander Tadashi Nakajima, who formed the Kamikaze unit on Cebu Island.

Vice Admiral Ōnishi inspects Kamikaze pilots.

Vice Admiral Ōnishi pours 'sake' (rice wine) for his pilots in a purification ceremony.

A group of Kamikaze pilots. The white scarves they all wear were also symbols of their purity.

By far the most popular aircraft for Kamikaze attacks was the Mitsubishi Zero fighter adapted, as here, to carry a 550lb bomb.

Zeros taking off for Kamikaze missions.

It will be noted that the one in the top photo is carrying a bomb but those in the bottom photo are not.
These are the fighters that would escort the suicide-attackers to their targets and return to base
to report on the results of the strike and the effectiveness of the tactics employed.

Other Kamikaze aircraft.
ABOVE: The Yokosuka Judy dive-bomber.
BELOW: Nakajima Jill torpedo-bombers.

Further Kamikaze aircraft.

ABOVE: Yokosuka Frances bombers.

BELOW: The Aichi Val dive-bomber. This had been replaced by the Judy on conventional missions but was widely used on suicide attacks.

The American landings on Leyte Island.

While supporting the Leyte landings, heavy cruiser HMAS *Australia* was struck by a Japanese bomber that damaged her foremast and bridge. This, however, was not an organized Kamikaze attack but one made on an individual impulse.

US escort carrier *St Lo* in the Battle of Leyte Gulf.

She defied the guns of Japanese battleships and heavy cruisers (ABOVE)
but was sunk by a Kamikaze Zero, reportedly flown by Lieutenant Yukio Seki (BELOW).

The Kamikaze successes at Leyte Gulf convinced the Japanese that these missions must continue.

ABOVE: Pilots are briefed prior to a sortie.

BELOW: A Zero about to ram US battleship *Missouri*. Though the photo is well-known, the attack caused minimal harm. Most Kamikaze strikes inflicted heavy damage and high casualties.

The largest warships sunk by Kamikaze attacks were three US escort carriers: *St Lo* at Leyte Gulf; *Ommaney Bay*, shown here during the Lingayan Gulf campaign; and *Bismarck Sea* at Iwo Jima.

Superfortress bombers over Japan. Their raids on Japanese cities inflicted appalling damage and loss of life.
One on Tokyo caused more fatal casualties than both the atomic bombs combined.

Emperor Hirohito inspects bomb damage in his capital.
He was horrified by the sufferings of 'my innocent people'.

Mitsubishi Betty bomber carrying an Oka ('Cherry Blossom') manned bomb.

A close-up of the Oka. Although it caused much trepidation, its successes were limited.
The Americans called it the Baka, meaning 'mad' or 'madman'.

The Kamikazes' opponents at Okinawa.

ABOVE LEFT: Admiral Raymond Ames Spruance, commander of the US Fifth Fleet.

ABOVE RIGHT: Vice Admiral Marc Mitscher, commander of Fifth Fleet's fast carriers, Task Force 58.

The Okinawa landings.

The last sortie of the Japanese super-battleship *Yamato*.

ABOVE: She is pounded by bombs and torpedoes from American carrier-based aircraft.

BELOW: She finally disintegrates in a colossal explosion. The size of this can be assessed by comparing it with that of her escorting destroyers.

The US Navy's most famous warship: Fleet carrier *Enterprise*.

She was in action throughout the Pacific War (ABOVE), but her distinguished career was
ended when she was badly damaged by a Kamikaze attack at Okinawa (BELOW).
She was struck on her forward elevator which, as can be seen, was blasted high into the air.

The end of the Second World War.

ABOVE: The underground conference room at the Imperial Palace where the decision was made to accept the terms of the Potsdam Declaration.

BELOW: The Japanese delegation arrives on board US battleship *Missouri*.

the flight to the target would be shorter than usual, it would not be too much for Nakano's strength, and since he was a fine pilot and a fine leader, he was 'the ideal man' for the task. The other four men selected, strictly on the basis of their flying ability, were Lieutenant Kunitane Nakao and Warrant Officers Kiichi Goto, Yoshiyuki Taniuchi and Masahiko Chihara. This was the occasion previously mentioned when all the pilots, as they prepared for take-off, shouted their thanks to Nakajima for having chosen them.

It was the earliest Kamikaze attack that went in a few minutes after noon, however, that was the most effective. One of the targets selected was battleship *New Mexico* which was playing host to two distinguished British officers. Admiral Sir Bruce Fraser was famous for having commanded the forces that sank the German battle-cruiser *Scharnhorst* in December 1943. In August 1944, he had taken command of the British Eastern Fleet in the Indian Ocean but Churchill, probably mistakenly, was determined that this, suitably renamed the British Pacific Fleet, should fight alongside the US navy in the final campaigns against the Japanese. Fraser had therefore come to the scene of action, eager to learn as much as possible about the conditions his warships would have to face, the effectiveness of Japanese assaults and the best ways of repelling these.

Also aboard *New Mexico* was Lieutenant General Sir Herbert Lumsden, an officer whose record included commanding an armoured division and later an army corps in the fighting in the deserts of Egypt and Libya. Unfortunately he had disagreements with both superiors and subordinates and returned to England in November 1942. A dashing cavalry officer and a first-rate amateur steeplechase jockey who had ridden in the Grand National, he was a type who appealed to Churchill and early in 1944, he was sent out to become Churchill's personal liaison officer with General MacArthur. It was a role in which he proved a great success, quickly gaining MacArthur's confidence and providing Churchill with much vital and helpful information.

At noon on 6 January, Fraser and Lumsden were on the port side of *New Mexico*'s bridge, watching the Americans pound the Japanese shore batteries and talking with the battleship's skipper, Captain Fleming. For no particular reason, Fraser decided to cross the bridge to get a different view of the proceedings from its starboard side. This saved his life. Moments later, a suicide bomber dived on *New Mexico*. It was hit and caught fire, but plunged on to strike the exact spot that Fraser had just left. Lumsden, Fleming and twenty-seven more were killed and eighty-seven wounded, but the admiral was unhurt. His subsequent report to Churchill did nothing to dispel the prime minister's concern about the effects of Kamikaze attacks, the more so because Churchill was shocked by Lumsden's death which he considered 'a loss to his country and to me personally'.

A second hit on *New Mexico* soon after 1430 caused little damage and no casualties, but battleship *California* which, like *New Mexico*, was engaged in bombarding the shore batteries, was less fortunate. Attacked by two Zeros, she shot down one at a safe distance, but the other, though hit repeatedly, struck her at the base of her mainmast, causing a huge explosion and furious fires. These were eventually brought under control and *California* continued to carry out her bombardment duties, but she had lost 35 officers and men dead and 168 wounded, of whom 13 later died of their injuries.

Less powerful warships also suffered severely. Light cruiser *Columbia* was hit by two Kamikazes and near-missed by a third. She had her two after 6in gun turrets put out of action and fires started that necessitated the flooding of her magazines, while thirteen of her crew died, with forty-four more being wounded. Nonetheless, she also remained in action.

So too did heavy cruiser *Louisville*, that had already been hit on the 5th. She shot down at least four attackers but a Judy bomber that broke through her gunfire crashed into the starboard side of her bridge, causing fires and other serious damage. She suffered eighty-eight casualties, thirty-two of them being killed outright or succumbing to their wounds later. Among these last was the flag officer aboard her, Rear Admiral Theodore Chandler.

Destroyer *Walke* was attacked by four Kamikazes. She shot down the first two at a safe distance, but the third crashed into her bridge, killing her CO, Commander Davis, among others and starting raging fires. Nonetheless, she not only managed to subdue the flames but shot down her fourth attacker before it could hit her. This may have saved *Walke* from destruction, for minesweeper *Long* was struck by two Kamikazes, and she capsized and sank. Minesweeper *Southard* was hit only once and survived, and the suicide pilots rammed two other destroyers and near-missed three more. Happily, damage and casualties in these were light.

Oldendorf's Australian warships did not escape the Kamikazes' attention either. *Shropshire*'s AA gunners hit an aircraft that dived on her out of the sun just in time; it narrowly missed her and crashed into the sea close to her starboard side. Australian destroyer *Warramunga* also fatally damaged a suicide attacker, but it kept going and rammed US destroyer transport *Brooks*, knocking down one of her funnels before smashing through the deck into her engine room. She came to a halt with fires raging, but *Warramunga* went to her assistance and after some ninety minutes of feverish activity was able to quell the flames and then tow *Brooks* away from the danger zone.

Naturally *Australia* was not neglected. At least a couple of suicide attackers were shot down when heading for her, but at 1734, another one, reported to be a Val dive-bomber, could not be stopped and duly rammed her. The fires that were started were swiftly brought under control, but fourteen men dead and twenty-six injured were added to her already high casualty list.

This was the Allies' worst day in the Battle of Lingayen Gulf, but the next three were not pleasant either. On 7 January, a very serious incident was narrowly avoided. The main body of Seventh Fleet was now approaching ready for the landings on the 9th and had been reported. A suicide attacker, evading the Combat Air Patrol, tried to ram light cruiser *Boise*, on board which was General MacArthur. Fortunately, AA fire claimed it at the last moment and it crashed into the water and exploded, close to its target but without doing any harm. Other raiders were downed at a safe distance and only one got through to ram a Landing Ship Tank which miraculously remained afloat and was towed to safety.

In Lingayen Gulf, the ordeal of the Bombardment Group continued, the Kamikaze Corps sinking minesweepers *Hovey* and *Palmer*. Amazingly, HMAS *Australia* was not targeted on this day; however, 8 January found her back in the firing-line, her attackers reported to be Frances bombers. One of these was shot down just short of *Australia* but skidded over the water into her side, causing minor damage. Then another, though also damaged, kept going and hit her on the waterline. Its bomb exploded, blowing a sizeable hole in her side; it caused flooding and listing, though the former was soon brought under control and the latter corrected.

As on the previous day, Kamikaze attacks were also made on Seventh Fleet's approaching amphibious forces. Despite a strong Combat Air Patrol and heavy anti-aircraft gunfire, some of the raiders managed, as usual, to break through the defences. Early that morning, one of them rammed escort carrier *Kadashan Bay*, its bomb blowing a huge hole in her side and so damaging her that she had to withdraw from the combat zone. Soon afterwards, a Kamikaze went into troop transport *Callaway* with a thunderous crash, but she still stayed afloat, though losing twenty–nine men killed. Finally, that evening, escort carrier *Kitkun Bay* was struck. A large fire was started and although it was eventually brought under control, *Kitkun Bay* lost sixteen dead and thirty-seven wounded and her extensive damage compelled her also to withdraw.

Despite the attentions of the Kamikaze Corps, however, Seventh Fleet's main body reached Lingayen Gulf on schedule and at 0700 on 9 January, all Kinkaid's transports were in position ready for the invasion of Luzon, while their supporting warships had begun a preliminary bombardment. The landings would meet strictly limited resistance, for General Yamashita had intended to fight only a delaying action on the beaches, preferring to make his stand in Luzon's mountainous interior. Vice Admiral Ōnishi and his followers, on the other hand, had no intention of allowing the invasion to be uncontested.

In view of past events, the Americans were under no illusions on this score and their vessels had practised laying down a massive 'anti-Kamikaze barrage' to protect themselves. This proved highly efficient throughout the day, despite one unhappy incident late that evening: battleship *Colorado* was struck on the bridge by a 'friendly' 5in shell and lost eighteen men killed or fatally wounded.

Once more, though, it proved impossible to thwart Ōnishi's warriors completely. At 0728, three Kamikazes attacking with the rising sun behind them were able to achieve surprise. The first tried to ram destroyer escort *Hodges* but presumably mistimed its run and only knocked her mast down before plunging into the sea and exploding. The second made no mistake. It crashed squarely into light cruiser *Colombia*, caused heavy damage and added another twenty-four men dead and ninety-seven wounded to her combat losses. Mercifully, the third attacker was hit by a blast of anti-aircraft fire and disintegrated into a mass of flaming fragments.

Not until just after 1300 did the Kamikazes again break through the AA barrage and this time there were only two of them, but a couple of Kamikazes could still do a great deal of damage. Both seemed to be heading as if drawn by a magnet towards the luckless *Australia*, but one hurtled past her to strike battleship *Mississippi* near the bridge instead, killing or wounding almost 100 men. *Australia* had already suffered more than 100 casualties and happily she would not increase that total on 9 January. Although the second Kamikaze did attack her, it missed her bridge at which it was apparently aiming and merely took off her radar and wireless aerials and knocked over the top third of her front funnel before going into the sea.

It was *Australia*'s last combat in the Second World War. That evening, she and the damaged American cruisers *Louisville* and *Colombia* were ordered to retire to Leyte Gulf. Here *Australia* effected temporary repairs before returning to her homeland for rest and rehabilitation. Vice Admiral Kinkaid, an officer not given to exaggeration, would describe her performance throughout the Battle of Lingayen Gulf simply as 'excellent'. Vice Admiral Oldendorf would declare that her conduct was 'an inspiration to all of us'.

In six days of intensive endeavours, the Kamikazes had inflicted terrible losses on their enemies, greatly worried Allied leaders and effectively ended the Americans' belief that they could master anything the Japanese could bring against them. Yet now the Kamikazes' greatest weakness once more became apparent. As already shown, they were a wasting asset. Though they still had a reserve of pilots, their recent efforts had reduced the available aircraft to a mere handful. Moreover, since General Yamashita had decided not to fight more than a delaying action for the Luzon Plain between Lingayen Gulf and Manila, it was clear that now the Americans were established ashore, it would not be long before they took over the main aerodromes that the Kamikazes had been using.

Vice Admiral Ōnishi thoroughly appreciated the situation and had reached certain conclusions. As was mentioned earlier, the Japanese air fleets in the Philippines had combined their resources with Vice Admiral

Fukudome as their official head. Ōnishi, who was much the stronger character, now persuaded Fukudome and members of his staff to leave Luzon and take charge of Japan's air strength in Formosa. They were carried there in Betty bombers and arrived in the early hours of 7 January. Ōnishi intended that once the Americans had landed on Luzon, he and all the remaining Kamikaze personnel would become foot soldiers and join the ranks of Yamashita's defenders.

Ōnishi believed he would not survive the fighting and since he was proud of his men's achievements and considered that the suicide tactics and the 'Kamikaze spirit' were important to Japan, he wished to ensure that the records of the Corps should not perish also. All documents relating to the Corps were collected and copies made of each. Then the originals were entrusted to Commander Nakajima and the copies to Lieutenant (junior grade) Shimizu and early on 8 January, they boarded Judys and flew to Formosa; independently so as to reduce the chances of interception. Fog caused Shimizu's machine to crash, seriously injuring him and killing his pilot, but Nakajima arrived safely. Just two days later, he was able to greet Ōnishi, Captain Inoguchi and his other fellow staff officers: Admiral Toyoda had decided that the Kamikaze personnel must be preserved and ordered them to Formosa as well.

Even after their leaders' departure, Kamikaze pilots in Luzon continued making sporadic attacks until they had expended their few surviving aircraft. Over the next few days they damaged half a dozen transports with heavy losses of life. The final attack came on the morning of 13 January, the day when MacArthur and Krueger set up their headquarters ashore; escort carrier *Salamaua* was hit, sustaining almost 100 casualties, 15 of them fatal. Then as many of the remaining Kamikaze personnel as possible were evacuated to Formosa by various perilous means.

Vice Admiral Ōnishi's own move to Formosa had been somewhat fraught. As his transport aircraft had approached Takao aerodrome, it had come under fortunately inaccurate fire from Japanese AA gunners and hardly had he left the base than it had been subjected to a fierce American air-raid. Ōnishi, however, was as full of fight as ever and set about forming a new Kamikaze unit out of the experienced pilots who had been brought out of Luzon and new recruits from the Kamikaze training centre already on Formosa. It was called the Niitaka Unit after a mountain that was the highest in Formosa and so at that time anywhere in the Japanese Empire. It formally came into existence on 18 January and three days later would be seen in spectacular action.

Its opponents were the vessels of Halsey's Third Fleet which had recently entered the South China Sea to savage Japanese merchantmen. When retiring from the area, Third Fleet struck at Formosa on 21 January. The Niitaka Unit promptly retaliated; three waves of suicide attackers, containing in all four Zero fighter-bombers, six Judy bombers and seven Zero fighters as escort taking off from Takao airfield. They were airborne just in time to escape another American strike against the base.

On their way to their targets, the Kamikazes were intercepted by American fighters which shot down one Zero and forced two others to turn back. Unfortunately, all these were fighters from the escort and the attackers duly arrived over Third Fleet. Here more were downed by the Combat Air Patrol but, as usual, some got through. A Zero crashed into the flight deck of fleet carrier *Ticonderoga*, setting ablaze the aircraft parked on it. Then a Judy also dashed itself into *Ticonderoga*'s flight deck and increased the fires to a raging furnace. Other Judys rammed light carrier *Langley* and destroyer *Maddox*. Both were put out of action briefly, but suffered only moderate damage. *Ticonderoga*, however, was in a bad way. Her damage control parties eventually mastered her fires, but she had 345 casualties, 143 of them fatal, and her severe injuries compelled her to retire to Ulithi and subsequently to the United States for repairs.

Yet while the men of the Kamikaze Corps could help the defenders of Formosa, there was no way in which they could help their forces in the Philippines. Still less could they hope to return there. They could only watch helplessly while the Americans proceeded with their reconquest of the islands. A whole series of landings were made in the Central and Southern Philippines, but General MacArthur's main attention was focused on the operations in Luzon. Progress towards the Philippine capital, Manila, was held up by fierce resistance. The aerodrome at Clark Field, the centre of a vast complex of bases, was reached on 25 January but not secured until the 31st. On that day also, an American landing was made in Manila Bay 40 miles south of the capital but it was 12 February before these troops could reach Nichols Field on the southern outskirts of the city.

Manila itself had been reached by the main US forces north of the city on the evening of 3 February. MacArthur had been confident it would not be held and Yamashita had not wished it to be, but the commander of the naval base, Rear Admiral Sanji Iwabuchi, was prepared to resist to the death and he had some 16,000 Marines to carry out his orders, plus about 4,000 soldiers who had retreated there. The Americans were compelled to use heavy artillery to assist their troops as they captured the city street by street and house by house. It was not until 3 March that resistance ended. Iwabuchi's defenders had died almost to the last man but they had killed 1,000 US soldiers and wounded 5,500 more; also as many as 100,000 civilians may have died, caught up in the general devastation. Most of Manila lay in ruins and its famous old walled Spanish section, appropriately named Intramuros, had been reduced to rubble. General MacArthur cancelled plans for a victory parade.

Nonetheless, with Manila, cruelly mauled though it was, in American hands, all responsible Japanese leaders accepted that the Philippines were irretrievably lost to them, though it would be some time before all their troops in the islands were killed or captured. General Yamashita with his remaining 60,000 men in fact held out in the north-east of Luzon, and tied down four American divisions until the end of the Second World War. Japanese resistance finally ended in March 1974, when Second Lieutenant Hirō Onoda, obeying an order from his former commanding officer, emerged from the jungle on the island of Lubang, south-west of Manila and north-west of Mindoro, still wearing his now tattered army uniform, and surrendered. He handed over his samurai sword, which was in pristine condition, his ammunition and two rifles in perfect working order. The sword was politely returned to him.

Notes

1. She was the second carrier of this name to fight in the Pacific War. Her predecessor, the much-loved 'Lady Lex', had been sunk in May 1942

during the Battle of the Coral Sea. For the confusion of historians, a number of American carriers – and other types of warship for that matter – in action in 1944 bore the names of vessels lost earlier in the conflict, among them *Lexington*, *Yorktown*, *Wasp*, *Hornet* and light carrier *Langley*.

2. Earlier in the month, Ōnishi had been flown to Tokyo in order to speed on the arrival of reinforcements for the Kamikaze Corps. He had been in such poor health that for his return flight he had had to be carried into his aircraft on a stretcher.

3. Cebu was subsequently invaded by the Americans on 26 March 1945 and had been secured by 18 April.

Chapter 5

Developments and Defences

S o the Philippines had been lost to Japan and, as her Navy Minister, Admiral Mitsumasa Yonai, stated after the war: 'When you took the Philippines, that was the end of our resources.' Yonai, like many other naval commanders, joined the ranks of those who urged that a continuation of the war was pointless and peace should be secured as soon as possible. Some of Japan's other leaders were less convinced and remained defiant, especially the War Minister, General Korechika Anami, who proposed to arm the country's entire population, men and women alike, to face any American invasion.

Yet Anami and his diehards were not completely remote from reality and while they refused to contemplate surrender, they were not averse to accepting peace, even if it implicitly acknowledged defeat. At the time of their greatest successes, the Japanese had been prepared for a compromise peace, albeit one very much in their favour. They now realized that peace would result in their being subjected to harsh terms, because in November 1943, the Cairo Declaration by Britain and the United States had promised China's Chiang Kai-shek that Japan would have to relinquish all captured territories. That Anami would have gone along with this is shown by his having supported attempts to persuade Russia to act as mediator between Japan and the Western Allies. The Russians, who had never forgotten or forgiven their defeat by Japan in 1905, would certainly have insisted on similar terms.

Unhappily, earlier in January 1943, at the Casablanca Conference, President Roosevelt, with the concurrence of Churchill, had demanded the 'unconditional surrender' of the Axis Powers, including of course Japan. Some historians have argued that this had no adverse consequences, but the military leaders who had to deal with them strongly disagree. Nimitz, for example, points out that the demand meant that 'Terms would neither be offered nor considered. Not even Napoleon at the height of his conquests ever so completely closed the door to negotiation. To adopt such an inflexible policy was bad enough: to announce it publicly was worse.'

One unfortunate result of this demand was that it contradicted the Western Allies' claim that their quarrel was with the leaders of the Axis states, not their peoples. Japan's history showed that those who surrendered could expect little mercy, and chilling utterances from senior American officers that killing Japanese was no different from killing lice and that after the war the Japanese language would be spoken only in hell strongly indicated that if Japan surrendered unconditionally, she could expect no mercy at all.

If any of Japan's leaders had been optimistic enough to doubt this view, it appeared to be confirmed when on 24 November 1944, Superfortress bombers from Tinian in the Marianas began a series of attacks on Tokyo, Nagoya, Osaka and Kobe that were openly stated as being designed to destroy not just factories but large areas of cities and large numbers of their inhabitants. General Curtis LeMay who controlled the bombers equally frankly admitted that if his country had lost the war he would probably have been 'tried as a war criminal'. The raids reached their horrible culmination on the night of 9/10 March 1945, when 300 Superfortresses devastated Tokyo, set more than 25,000 buildings ablaze, drove about a million homeless to seek shelter in the countryside and as LeMay cheerfully tells us, 'scorched and boiled and baked to death' at least 83,000 civilians.

These raids did inflict heavy blows on Japan's already crumbling economy, but politically their effect was entirely negative. They did not break the will of the Japanese people. They did infuriate several important Japanese who had hitherto been wavering, to such an extent that they became supporters of General Anami; Admiral Toyoda was one of them, a matter of some importance when he became Chief of Japan's Naval General Staff and, like Anami, a member of the six-man Supreme War Council. They also ensured that the moderate Japanese leaders who sincerely desired a speedy peace did not dare to advocate it openly as long as it could be bought only by unconditional surrender.

It is only with this background in mind that the attitude of Vice Admiral Ōnishi can be appreciated. It will be recalled that on 6 January 1945, he had announced that once the Americans had secured their landing on

Luzon, he and all the surviving Kamikaze personnel should become foot soldiers in order to assist Luzon's ground defenders. Captain Inoguchi had then urged that he should instead return to Japan, where he could play an invaluable part in directing the war effort. Ōnishi had replied: 'Victory is now impossible, even if I did return to the homeland.'

This observation should not be given too much weight. Ōnishi's conversation with his chief staff officer had revolved around the defence of Luzon and it may be that he meant only that victory on that island was now impossible. Equally of course it is likely that, being a very experienced naval airman, he was well aware that without the Philippines, Japan had no chance of gaining the favourable peace that had been her war aim. In either case, though, he was convinced that the fighting must continue, for, as we know, when he was ordered to Formosa by Admiral Toyoda, he at once established a new Kamikaze squadron.

When the Niitaka Unit had officially come into existence on 18 January, Ōnishi had addressed the men who would fly its Zeros and Judys. We are told by Commander Nakajima that he ended his speech by declaring: 'Even if we are defeated, the noble spirit of the Kamikaze attack corps will keep our homeland from ruin. Without this spirit, ruin would certainly follow defeat.'

Ōnishi's remark was no doubt a reflection of the old samurai adage that defeat was not in itself dishonourable as long as it could be redeemed by acts of physical or moral courage. In addition, however, it would seem to indicate that Ōnishi believed that, while Japan would certainly have to accept harsh terms when peace was concluded, as long as she continued to fight bravely and effectively, she would not be destroyed but would survive with her honour intact. It would not be stated directly and perhaps was not fully realized, but in practice from this time onwards, the Japanese armed forces and the Kamikazes in particular would be fighting to save their country from unconditional surrender.

In the coming struggles, the only advantages the Japanese had were the stubbornness of their soldiers on the defensive and the determination of their Kamikazes on the offensive. That the Kamikazes had already accomplished far more than could possibly have been achieved by orthodox air attacks was obvious to all and henceforward there was rarely any question of whether suicide attacks should be continued. On the contrary, ways were sought of extending such tactics into different spheres of activity.

For example, in May during the Okinawa campaign, the Japanese would introduce the concept of 'suicide commandos'. The aerodrome at Yontan which was already in American hands was approached by five Japanese aircraft carrying these commandos, and although four were shot down, the remaining one landed and its passengers poured out. All were killed by the defenders but not until they had wrecked seven warplanes, damaged twenty-six others and destroyed 70,000 gallons of aviation fuel. This, though, was more in the nature of a 'banzai charge' than a special attack operation.

Much more akin to Ōnishi's aerial samurai were the suicide missions of Japan's surface navy and indeed sub-surface navy, at least in intention. The surface weapon used was the dramatically named 'Shinyo' or 'Ocean Shaker' that the Americans more realistically called the 'Suicide boat'. It was a fast motor-boat with a one-man crew, at first made out of light wood, although later a version with a steel frame appeared. Its bows were packed with a huge charge of TNT, or later two depth-charges of similar power, and its crewman's task was to ram its target, whereupon the explosive would be detonated.

By the end of the war, some 6,000 Shinyos had been built but their achievements were meagre. They first attacked American vessels in Lingayen Gulf on the night of 9/10 January and made subsequent attacks during the Americans' reconquest of Luzon, causing a very few losses among auxiliaries and landing-craft. It was intended that the Shinyos should play a major part in the defence of Okinawa and some 400 were sent to the Kerama Retto, a group of islands 15 miles west of Okinawa's southern point. Sadly for the Japanese, the Americans made a preliminary landing on Kerama Retto on 25 March, secured it by the 27th, and captured all the Shinyos. There were still a number left on Okinawa itself and after dark on 31 March, fifty of these attacked US amphibious craft making for the island. All were destroyed after scoring a single hit on a Landing Ship Medium. A few minor Shinyo missions were carried out later, but caused only slight damage to cargo ships and auxiliaries.

The Japanese contemplated the use of midget submarines, similarly designed to ram enemy vessels and with TNT packed in their bows, but none of these would ever see action. A variation, however, would be employed. This was the 'Kaiten' – 'Turn of Fate' or 'Turn toward Heaven' – or so the Japanese named it, though the Allies gave it the more accurately descriptive title of the 'Human Torpedo'.

It was not the first time that the Axis powers had produced 'human torpedoes', for this had been the name given to the underwater craft used by the Italian 10th Light Flotilla in the Mediterranean. Known also as 'Chariots', these were miniature submarines, the two-man crew of which sat astride them wearing breathing apparatus. They were usually carried by orthodox submarines close to their objective, to which they then proceeded on their own. On reaching it, the explosive warhead of the chariot was detached, a time-fuse was set and the warhead clamped to the target's keel. On the night of 18/19 December 1941, Italian human torpedoes blew huge holes in the hulls of the British battleships *Queen Elizabeth* and *Valiant* at anchor in Alexandria Harbour and put them out of action for many months.

While these Italians were undoubtedly very brave and skilful men and their missions extremely daring and dangerous, they were in no sense suicide raiders. They had every intention of surviving if they could and the delayed-action fuses on the explosives gave them plenty of time to get clear. By contrast, when the Kaiten struck home, there was no chance for its operator to escape and he would perish with his craft and his victim.

Designed by a couple of young naval officers, Lieutenants Hiroshi Kuroki and Sekio Nishina, the Kaiten really was a torpedo. It was an adaptation of the famous 'Long Lance' carried on Japanese warships: a horror that was propelled by liquid oxygen, enabling it to carry a warhead twice the size of any possessed by other nations at a greater speed over a far longer distance. The Kaiten was a 'Long Lance' controlled by a pilot who sat in a miniature cockpit on top of it equipped with a short and rather crude periscope.[1] Originally an escape hatch was provided so that the pilot could leave his Kaiten when it was about 50 yards from its target. In the frenzy of excitement and enthusiasm that followed the first news of Ōnishi's aerial samurai, however, many sailors clamoured to be allowed to sacrifice themselves in action as the pilots were doing. The escape hatch was discarded, making the Kaiten a true suicide weapon.

Like the Italian Chariots, the Kaitens had to be carried to within a short distance of their targets by larger submarines, I-boats as the Japanese ones were called. On 19 November 1944, six Kaitens and their parent I-boats arrived outside the US base at Ulithi and, in the early hours of the following morning, the human torpedoes made their attack. They were led by Lieutenant Nishina who, rather morbidly, was accompanied by the ashes of his colleague Lieutenant Kuroki who had been killed on 6 September testing the Kaiten prototype. The defenders were alert and five of the Kaitens were sunk before they could inflict any harm but, like Ōnishi's aerial Kamikazes, one Kaiten could cause considerable damage. It struck tanker *Mississinewa* which exploded into a roaring mass of flames and went to the bottom with the bodies of 150 of her crew.

It seemed a good beginning but from then until the end of June 1945, a whole series of Kaiten raids were carried out in widely separated locations, including Ulithi again, the Marianas, Iwo Jima and Okinawa. Their only results were the loss of all the Kaitens that had been launched plus others that had still been on board the ten I-boats that were also sunk in the course of these operations. Not until July, when Japanese submarines embarked on a final offensive, did the Kaitens find another victim. On the 24th, one struck destroyer escort *Underhill* guarding a convoy to the Philippines. It tore a great hole in her side and she sank almost at once with the loss of 112 seamen.

While the Kaitens had proved perhaps slightly more successful than the Shinyos, the amount of time, material and money expended on them both, not to mention on various projects that never matured, presents a picture of muddled thinking on the part of some of the Japanese leaders. The more able of them must surely have become convinced by this time that the only effective suicide attacks were those made by aircraft and be looking rather desperately to the Kamikaze Corps to provide some relief from their woes.

The Corps faced new opponents after January 1945, on paper at least. Kinkaid's Seventh Fleet was protecting American troops landing in various parts of the Central and Southern Philippines and Australian troops landing at Tarakan, Brunei Bay and Balikpapan in Borneo.[2] Third Fleet had ceased to be, but only because it had been transformed into Fifth Fleet. In June 1944, it had been decided that the US Central Pacific Fleet should be commanded alternately by Spruance and Halsey while the one not in command stayed at Pearl Harbor with his staff, planning his own next assault, thus greatly reducing intervals between operations. Spruance and his Fifth Fleet had won the Battle of the Philippine Sea in June. Halsey had taken over on 26 August, whereupon his command became the Third Fleet and his fast carriers ceased to be designated Task Force 58 and became Task Force 38.

Now since 27 January 1945, Spruance had again taken over from Halsey and the Kamikaze Corps would therefore be confronted by the US Fifth Fleet and its Task Force 58. These were just as powerful as Third Fleet and Task Force 38 had been and would prove to be better able to defend themselves, for during the preceding months, the Americans had learned many lessons and devised a number of countermeasures to reduce the deadly effectiveness of the special attack airmen.

One obvious step was to raid the Kamikazes' bases and prevent them from ever taking off. This had been done in the past, but although the strikes had destroyed Japanese aircraft on the ground and caused some disruption and confusion, they had not prevented the great majority of suicide attacks from proceeding according to plan. In the future, still greater efforts would be made and *The United States Strategic Bombing Survey (Pacific War)* reports that in mid-April, at the request of Admiral Nimitz, 2,000 Superfortress sorties were diverted from raids on Japanese cities so that they could hit the Kamikazes' airfields instead. Despite this, however, another six weeks would elapse before the suicide attacks slackened and then for other reasons.

Far more effective were the defensive tactics that the Americans had worked out. In order to give as early a warning as possible, it was decided that radar-equipped 'pickets' would be stationed in all directions around and at distances up to 100 miles away from a landing beach or a task force at sea. These pickets would usually be destroyers, destroyer escorts or mine-sweepers, often accompanied by landing craft with powerful AA armaments. They also controlled their own Combat Air Patrol which they could use against hostile intruders. In addition, any US aircraft sent out on a mission were directed to fly over a particular picket station on their return. Then its CAP could deal with any Kamikazes or indeed conventional Japanese aircraft that were trying to follow the Americans back to their carriers. Moreover, any aircraft heading for the carriers other than from the direction of the chosen picket were known to be hostile.

Once warning had been given, the Americans knew that the only way they could be sure that the Kamikazes would not cause havoc was by their fighters shooting them down at a safe distance from their intended victims. As well as the CAP over the pickets, a landing area or a naval force would naturally possess its own CAP and in December 1944, *Lexington* and *Ticonderoga*, followed later by other fleet carriers, increased the number of their Hellcats by about twenty, while considerably reducing that of their Helldiver bombers. The Helldivers had in any case proved somewhat disappointing because they were not as structurally sound as the Dauntlesses they had replaced, so could not dive too steeply without losing their wings. Since by now the Hellcats had been modified to carry bombs, this action in fact increased the carriers' striking power as well as the strength of their interceptors.

Nor had the Americans neglected the improvement of their warships' gunfire. Anti-aircraft shells with the deadly proximity-fuses had reached all vessels by this time and large amounts of additional AA weapons were being fitted. The number of warships had increased as well and the Kamikazes would find themselves facing a dense and lethal 'wall of steel'. Nonetheless, experience had shown that a Kamikaze might be hit by a shell of anything less than 5in calibre, might even be set on fire, yet could still continue its dive onto its target. Therefore the Americans, realistically and wisely, had also considered ways of reducing the damage and casualties caused when a Kamikaze did strike home.

Damage control was a subject that the Americans had studied since mid-1942. The losses of the original *Lexington* in the Battle of the Coral Sea in May and the original *Yorktown* in the Battle of Midway Island in June had been followed on 9 August by a crushing defeat at the Battle of Savo Island, which saw four heavy cruisers go to the bottom: three American and HMAS *Canberra*. As a result, flammable material was banned from all warships, wooden, heavily-upholstered furniture was removed from wardrooms, and layers of paint and linoleum were scraped off bulkheads and decks down to the bare steel. 'Day and night for the rest of 1942,' reports Professor Morison, 'sounds of chipping hammers were never still.'³ Better fire-fighting equipment was introduced, particularly the 'fog nozzle' inspired by the New York City Fire Department that sent out a mist of water vapour and quenched flames far more effectively than the solid stream from hoses.

In addition, intensive training of every ship's damage control parties was commenced. Exercises were held at which they could practise their damage control and fire-fighting schools were set up at which experienced firemen from New York or Boston acted as instructors. Eventually the damage control personnel of every new warship would attend one of these schools before she went to sea. The benefit of the new attitudes would become apparent as early as 30 November 1942. At the Battle of Tassafaronga, four US heavy cruisers suffered damage that would have resulted in the loss of all of them had it occurred a few months earlier. Yet only the unlucky *Northampton* capsized and sank. The others were out of action for nine months or longer, but survived to fight again: 'What an improvement in damage control methods since the Battle of Savo Island!' rightly exclaims Professor Morison.

Thereafter the Americans worked continuously to further improve their damage control methods and the Kamikaze attacks stimulated their efforts. Foam generators used for smothering flames were supplied to every warship; on the decks of aircraft carriers there was one every 100ft. Mobile pumps were similarly provided. Fire-proof clothing enabled men to move into the heart of the flames with impunity. Portable oxyacetylene torches assisted the rescue of sailors who had been trapped. A new type of naval auxiliary, the Salvage Vessel, was introduced, specifically to help combat fires on other ships.

In short, the US navy had taken every possible step to defend itself from and reduce the effectiveness of the Kamikaze Corps. It was now up to the Corps to see if it could surmount the obstacles confronting it. This was a matter of desperate urgency, for now that they had regained the Philippines, the Americans were bound to advance against Iwo Jima and Okinawa, the last strongholds between them and the islands of Japan, and then on to the homeland of their enemies.

The leaders of the Corps realized that it would have to be reorganized if it was to meet the challenge and set about doing this. On 11 February 1945, the Japanese Fifth Air Fleet was formed in Kyushu, the most southerly of Japan's larger islands, under Vice Admiral Matome Ugaki, of whom much more will be heard later. His 600 warplanes were dispersed among thirty-six airfields, and American air-raids could not hope to neutralize, let alone eliminate, all of these. Before Ugaki could take any positive steps, however, on 16 February, aircraft from Fifth Fleet's carriers made the first naval air strike on Tokyo since that by Lieutenant Colonel Doolittle's Mitchells in April 1942. Bad weather and large numbers of Japanese fighters prevented the infliction of serious damage, but this mattered little. On the same 16 February, eight of Fifth Fleet's battleships and five of its heavy cruisers, supported by warplanes from its escort carriers – transferred from Seventh Fleet – began a massive bombardment of Iwo Jima.

Iwo Jima is an island in the Volcano Group, 5 miles long and 2.5 miles across at its widest point. The Americans desired its capture not only to deprive their enemies of a land and air base blocking the advance to the Japanese homeland, but because it had airfields from which the Superfortresses raiding Japan could be given a fighter escort and at which damaged bombers could land rather than having to make the long journey back to Tinian. It may be recalled that in July 1944, Iwo Jima's few defenders could only wait apprehensively for an invasion that they had no chance of resisting, but the Americans had missed their opportunity. In February 1945, it was a very different story.

Command of Iwo Jima had been entrusted to Lieutenant General Tadamichi Kuribayashi who, according to Major Frank Hough in *The Island War*, was the only Japanese commander 'to whom high Marine officers could accord genuine professional respect.' He had designed an impressive system of inter-connecting fortifications, joined up by tunnels and with their surface positions splendidly camouflaged. From these his garrison of 21,000 brave, capable and well-trained fighting men could offer a terrifyingly effective resistance.

American Intelligence was not unaware that Iwo Jima would present a formidable obstacle and every attempt was made to 'soften it up' prior to the date of its invasion. Starting on 8 December 1944, Liberators from the Marianas bombed the island on every single day and from 31 January 1945, on every single night as well. On 16 February, a continuous naval bombardment joined in the assault and on the 19th, the 4th and 5th US Marine divisions went ashore under a massive barrage from Fifth Fleet's heavy gunnery units and constant attacks by Fifth Fleet's aircraft including those from its fast carriers, back from their strikes on Tokyo.

Unfortunately, neither air nor naval bombardments could inflict more than minimal damage on Kuribayashi's well-sited, well-protected and brilliantly concealed defences. The Marines – 3rd Marine Division reinforced the others on 24 February – endured a ghastly ordeal. They lost almost 6,000 dead, missing or fatally injured, more than 17,000 wounded and in excess of 1,600 'combat fatigue casualties'. They earned twenty-four Congressional Medals of Honor, and they captured Iwo Jima. By 16 March, most of its defenders, including Kuribayashi, were dead, 216 had been captured, and the island was declared secure. At dawn on the 26th, however, 350 Japanese emerged from hiding to make a 'banzai charge' that caused 172 American casualties, 53 of them fatal, before they were wiped out. Some American optimists had predicted that the conquest of the whole island would only take four days.

During their struggle, Kuribayashi's warriors had received precious little help from their homeland and on the only occasion when any materialized it came, inevitably it seems, from the Kamikaze Corps. The Fifth Air Fleet had been talking about a suicide raid on the American base at Ulithi but no action was taken until 16 February, when Captain Sugiyama, commander of 601st Air Group, received orders from his superiors to form a new Kamikaze unit. He asked for volunteers two days later and, as so often happened, was forced to make a choice from among the large number of those who enthusiastically offered their services.

By 19 February, the new Kamikazes were ready for action, but by then all attention had been directed elsewhere and it was against American vessels in the vicinity of Iwo Jima that they would make their assault. This they did in the late afternoon and evening of 21 February, the first major Kamikaze strike since the one against Third Fleet off Formosa exactly one month earlier, and one made by mixed formations of bombers and fighters, all under the overall control of Lieutenant Hiroshi Murakawa, who was appointed because of his great experience in more orthodox forms of warfare. They struck in waves; the tactic whereby they would drop their weapons first and then try to ram was again adopted, and so great was their enthusiasm that the pilots of those fighters supposed to be acting only as escorts, on their own initiative and contrary to orders, also made suicide dives.

Every single aircraft that took part in the raid was therefore lost, but not in vain. The first wave, consisting of eight Zeros, encountered Hellcats which shot two of them down, but the remaining six attacked fleet carrier *Saratoga*. They dropped their bombs, scoring three hits; then they dived at her, one crashing into her flight deck while another struck her near the waterline, tearing a huge hole in her side.

Later waves came in so close together that their attacks seemed almost continuous. A cargo ship and a Landing Ship Tank were hit and the latter sank later, but both of them had comparatively few casualties. *Saratoga*, however, suffered far from minor losses when, for the second time, a Kamikaze smashed into the middle of her flight deck. Huge fires were started and although they were eventually mastered, *Saratoga* had to withdraw, ultimately to the United States. She lost 123 of her crew killed and 192 wounded, and 42 of her aircraft were destroyed. Moreover, her injuries proved so severe that she took no further active part in the war, being used thereafter only for training purposes. In 1946, she was sunk by an atomic bomb during the American tests at Bikini Atoll.

At much the same time as *Saratoga* was hit, eight Kamikaze torpedoplanes attacked a pair of American escort carriers. Of the six that went for *Lunga Point*, five were shot down and any torpedoes they launched missed. The remaining aircraft which had already dropped its weapon tried to ram her. It failed to hit her squarely and skidded along her flight deck before going into the sea where it exploded, shrapnel causing some damage to her hull but no casualties.

Escort carrier *Bismarck Sea* was less fortunate: two aircraft crashed into her only seconds apart. Both exploded, causing serious casualties and starting fierce fires. It may be that they had both still been carrying their torpedoes, for sailors on nearby vessels reported that they were temporarily blinded by the brightness of the explosions. In any case, *Bismarck Sea* was doomed. Her fires could not be quenched, ammunition began to detonate, and finally her after magazine blew up, tearing off her stern. 'Abandon ship' was ordered and she capsized and sank, taking with her 318 of her crew.

Despite the fact that this operation had sunk an escort carrier and knocked a fleet carrier out of the war – which in Japan's present position was just as good – no further Kamikaze attacks were made on the US vessels around Iwo Jima. Probably this was because it was felt that the distances involved were too great. Yet at the same time, the plan for a suicide raid on Ulithi was revived. This appears astonishing at first glance, for Ulithi is in the northern Caroline Islands south-west of the Marianas, 1,400 miles away from Kyushu, far more than Iwo Jima. Vice Admiral Ugaki, however, knew from Intelligence reports that Fifth Fleet's carriers had retired to Ulithi and he hoped to catch them at anchor and inflict another Pearl Harbor.

Accordingly on 10 March, twenty-four long-range Frances bombers took off for Ulithi, only to be recalled on receipt of an inaccurate message that there was only one carrier there. The error was corrected, and next day the bombers set out again to strike at the fifteen 'flat-tops' now reported to be at Ulithi. They were bedevilled by adverse head-winds, rain-squalls and engine malfunctions of various kinds. Several came down in the sea and most of the rest were forced to turn back. Only two, both desperately short of fuel, reached Ulithi.

By this time, night had fallen but the base was brightly lit, for the Americans had not imagined that they would be in any danger from an air-raid. Carrier *Randolph* was particularly brightly illuminated because she was taking ammunition aboard, and one Frances crashed into her. It was so short of petrol that it did not ignite in flames when it struck, as usually happened, but its bomb exploded, causing damage that put *Randolph* out of action for a fortnight, killed 25 men and wounded 106 more. All lights were then quickly extinguished, but the pilot of the remaining Frances thought he had located a carrier and dived, spectacularly but uselessly, into what was in reality a small islet. Next day, a speedy Myrt 'recce' aircraft flew over Ulithi and reported the mission had failed. Ugaki, who took full responsibility, never repeated it.

The organizers of the Kamikaze Corps reached a number of conclusions as a result of the raids at Iwo Jima and Ulithi. It seemed clear that very long-range missions were impractical and it was better to operate when their pilots only had a comparatively short flight to their targets; this presented no problem for the Japanese knew that their enemies intended to strike first at Okinawa and then at Japan's home islands. It also seemed that a single raid, however successful, had only a temporary effect. What was needed was a continuous series of raids that might really reduce the Americans' strength and confidence. Moreover, these should be made in very large numbers so that their pilots could hope to swamp and thereby overcome the improved American defences.

It was therefore necessary that the Kamikaze Corps should be drastically increased in size by reinforcements of men and aircraft. If the aircraft could be improved so as to counter the improvements made by the Americans, so much the better. As it happened, a new and potentially formidable suicide weapon was just ready to be revealed.

Among those who had advocated the use of suicide attacks even before the formation of the Corps was a young naval ensign and pilot of a transport aircraft named Mitsuo Ota. A university graduate with a fine mind, he had become convinced early in 1944 that conventional bombers could accomplish little and were being shot down at an unacceptable rate. He believed the solution was the creation of what might be called a manned flying bomb, or perhaps more accurately glider-bomb, that could be carried beneath a standard bomber and released a short distance from its target, on which it would dive with unstoppable speed. The pilot, of course, would have no chance of survival.

In the late summer of 1944, Ota, with the aid of the Aviation Research Department of Tokyo Imperial University, drew up preliminary blueprints of his glider-bomb. These were carefully studied during the autumn months and the possibilities of using such a weapon received strong support. Particularly enthusiastic was Captain Motoharu Okamura, a veteran naval pilot who, like Ota, had come to believe that the only way for Japan to turn the tide of war was by resorting to 'crash-dive tactics'.

Accordingly, the project received the 'go-ahead' and by the end of October, the first glider-bombs had been built. By March 1945, they were ready to be used by the 721st Air Group, a special Kamikaze unit commanded by Okamura. Called the Oka, meaning 'Cherry Blossom', a symbol of purity in Japan, the manned bomb was a fraction under 20ft long, had a wingspan of almost 16ft 6in and its nose was packed with 2,645lb of explosives.

It could neither take off nor land on its own, so would have to be carried to within 20 miles of its proposed target by a modified Betty with which the suicide pilot could communicate through a telephone circuit. It would then be cast off and go into a glide until within sight of its intended victim, when its pilot could use rockets in its tail to increase its speed to at least 600, perhaps as much as 650 mph.

With its small size and enormous speed the Oka should be almost impossible to intercept or to hit with AA fire. It appeared therefore to present a terrible threat and indeed was regarded by the Americans with more apprehension than the 'normal' Kamikazes. Yet the Oka had several disadvantages. Its mother-plane, the Betty, was very vulnerable to interception by US fighters until the time that it released its Oka. If and when it did, the Oka's pilot would find it extremely difficult to control his manned bomb and the faster it went, the more difficult this became. The Americans, partly admittedly to disguise their fears, called the Oka the Baka, this being the Japanese word for 'mad' or 'madman'. Whether or not it would prove an appropriate designation remained to be seen.

Meanwhile on 1 March 1945, a number of training units at various bases throughout Japan were banded together to form the Tenth Air Fleet. This had a strength of 400 aircraft and it was intended that it should be used as a reserve for Fifth Air Fleet and its pilots should fill any gaps in this as and when needed. Then it was 'suggested' that the Fifth and Tenth Air Fleets should turn their various formations into Kamikaze units and a massive drive to increase the number of suicide pilots was begun.

In the early days of the Kamikaze Corps, as we have seen, the pilots had been genuine volunteers and its organizers had been at pains to ensure that no pressure was put upon them. Now different attitudes were adopted. Strident propaganda broadcasts praised the achievements of the special attack pilots and hailed them as the saviours of their country. Kamikaze Corps staff officers visited bases to lecture the airmen on the successes gained in the Philippines. Meetings were held at which university students were urged to offer their services. Inevitably there was a good deal of 'peer pressure', with men being bullied or shamed into volunteering and doing so doubtfully and hesitatingly.

Furthermore, whereas the first Kamikaze volunteers were given no unusual attention or privileges and frequently lived in spartan and not very comfortable conditions, these latest recruits received special treatment. The civilian population showered them with praise and presents and regarded them with exaggerated respect. They were young men who were not used to such deference and some, to the regret of the founders of the Kamikaze Corps, lost the dignity of their predecessors and became unpleasantly conceited and arrogant.

Also in March 1945, another move was made that in the short term would increase the numbers of the Kamikazes but would later lead to problems and regrets. Even before the formation of the Kamikaze Corps, there had been occasions when pilots of Japan's Army Air Force had attempted to ram US warships. The earliest, it appears, was on 27 May 1944 at Biak Island just north of New Guinea. Major Katsuhige Takada, commanding a unit of twin-engined Kawasaki Nick fighter-bombers, attempted to hit destroyer *Sampson* but was struck by AA fire and came down at a safe distance away. This, however, was clearly an 'impulse' attack of the kind previously described and Takada's observer, Sergeant Major Motomiya, in fact survived and was taken prisoner.

After the formation of the Corps, other army pilots seem to have made similar 'impulse' attacks and it has been suggested by Peter C. Smith in his *Kamikaze: To Die For The Emperor* that some of those assaults reported to be by Navy Air Force Vals were really made by Army Air Force Sonias which, as was mentioned earlier, were very similar in appearance. The Army Air Force's leaders, however, had hitherto rejected the use of suicide tactics. Now, with their country in peril, they felt they must make sacrifices similar to those of Japan's naval airmen. They proposed to form suicide squadrons of their own under Lieutenant General Miyoshi, to be known as 'Tokubetsu' or 'Special Units'.

At first, all went well. Army fliers volunteered for suicide duties in sufficient numbers; army fighters, Nakajima Oscars, were adapted to carry bombs in the same way as Zeros, and it was hoped that a new suicide aircraft that had just been designed could be used by the Tokubetsu (though in fact it never was).[4] Within a couple of months, however, matters had gone badly wrong. The supply of army volunteers began to dry up and despite the protests of the officers directly commanding the Tokubetsu, the army chiefs began to direct whole formations to carry out suicide attacks, without any of the men having volunteered.

So great was the unselfish devotion to duty of the Japanese fighting men that almost all these enforced sacrificial offerings carried out their orders and even came to accept that only by such tactics could they perhaps save their country from total disaster. After the war, Lieutenant General Kawabe, who as army deputy chief of staff at Imperial General Headquarters was ultimately responsible for the suicide missions of Army Air Force units, assured an interrogator that 'Everyone who participated in these attacks died happy in the conviction that they would win the final victory by their own death.' If we change 'happy' to 'consoled', he was probably not far wrong.

Nonetheless, compulsory suicide was quite contrary to the original ethics of the Kamikaze Corps, and many of its early supporters felt that the nobility and 'purity' of their cause had been polluted. There were a few ugly incidents. Some pilots tried to dull their fears with drink and were still drunk when they flew their last mission. Others returned to base, insisting they could not find any potential targets. An admittedly very small number wore parachutes and were prepared to bail out and be captured. One is reported to have vented his feelings by shooting up his senior officers' quarters as he took off. It is only fair to add, however, that all these men put together made up a minute proportion of the Kamikaze strength. As Captain S.W. Roskill in the British Official History of *The War at Sea* confirms: 'Most of the conscript crews seem to have set out with the same selfless dedication as the volunteers.'

It should also be recorded that the pressure put on naval units and the orders given to those in the army only came later. In March 1945, for the last time, the Kamikaze Corps received a large intake of genuinely enthusiastic volunteers. These began to congregate on Kyushu, most southerly of Japan's main islands, because it was from there that the defence of Okinawa could best be undertaken and the Japanese rightly anticipated that it was against Okinawa that the next American onslaught would fall.

So Ugaki's Fifth Air Fleet was steadily strengthened by reinforcements from its reserve formation, Tenth Air Fleet, and also from Third Air Fleet which had been entrusted with the protection of Japan's eastern areas. Captain Okamura's 721st Air Group with its Oka manned bombs moved into Kyushu as well, taking up residence in its largest airfield at Kanoya. Kyushu also received the first batch of Lieutenant General Miyoshi's Army Air Force Kamikazes and, despite the bad feeling, amounting almost to active hostility, between Japan's fighting services, they were willing to be placed under Fifth Air Fleet's control. The Kamikaze Corps was thus ready to fight for Okinawa and at last was of a strength that would enable it to deliver massed air-raids that might yet overcome the improved defences of the United States navy.

Notes

1. Improved versions of the Kaiten were designed later. These had a crew of two and were larger and faster with a bigger cockpit and a longer and much better periscope. Very few, however, had been built by the time the war ended and none were ever sent into action.
2. All these objectives had been secured by the end of July 1945 except for Mindanao, where the Japanese, as at Luzon, held out until the end of the war. Kinkaid, incidentally, became a full admiral in April; a promotion well deserved and, one might suggest, well overdue.
3. Sadly, these particular precautions *had* been forgotten again by the Royal Navy by the time of the Falklands conflict in 1982.
4. This aircraft was the Nakajima Ki-115, known as the 'Tsurugi' or 'Sabre'. It was a single-engined monoplane that carried a bomb bolted to its fuselage and was constructed of wood, not metal, making it cheap and easy to mass-produce. Unfortunately, its performance proved poor and its handling qualities worse. A number of pilots were killed testing it and although more than 100 were built, none of them saw combat, which is why it was never given a code-name by the Allies.

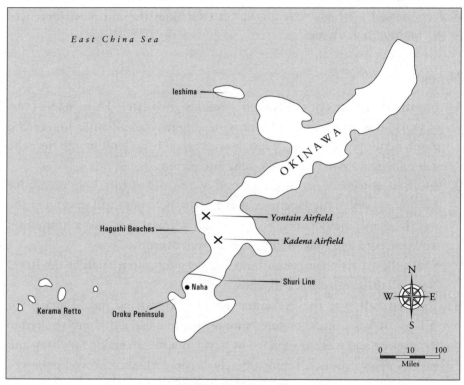

Map III – Okinawa.

Chapter 6

Floating Chrysanthemum

The massed air-raids would be called 'Kikusui' and the Kamikaze pilots who carried out these and other suicide operations at Okinawa would collectively be known as the Kikusui Force. The word means 'Floating Chrysanthemum'. Like the cherry blossom, the chrysanthemum flower is a symbol of purity in Japan – the Imperial crest is a stylized chrysanthemum – and that it was described as floating was a reference to the belief that the suicide volunteers would obtain purity by their sacrificial attacks on enemy ships.

Overall control of the Kamikaze operations in general and of the Kikusui in particular still rested with Vice Admiral Takijirō Ōnishi. In March 1945, he was appointed vice chief of the Naval General Staff and moved to the Combined Fleet Headquarters at Hiyoshi, south of Tokyo. Trusted subordinates also took up new positions which gave them responsibilities connected with the defence of Okinawa: Captain Inoguchi, for instance, was on the staff of Tenth Air Fleet; Commander Nakajima would join that of Captain Okamura's Ota Group. The most important appointment, apart perhaps from that of Ōnishi, however, was the one in February already noted: Vice Admiral Matome Ugaki as the leader of Fifth Air Fleet.

Like Ōnishi, Ugaki had been an admirer of Admiral Yamamoto: indeed at the time of Pearl Harbor – he then held the rank of rear admiral – he had been Yamamoto's chief of staff. He had kept that post until Yamamoto was killed by Lockheed Lightning fighters from Guadalcanal that shot down his Betty over Bougainville on 18 April 1943. Ugaki had been following the Imperial Navy's commander-in-chief in a second Betty. This too was attacked and came down in shallow water near the coast. Ugaki was injured but survived. Later he had taken command of Battleship Division One – *Yamato* and *Musashi* – and had fought in the Battles of the Philippine Sea and Leyte

Gulf. Now at the age of 54, the reorganization previously described made him in effect commander-in-the-field of the Kamikaze Corps.

It was not Ugaki, though, who made the first move in the struggle for Okinawa; it was Vice Admiral Marc Mitscher. He had commanded Task Force 58 – Fifth Fleet's carriers – in the Battle of the Philippine Sea and Task Force 38 – Third Fleet's carriers – in the Battle of Leyte Gulf. Now he was back in control of the eleven large and six light 'flat-tops' of Task Force 58, and on 18 March they made preliminary strikes on airfields in the Japanese homelands, causing considerable harm. Naturally the Japanese retaliated with attacks by both Kamikazes and orthodox bombers. The latter inflicted minor damage on *Enterprise* and *Yorktown*, while *Intrepid*, which the Kamikazes had neglected recently, was now attacked by one. She shot it down but debris and burning fuel killed two men and wounded forty-three others.

Next day, Mitscher's airmen concentrated on the docks at Kure and Kobe, but met with effective resistance from the new Kawanishi George fighters that proved far superior to the now aging Zeros. The Americans' own Combat Air Patrol also put up a resolute defence, holding off most of the counter-attacks made on their carriers, with one crucial exception. As Task Force 58 was preparing to launch fresh raids on Japan, five Judys that had eluded the CAP hurtled down on carriers *Wasp* and *Franklin*, scoring one bomb hit on the former and two on the latter. They came so low that *Essex* was also slightly damaged by 'friendly' fire and with such reckless daring that the Americans believed them to be suicide attackers.

It is now generally accepted that this was not the case. Although the Judy was the most popular choice for suicide operations apart from the Zero, it was also an extremely fine dive-bomber in its own right. There had been many previous occasions when Kamikazes had dropped bombs at their targets and then tried to ram them, but on this occasion only bombs struck home. All the Judys were downed by AA fire and there was no instance of any of them hitting a US warship or even near-missing one. There is thus every reason for believing they were not Kamikazes.

Yet it may be that that is not the whole story. We know from Japanese accounts that the Kamikaze Corps had plenty of Judys on its strength and indeed on the following day, 20 March, twenty of these were directed against Task Force 58, although they were thwarted by the Hellcats and only succeeded in damaging destroyer *Halsey Powell* and, oddly enough, submarine *Devilfish* which was caught by surprise on the surface. Going back to the 19th, we also know that several Kamikaze missions were flown on that date as well. From these, fourteen aircraft did not return and those that did, presumably the escorting fighters, claimed that two carriers had been damaged. It is just possible, therefore, that *Wasp* and *Franklin* were victims of the Kamikaze Corps, though not of its usual suicide dives.

Whatever the case, the Americans suffered heavily on 19 March. *Wasp* was able to continue operations, but had 370 casualties, 101 of them fatal. Both the bombs that hit *Franklin* landed on her flight deck where her aircraft were just taking off, setting these ablaze. Both then burst through the flight deck into the hangar, where they exploded, causing further fires and leaving her crippled and listing sharply to starboard. Of her crew, 724 died and 265 others were injured.

Even so, there was one aspect of this tragedy that could give the Americans hope for the future. *Franklin*'s damage was far worse than that suffered by the original *Lexington* or the original *Yorktown*, but they were at the bottom of the sea and she was still afloat. She was towed from the danger zone by heavy cruiser *Pittsburgh*, protected by the rest of Mitscher's carriers, and ultimately made her way back to the United States for repairs. It was clear that the standard of American damage control parties was now so high and the efficiency of their latest fire-fighting equipment so great that they could mitigate many a grim misfortune in the fighting to come.

On 21 March, there was another incident that would have given the Americans reassurance for the future if they had only known about it. In the course of their operations against Japan, Mitscher's carriers had destroyed 161 enemy warplanes but at the cost of 116 of their own aircraft. The Japanese had considerably overestimated these losses and the effects of their counter-attacks. They believed that Task Force 58 had been seriously weakened and was retiring with several cripples to look after. It seemed to Vice Admiral Ugaki that this would give him an ideal opportunity of directing against the Americans the new weapon he had acquired: the Oka manned bomb.

Accordingly, a force of eighteen Bettys was quickly gathered under the direction of Lieutenant Commander Goro Nonaka, a veteran torpedo-bomber pilot. All the Bettys, except two that had been made responsible for the squadron's navigation and communications, were carrying Okas. The crews of the Bettys and the pilots, led by Lieutenant Mihashi, who were to fly the Okas, were all ready and eager for a chance to see action.

Captain Okamura, however, was not eager. It is a telling comment on the weaknesses of the Oka that he felt Nonaka's squadron would only be able to carry out its mission if it had a very strong fighter escort. He was told that fifty-five Zeros could be provided. In fact, problems with keeping these serviceable would reduce the number to thirty but in any case Okamura was not happy even with fifty-five, warning Ugaki's chief staff officer, Rear Admiral Yokoi, that this was not enough. Yokoi was willing to cancel the operation but Ugaki, when asked for his approval, declared bluntly: 'If the Oka cannot be used in the present situation, there will never be another chance of using it.'

Okamura was frankly horrified by this decision. He knew that the mission would at best be a very difficult one and at worst would lead to his men going to a useless death. He therefore felt honour-bound to command it himself and advised Nonaka accordingly. Nonaka had already rejected a request from one of his officers, Lieutenant Kai, to lead the raid in his place and although Japanese obedience to orders was proverbial, he refused point-blank to accept Okamura's instructions. He protested furiously that it was his right to be at the head of his squadron and to suggest otherwise indicated a lack of confidence in him. Okamura acknowledged the justice of this attitude and, it is said, watched the Bettys take off with tears in his eyes.

There had been ample reason for Okamura's uneasiness. Some 60 miles from their objective, the formation was intercepted by fifty Hellcats from *Hornet* and light carrier *Belleau Wood*. Despite the efforts of the Zeros, fifteen of the Bettys were quickly shot down, as were twenty of their escort. Nonaka's Betty and two others managed to escape destruction temporarily by taking refuge in thick cloud cover, but the Hellcats were determined to let none escape. They were ready for the Japanese when they emerged and downed these last three bombers as well. The raid had been a total failure.

It was a failure with grim implications for the Japanese. Though it appears that the Americans did not realize the importance of what they had achieved, it was clear to Ugaki and others that the Oka was not the war-winner that some had promised. It would be used in the defence of Okinawa but only as one part of larger raids and, as will be seen, its successes were strictly limited. Attempts were made to design improved marks of Oka that would, for instance, be able to reach the target on their own without the aid of a mother-plane, but none of them were forthcoming before the end of the war.[1]

Ugaki would therefore have to rely on his mass Kikusui attacks, but his actions against Mitscher's carriers had cost him sixty-five aircraft. Other potential reinforcements had been destroyed on the ground during the American raids and these had also damaged facilities and disrupted communications. As a result, Ugaki would be unable to mount his first Kikusui raid until 6 April. Yet, as previous occasions had proved, preventative strikes could hamper and delay the Kamikazes but never completely check their activities. The Americans would find no lack of unwelcome attention when they closed in on Okinawa.

This they did on 25 March, with air-raids from Mitscher's carriers. *Wasp*, like *Franklin*, had left the combat zone to effect repairs, but Mitscher still had the aircraft of nine fleet carriers and six light carriers with which to pound the Japanese defences. Next day, aircraft from Fifth Fleet's eighteen escort carriers joined in the assault, while Fifth Fleet's heavy gunnery units added their weight of shells to the bombardment. On the following day, the Kerama Retto was secured, and on the day after that, the four carriers and supporting warships of the British Pacific Fleet arrived. Designated Task Force 57, they were placed under Spruance's command and given the task of neutralizing airfields on Formosa and the Sakishima Islands between it and Okinawa, to prevent aircraft from them intervening in the Okinawa battle.[2]

During these preliminaries to the landings on Okinawa, which were due to take place on 1 April, the Kamikazes, as expected, did their best to cause trouble and were responsible for various degrees of damage to battleship *Nevada*, light cruiser *Biloxi*, four destroyers, a destroyer escort, a destroyer transport and some naval auxiliaries. Their efforts reached an appropriate culmination on 31 March, when one attacked heavy cruiser *Indianapolis*, Admiral Spruance's own flagship. It struck her near the stern and went on into the sea, but its bomb penetrated her deck before exploding, blew two holes in her hull and wrecked her propellers. Yet another fine ship had to be withdrawn from the combat area to carry out extensive repairs.

Admiral Spruance transferred his flag to battleship *New Mexico*, from the bridge of which he watched as Fifth Fleet's 1,300 amphibious vessels, including 430 big troop transports, moved in towards Okinawa on 1 April. On board were 182,000 men of the US Tenth Army, commanded by Lieutenant General Simon Bolivar Buckner, and their objective was the 6-mile-long Hagushi beaches on Okinawa's west coast.

Since a successful invasion here would enable the Americans to make a quick capture of the aerodromes at Yontan and Kadena, it was correctly believed that Japanese Intelligence would have foreseen this move. Spruance and Buckner therefore anticipated that the landings would be bitterly resisted. In reality, Lieutenant General Mitsuru Ushijima, who commanded Okinawa's defenders, had decided, perhaps unwisely, that he would not fight for the beaches. Nor would he do more than delay the loss of that part of the island – about three-quarters of it – north of the beaches. Instead he would concentrate his men in the southern section of Okinawa north of its capital Naha, where the natural obstacles of steep hills and narrow ravines had been strengthened by man-made fortifications that were mutually supporting and, as at Iwo Jima, connected by underground tunnels.

Consequently, the American landings met with virtually no opposition. The two airfields were quickly seized and by noon of the following day, the invaders had broken right across the island to its east coast. The only real resistance was attempted by the Kamikazes and they were largely unsuccessful. One suicide aircraft crashed into a gun turret of battleship *West Virginia* but caused only minor damage. Another went for light cruiser *Birmingham* but was hit by AA fire just in time and went into the sea astern of her. An Oka raid was also sent out on 1 April, but again achieved nothing whatsoever.

Indeed, by an odd irony, the Kamikazes did most harm to vessels not involved in the actual invasion. In an attempt to distract attention from the real beachhead, a small force, called the Demonstration Group, had made a mock landing on Okinawa's south-east coast. This was attacked by Kamikazes which hit a transport and a Landing Ship Tank, killing forty men and injuring twenty-seven others. Then, in the late afternoon, with

50,000 US troops now ashore, two of the big transports that were already retiring were also hit, adding another twenty-one dead to the total of the suicide pilots' victims but having no effect on what has been called 'the most successful amphibious landing of the war.'

With the Americans established on Okinawa, Vice Admiral Ugaki got ready to deliver his first Kikusui which he and others hoped might deal such terrible blows that Japan could still hope for at least an honourable peace. It took time to gather the huge numbers desired, since reinforcements had to come from all parts of Japan and once in Kyushu had to be dispersed widely and concealed under trees or camouflage of various kinds to escape the prying eyes of American reconnaissance aircraft, not to mention strikes by Fifth Fleet's warplanes. As was stated earlier, therefore, it would be 6 April before the Kikusui could be launched.

In the meantime, Ugaki continued to harry the Americans over the next few days with suicide raids, minor in comparison with what was to follow, but adding to the strain on the men of Fifth Fleet. A Kamikaze crashed into the bridge of destroyer transport *Dickerson*, killing fifty-one of her crew and so damaging the ship that it was accepted she was beyond repair and the Americans scuttled her. Escort carrier *Wake Island* and four transports were also hit; all survived with various degrees of damage and more good men lost.

Then on 6 April came the first and largest Kikusui. In a series of waves, 355 Kamikazes, though the figure probably includes the escorting fighters, and about the same number of conventional attackers headed for Okinawa. They included eight Oka-carrying Bettys, but it seems that five of these were shot down before they could release their Okas and none of the remaining manned bombs made any hits. More significant was the fact that at least 125 of the aircraft sent out by Vice Admiral Ugaki came from Japan's Army Air Force and among the types of warplane used on suicide missions there could now be included bomb-carrying Nakajima Oscars, twin-engined Kawasaki Nick fighters and Mitsubishi Hamps, a variant of the Zero with clipped wings, built for the army.

It appeared inevitable that so many suiciders must cause a great deal of death and destruction, which they did! It was also entirely understandable that the sheer size of the onslaught rocked American morale and led to some anxious discussions as to how long it would be possible to survive assaults of this nature. These concerns led to an eager acceptance at face value of the inflated claims of American pilots and, on the other hand, a decision to keep silent about American losses, for the first time in the war.

Yet despite all the harm for which the Kamikazes had been responsible, there were several reasons why the Americans could anticipate that the future would bring hardship and suffering but also an ultimate triumph. For a start, it seemed unlikely that the Japanese had the resources to make other raids on a similar scale. Nor did they. The second Kikusui, which took place on 12 April, saw the number of Kamikazes employed fall from 355 to 185, and this was more than could be found for later missions. The Kamikaze Corps had made its greatest effort on 6 April, but it would never be repeated.

Furthermore, the injuries the Corps had inflicted, though horrible, were nothing like as great as its organizers had hoped and optimistically claimed. Nor had they been inflicted where they would be most valuable. If anything had really been demonstrated by the first Kikusui, it was that the new defensive tactics that the Americans had adopted were capable of mitigating the effects of the most massive raids the Kamikaze Corps could hope to mount.

Of all the American defensive measures, the most valuable on this and other occasions was undoubtedly the stationing of destroyers and smaller craft well away from Task Force 58 and the Fifth Fleet vessels directly supporting the Hagushi beachhead which were the Kamikazes' two main objectives. Bad weather on the morning of 6 April delayed the start of the Kikusui, but the afternoon would see frenzied action and the first US warships involved were the picket destroyers north and north-east of Hagushi: *Bush*, *Colhoun* and *Cassin Young*. At about 1400, their radar detected the advance guard of Ugaki's warriors heading for Okinawa. They gave due warning to the rest of Fifth Fleet and directed fighters from various Combat Air Patrols to intercept the intruders.

They also performed a greater service involuntarily. Ugaki had personally warned his fliers to concentrate on their major targets, the American carriers and battleships, especially the carriers, ignoring smaller warships. 'Do not be misled by your enthusiasm,' he is reported as saying, 'do not attack the first ship you see.' Several of his formation leaders, however, disobeyed orders and did attack the first ships they saw, which were of course the unlucky radar pickets.

It was most unusual for Japanese officers to disregard instructions in this way, but their motives are understandable. They realized that the picket destroyers had been the source of the warnings given to their enemies and the reason for the interceptions made by US fighters which began as early as 1430. If they eliminated the pickets, therefore, their later waves might have a better chance of achieving surprise and breaking through to the really important targets. It might also be that certain cynical realists grimly appreciated that they might well not break through themselves and it would be sensible to die usefully by sinking some American warships, if only minor ones.

So the US destroyers were subjected to especially savage Kamikaze assaults. Nor was it only those in the outlying pickets that suffered, for the Americans had established an 'inner ring' of destroyers, again on radar watch, to give warning to the larger warships; these also felt the Kamikazes' wrath. In his Official History, Professor Morison, who was with Fifth Fleet during the Okinawa campaign, gives a breathtaking account of the pickets' ordeals.[3]

The first assault was made by the now elderly Vals which, incidentally, had dispensed with air-gunners so as to increase their performance and had only the pilots on board. Shortly before 1500, two of them went for destroyer *Bush* but she shot both of them down at a safe distance. *Bush* had once survived a very heavy orthodox attack during the Leyte campaign, but this time the odds against her were too great. At 1513, a modern Jill torpedo-plane, carrying not a torpedo but a bomb, came in fast and low. Professor Morison takes up the story:

Commander Westholm promptly swung ship to bring it abeam and unmask his main battery. Fire was opened at a range of 7,000 to 8,000 yards. The plane jinked and weaved at an altitude of 10 to 35 feet above the water, and although every gun on the destroyer was firing, it kept coming and crashed between the two stacks. The bomb exploded in the forward engine room, killing every man there, and most of those in the two fire rooms. Flooding started immediately and *Bush* took a 10-degree list, but escaping steam smothered the fires and power was regained as the auxiliary diesel generator cut in. Handy-billys were used to control the flooding, the wounded were treated on the fantail or in the wardroom and although the ship had gone dead, everyone expected to save her, and all hands cheered when a CAP of four planes appeared overhead.

Bush was in a very dangerous position, however, for not only was she dead in the water and listing, but her 5in guns had been jammed and could not be brought to bear on any new attackers. Other waves of aircraft kept coming into view and Commander Westholm adopted the unusual course of ordering 150 men to go overboard where they would be less liable to be harmed, and putting out knotted ropes so that they could get back on board if and when it was safer to do so.

Meanwhile, news of *Bush*'s peril had become known. Formations of fighters were sent to help protect her and did destroy a considerable number of enemy aircraft. Destroyer *Colhoun*, the vessel nearest to *Bush*, steamed to her aid as fast as possible, only to come under attack herself. She shot down three Zeros in quick succession but a fourth was only spotted at the last moment as it dived at *Colhoun*'s port bow. Commander Wilson ordered an emergency turn, but he was just too late:

> The plane, already aflame, hit *Colhoun*'s main deck, killing the gun crews of two 40-mm mounts. Its bomb exploded in the after fire room, killing everyone there and rupturing the main steam line in the forward engine room. Lieutenant (jg) John A. Kasel, the engineer officer, opened the cross-connection valve before diving for the bilge, so the after engine room had steam and a speed of 15 knots was maintained.

This quick action brought only temporary relief. Further Kamikazes hurtled into the attack. *Colhoun* shot down two Vals but at 1717, a Zero smashed into her forward fire room and exploded, wrecking both her boilers, tearing a hole, 20ft long, in her hull below the waterline and starting the usual dreadful fires. One of her 5in guns was knocked out and all power was lost, with the result that the remaining 5-inchers could only be aimed manually, an appallingly difficult and exhausting business, so that *Colhoun*, like *Bush*, had lost much of her ability to defend herself. Worst of all, she also lost all forward movement and, again like *Bush*, was left dead in the water.

It might have been sensible for the Japanese to have left *Bush* and *Colhoun* crippled and drifting, but it seems their blood was up and they were determined to sink the ships that had sent out early warnings and thereby threatened the success of their whole operation. They made repeated efforts to do so. *Colhoun* shot down another Zero but then came under attack from a couple of dive-bombers:

> One, a Val, caught its wing in the after stack, caromed on No. 3 gun, knocking off its gas tank which burst into flames, and then bounced off main deck into the water. There the bomb exploded, knocking a 3-foot-square hole below the waterline and so deluging the after part of the ship with water that all fires were extinguished and everyone on the fantail was washed overboard.

Meanwhile, the second dive-bomber, another Val, hit by 40mm fire, pulled away from *Colhoun* and rammed *Bush* amidships instead, all but cutting her in half. Yet the men who had previously gone overboard climbed up to her deck again and her fires had almost been brought under control when one more Kamikaze, this time a Zero, made its dive:

> For the last time the 20-mm and 40-mm guns of *Bush* spoke. The Kamikaze cleared her by five feet, gained altitude, did a wingover, came in again, and crashed her port side at 1745, starting a terrible fire and killing or fatally burning all the wounded in the wardroom. A handy-billy, shifted to this fire, was no better than a garden hose on such a blaze; the entire forecastle was enveloped in flames, and ready ammunition began to explode.

It was the final blow. At 1830, *Bush* broke in half, her bow and stern rose skyward, then her fires were at last quenched as she slid beneath the waves.

Commander Willis, head of the destroyer division of which *Bush* was part, six other officers and eighty-seven men were killed or died later, mainly from burns.

Colhoun did not long survive *Bush*. An army Hamp from a later wave of suiciders made one last attack. It was hit and set on fire and although it rammed *Colhoun*'s port side, she was so damaged already that this made little difference. By now destroyer *Cassin Young*, which had herself been attacked several times but escaped unhurt, had reached the scene, but *Colhoun*'s fires steadily worsened and her stern sank ever lower. All that *Cassin Young* could do was rescue swimmers in the water and take off the remainder of *Colhoun*'s crew. Thanks to her prompt assistance, *Colhoun*'s casualties were only thirty-five dead and twenty-one wounded, but with all her survivors safely on board *Cassin Young*, she was finished off by American gunfire.

Bush and *Colhoun* had not perished in vain. It had taken a total of seven hits to eliminate them and they had shot down eight other Kamikazes. To these must be added the aircraft destroyed by US fighters protecting *Bush* and *Colhoun* and those downed by fighters alerted by the warnings *Bush* and *Colhoun* had given. The American fighter pilots and the devoted deck-crews who kept them airborne were completely exhausted by the time darkness brought the Japanese assaults to an end, but there was not one wave of attackers that they did not disrupt. To give one example, the first formation to arrive at the Hagushi bridgehead – at 1710 – had taken off with twenty aircraft: army Nicks and navy Vals flown by army pilots. Just five reached Hagushi and all were shot down by AA fire before they could make their suicide dives.

Yet despite the interceptors' efforts, as the Japanese had hoped, it proved impossible for them to deal with all the huge numbers of attackers that Ugaki had thrown against them. Moreover, the supply vessels of Fifth Fleet which Ugaki had selected as his men's secondary targets after the carriers were operating in an area that stretched from the Hagushi bridgehead to the Kerama Retto, while many of Fifth Fleet's support groups were still further spread out along the whole west coast of Okinawa. Even Fifth Fleet could not hope to provide enough cover for all of them.

One of these groups which was particularly vulnerable consisted of minesweepers *Emmons* and *Rodman* which were operating to the north of

Okinawa, right in the path of the Kikusui raiders who would sight them earlier than any other US vessels except the radar pickets. They did have the protection of a CAP of Corsairs, a type of naval fighter that had first seen combat from an American carrier in January 1945, though they had been provided to the British and served on British 'flat-tops' for almost a year before then. When the Kamikazes attacked, the Corsairs shot down about twenty of them but could not intercept them all. One hit *Rodman* and caused considerable damage. Poor *Emmons* was hit five times: on the bow, on the bridge, on the superstructure and twice on the stern which blew off her rudder. She sank in a mass of flames.

Kamikaze hits reduced some of the vulnerable supply ships to flaming wrecks as well. A Landing Ship Tank loaded with fuel oil burned for twenty-four hours before sinking, while two cargo ships carrying ammunition drifted helplessly, shaken by explosions, until finished off by American gunfire before they could harm other vessels. Ugaki's men also struck several more Fifth Fleet destroyers, but the injuries inflicted were greatly reduced by the effectiveness of the Americans' damage control systems and fire-fighting equipment. *Morris* and *Mullany* were set on fire, *Hyman's* forward engine room was flooded, *Bennett, Harrison, Haynesworth, Howorth* and *Hutchins* were all hit, as were destroyer escorts *Witter* and *Fieberling*. Every one of them survived.

The most extraordinary demonstration of American efficiency in this department was shown in a raid late in the day on another pair of destroyers. This consisted of ten army Oscar fighters and two navy Kate torpedo-planes probably flown by army pilots and, like the Jill that had been the first to strike *Bush* nearly three hours earlier, each carrying a bomb, not a torpedo. They came in at very low-level and thereby avoided any detection by radar. They were getting close to Fifth Fleet's Bombardment Group when, at 1753, alert lookouts on *Leutze*, one of the 'inner ring' of picket destroyers protecting the heavy warships, sighted them, gave warning of their approach and opened fire on them, quickly followed by every other ship in the vicinity. The commotion attracted the attention of American fighters which also intervened and shot down four of the suiciders.

Surprisingly, with battleships and cruisers near at hand and plainly visible, the remaining Kamikazes ignored them in favour of attacking the picket destroyer line. It has been suggested that the army fliers were not good at warship recognition, but one would have thought that sheer size would have told them which were the most worthwhile targets. More likely, therefore, now that warning had been given, they simply concentrated on the warships nearest to them which they knew they would be able to reach.

Rather unfairly, the Kamikazes did not strike first at *Leutze* which was the vessel that had prevented their achieving surprise – probably they did not know this – but engaged instead two other warships nearby: destroyer *Newcomb* and minesweeper *Defense*. The minesweeper was the lucky one. She shot down one Kamikaze and although struck by not one but two others, she sustained only slight damage.

Newcomb was the unlucky one. One Oscar was shot down just in time. Another Oscar hit her after funnel which was knocked over the side. It was a Kate that hit her hardest. It smashed into her amidships and its huge bomb went off with a tremendous explosion that wrecked both engine rooms and the after fire room, cut off all sources of power and, as so often, started furious fires. Professor Morison quotes *Newcomb*'s skipper, Commander McMillian, to tell us what happened next:

> With intentions of polishing us off, a fourth plane raced toward *Newcomb* from the port beam and although under fire by her forward batteries came through to crash into the forward stack, spraying the entire amidships section of *Newcomb*, which was a raging conflagration, with a fresh supply of gasoline.

As *Newcomb* all but disappeared under a sheet of flame and columns of smoke, watchers on vessels nearby, who included Professor Morison on battleship *Tennessee*, concluded that the destroyer was doomed, but her crew thought otherwise. Lieutenant (junior grade) Owens led a damage control party that put out a fire in a magazine. Surgeon Lieutenant McNeil carried wounded men to safety, then worked all night to heal their injuries. Fireman Nemeth was killed by the flames while securing steam lines. Machinist's Mate Tacey died trying to rescue men whom the flames had trapped. In all, forty of *Newcomb*'s crew died and twenty-four were wounded.

Lieutenant Grabowsky, in command of destroyer *Leutze*, also thought *Newcomb* was fatally injured, so brought his ship alongside her and prepared to lower boats to rescue her crew. On discovering that they had no intention of leaving her, he and his men set to work helping to fight her fires. Then, at 1815, another Oscar dived on *Newcomb* heading straight at her bridge. One of *Newcomb*'s 5in guns, firing in local control, put a shell into the Oscar's cockpit, presumably killing the pilot. Yet the death of the man flying it did not always stop the dive of a suicide aircraft. As if still under control, the Oscar swung away from *Newcomb* and crashed onto the stern of *Leutze*, where it exploded:

> Now *Leutze* too was in trouble. A fire sprang up in the after ammunition handling room. While one of her repair parties continued fighting fires aboard *Newcomb*, the other two attempted to check flooding on their own ship and jettisoned topside weights. Steering control was lost with the rudder jammed hard right. Seventeen compartments laid open to the sea by the Japanese bomb let in so much water that *Leutze* began to settle. Destroyer *Beale*, with all fire hoses streaming, now closed the disengaged side of *Newcomb*; and not until then did *Leutze* signal 'Am pulling away, in serious danger of sinking.'

Happily, it was not as bad as that. *Leutze* had been crippled, but her damage control parties mastered the fires and the flooding and kept her afloat. She had a casualty list of forty-one, but only seven of these were fatal. Tough little *Defense*, the crew of which seem to have been uplifted rather than disheartened by their own clash with Kamikazes, took her in tow and brought her safely to Kerama Retto.

Newcomb also reached Kerama Retto, towed by fleet tug *Tekesta*. She was low in the water, her superstructure blackened by fire, one funnel missing, the other at a drunken angle, and her deck described as having 'the contour of a roller coaster'. Yet she too was still afloat. It was even considered that *Newcomb* and *Leutze* could be repaired. In fact they had not been by the war's end and were scrapped soon afterwards, as were several other cripples. This, though, in no way detracts from the credit due to the skill and courage of their damage control and fire-fighting personnel.

A total of 466 American officers and men were killed by the first Kikusui and 568 others were wounded, often badly and horribly. No wonder the Americans were shaken. Yet considering the scale of the Kamikazes' efforts, what in retrospect appears most remarkable is the way the Americans' defensive tactics, particularly their picket destroyers, had prevented the infliction of really important damage. Vice Admiral Ugaki had ordered his men to make Fifth Fleet's aircraft carriers their primary targets and had expressed the view that if enough of them could be sunk or knocked out of action, it would 'restore strategic equilibrium'. There were 355 aircraft present to carry out his wishes, but only about thirty even sighted the US 'flat-tops' and most of these were shot down by the Combat Air Patrol before they could attack. They scored no hits, and near misses on light carriers *San Jacinto* and *Cabot* caused only minor damage and no casualties.

Indeed, for all its tactical successes, the first Kikusui had been a strategic failure and the consequences of this would become apparent as early as 7 April and be felt most severely by the remnant of Japan's surface navy. Admiral Toyoda had decided that he must make another attempt to turn the tide of war by slaughtering the US naval units supporting the landings on Okinawa, thereby wrecking the Americans' supply system and leaving their troops vulnerable to a counter-attack by Okinawa's defenders. He had taken a similar gamble at the time of the landings on Leyte but his Operation SHO had taken place in very different circumstances from his present planned Operation TEN. Even the code-names given to them reflected this difference. 'Sho' means 'Victory' and Toyoda had had a reasonable chance of achieving this. 'Ten' means 'Heaven' and Toyoda would need heaven-sent luck if he was to triumph this time.

For a start, Operation SHO had been meticulously planned in detail and although badly outnumbered, Toyoda had been able to send out a strong force of warships. Operation TEN had only been conceived a day or so earlier as a result of violent agitation by Toyoda's fanatical chief operations officer, Captain Shigenori Kami, and there had been no time for detailed plans or clear instructions. In addition, there was only one naval squadron available with which the mission could be carried out.

Admittedly this squadron was built around an impressive centrepiece: the surviving super-battleship *Yamato*. If she could reach the Hagushi beaches, her 18.1in guns should cause havoc among the US transports and any warships defending them. On the other hand, in the Leyte Gulf fighting, *Yamato* had performed miserably in her encounter with Seventh Fleet's escort carriers and then she had had the support of 3 other battleships, 6 heavy cruisers, 2 light cruisers and 11 destroyers. For her sortie against Fifth Fleet at Okinawa, she would be accompanied only by light cruiser *Yahagi* and eight destroyers and would face a vastly superior force that would be bound to overwhelm her eventually by sheer weight of numbers.

Toyoda realized this. It had been his plan at Leyte Gulf that once his battle fleet had savaged the landing beaches and their supporting vessels, it should retire through the Surigao Strait, but he knew there could be no escape for *Yamato*. It was decreed that she should fight until she was sunk or was too badly damaged to continue, in which case she should be beached on Okinawa and her men should join Lieutenant General Ushijima's defenders. They would not be equipped for land fighting, but it was casually assumed that they would find plenty of dead American soldiers from whom they could acquire any weapons needed.

Since it was accepted that *Yamato* would not return from her mission, her squadron was retitled 'First Special Attack Force', again it seems on the advice of Captain Kami. 'Special Attack' was the polite name given to Kamikaze operations, and inevitably this operation has been described as a super-Kamikaze mission or a Kikusui at sea. It was really more like a naval banzai charge where the men of a unit in a hopeless position would hurl themselves on their enemy to kill and be killed. Certainly Kami, who constantly urged his seniors and associates alike to show 'a true samurai spirit', referred to Operation TEN in these terms. So did Ushijima, though he declared that 'banzai charges should be left to soldiers' and advised the navy against attempting one.

There were plenty of naval officers who disapproved equally strongly. Vice Admiral Seiichi Ito who commanded the *Yamato* force made no protest, perhaps not wanting to appear unwilling to participate in an obviously perilous action, but his chief staff officer Rear Admiral Nobii Morishita, *Yamato*'s captain Rear Admiral Kosaku Ariga, the commander of the escorting warships Rear Admiral Keizo Komura and *Yahagi*'s skipper Captain Tameichi Hara were all less restrained. As fighting men, they were prepared to face death if necessary, but they believed that Operation TEN would result in the useless sacrifice of a battleship that, because it bore an ancient name for Japan with patriotic and religious significance, was regarded by many as an integral part of the country.

Admiral Toyoda, however, remained inflexible and the traditional obedience of Japanese officers, as of the samurai before them, reasserted itself. They accepted their orders and, as Ariga declared, would do all they could 'to make the operation a success'. After the war, Toyoda would say that his decision to sacrifice *Yamato* had been the hardest of his life, but he had no regrets: 'If there was still a slim chance of success, we had to do everything to help our troops at Okinawa.' In the last resort, it was better that *Yamato* perish in action rather than skulk uselessly in harbour and, if the worst happened, be tamely surrendered to the victors.

Despite this attitude, it was not the only or even the main aim of Operation TEN that *Yamato* go down fighting bravely, as has often been stated; the main aim was to defeat the Americans. This was constantly reiterated by the officers responsible for the battleship's mission or attempting to carry it out. Toyoda's final signal to his 'First Special Attack Force' ordered it 'to fight gloriously to the death to completely destroy the enemy fleet, thereby establishing firmly an eternal foundation for the empire.' Rear Admiral Ariga, *Yamato*'s captain, promised his men: 'Our guns are going to sow destruction among our adversaries.' Captain Hara of *Yahagi* specifically told his crew: 'I wish to emphasize that suicide is not the objective. The objective is victory.'

Of course if *Yamato* was going to gain a victory, if her 18.1in guns were going to destroy American shipping off Okinawa, she would first have to get there. The reason why so many officers felt that Operation TEN could not succeed was precisely because they doubted *Yamato*'s ability to do so. Their concerns were well-founded. *Yamato* would have to face the carriers of Task Force 58 and although two fleet carriers and one light carrier had retired to refuel, Vice Admiral Mitscher still controlled seven large and five light 'flat-tops' with a total of 986 aircraft.

Toyoda had faced a similar problem in the Battle of Leyte Gulf but then he had had a brave, skilful and well-led decoy force that could and did lure Third Fleet's carriers away from *Yamato* and the other Japanese battleships.

If he was to protect his present striking force from Mitscher's airmen he would have to adopt other methods. He did, in fact, take a number of steps which he believed, not unreasonably, would give his warships at least a chance of reaching Okinawa.

For a start, *Yamato*'s great guns had been provided with a new anti-aircraft shell, the 'San-Shiki' or 'Beehive'. This was packed with layers of 25mm incendiary bullets, about 6,000 in all, and had a fuse in the nose by which it could be timed to explode in front of an aircraft formation, when it would scatter its incendiaries over a wide area like the blast of a shotgun. Secondly, it was hoped that surprise might be achieved. Toyoda had originally intended that the *Yamato* force would race directly towards Okinawa but Vice Admiral Ito convinced him that it would be wiser to steam south of Kyushu heading first westward, then southward, during the daylight hours of 7 April, before finally turning eastward to make a dash for Okinawa timed to arrive before dawn on the 8th.

Most of all, though, Toyoda was counting on the assistance of the Kamikaze Corps. Vice Admiral Ugaki was one of the few senior officers who gave an unqualified welcome to Operation TEN. He was confident that his first Kikusui on 6 April would 'knock out enough carriers to draw the enemy's sting'. Then on the 7th, he would throw as many of his remaining aircraft as possible against Mitscher's 'flat-tops' and his Kamikazes and the *Yamato* force would distract attention from each other, so that the Americans wouldn't 'know which way to turn'.

None of these hopes would be fulfilled. The San-Shiki shells were not popular with *Yamato*'s gunnery officers because they damaged the rifling of the 18.1in gun barrels if used too often. Moreover when fired they discharged a thick mass of smoke that hampered the more orthodox AA gunners. To make matters worse, the weather was bad and the American airmen made skilful use of cloud-cover to conceal their presence before delivering surprise attacks. There are reports of the new AA weapons being used in the resulting combats but only occasionally and, it seems, without effect.

Equally ineffective were the efforts of *Yamato* and her escorts to evade detection. American Intelligence had intercepted messages regarding their sailing and since the Japanese naval code had been broken, their destination was revealed and warning passed to Spruance and Mitscher. During the night of 6/7 April, US submarines sighted the *Yamato* force and reported its progress. At dawn on the 7th, reconnaissance aircraft left the US carriers to look for it. They sighted it as early as 0822, and thereafter American scouts kept it under constant observation.

Perhaps the greatest disappointment for Toyoda was the inability of the Kamikaze Corps to achieve its promises. As we have seen, the Kikusui of 6 April did not knock out or even seriously injure any American carrier and this left *Yamato* hopelessly exposed. It is not true, as has been stated, that there was no co-operation between the Japanese warships and Ugaki's airmen on the 7th. In fact the American strikes on the battleship and her companions and the major Kamikaze attacks on Mitscher's carriers both began at about 1230. So great had been the Kamikazes' losses on the 6th, however, that it was just not possible for them to mount raids of anything like the same strength as those of the Americans and they never succeeded in diverting the Americans' attention away from the *Yamato* force as both Toyoda and Ugaki had hoped.

It is difficult not to feel sympathy for the hapless Japanese seamen. They were without any fighter protection, which Ugaki could not provide in addition to the offensive actions he had undertaken on 6 and 7 April. They faced wave after wave of air strikes by Helldiver bombers, Avengers – some armed with bombs but most with torpedoes – and Hellcat and Corsair fighter-bombers. Their AA gunners, overcome by the sheer numbers of their tormentors, could shoot down only ten of these, though five others had to 'ditch' for various reasons. They could only endure as their splendid, beautiful ships were battered to destruction.

Inevitably the heaviest attacks fell on *Yamato* but her escorts were not neglected either. Mitscher was determined not to concentrate on one target as had happened when *Yamato*'s sister-ship *Musashi* had been sunk in the Battle of Leyte Gulf. He did not want to sink just *Yamato*, he wanted to sink every single ship in the First Special Attack Force.

Mitscher's pilots carried out his wishes. Of the 8 Japanese destroyers, 2 were sunk outright, 2 were crippled and finished off by Japanese gunfire or torpedoes and 3 of the remaining 4 were damaged. Tough little light cruiser *Yahagi* received almost as much attention as *Yamato*. It is believed that she was hit by twelve bombs and possibly five torpedoes. At 1405, burning furiously and shaken by explosions, she capsized and sank.

As for *Yamato*, she was probably struck by as many as twelve torpedoes and eight bombs. While smoke and flames poured out of her, water poured into her, especially on her port side which had taken most of the torpedoes. Despite counter-flooding, she began to list and this became ever steeper as her damage was increased by several very near misses from bombs. Her speed dropped lower and lower. A torpedo hit on her stern jammed the rudder and she began to turn in circles. Then all power failed and her great gun turrets jammed as well. The order was given to 'Abandon ship'. At 1423, *Yamato* turned over completely and sank almost at once. As she did so, her after magazine exploded. A colossal column of smoke, visible over 100 miles away, rose thousands of feet into the sky. For all practical purposes it marked the end of the Imperial Japanese Navy.

Total Japanese casualties in the Battle of the East China Sea, as this episode was entitled, were 4,250 officers and men, more than 3,050 of them from *Yamato*. When the battleship's list became too steep to be corrected, Vice Admiral Ito shook hands with his staff officers, ordered them to save themselves, then locked himself in his cabin to await his inevitable end. *Yamato*'s captain Rear Admiral Ariga and two other officers tied themselves to parts of the bridge to ensure that they went down with their ship.

Despite these actions, there was clearly no intention of the mission becoming the sort of mass suicide that had happened in the days of the samurai or even a true banzai charge in which those making it usually perished almost to a man. There were plenty of survivors from the *Yamato* squadron. The remaining destroyers rescued as many crewmen from the vessels sunk as they could. Even from *Yamato*, 269 men were saved, including Ito's chief staff officer, Rear Admiral Morishita, and the battleship's executive officer (first lieutenant) Captain Jiro Namura. From the escort vessels Rear Admiral Komura and Captain Hara also survived.

Nor did those destroyers still afloat ever consider pressing on to Okinawa. They sensibly returned to Japan and their action was fully approved by Admiral Toyoda and even the belligerent Captain Kami. Destroyer *Suzutsuki*, hit by several bombs and a stray torpedo, had lost some 20ft of her bow. She crawled back on her own, stern first, steered by her propellers, and she came home safely.

While Mitscher's airmen were sinking enemy warships, the carriers from which they came and their own supporting vessels were fighting off enemy warplanes. Vice Admiral Ugaki had been able to assemble 114 aircraft. Of these, sixty were escorting fighters and those detailed to make crash-dives – Zeros and Judys, the latter carrying only the pilot – were not well coordinated. Nonetheless, they harried the Americans with a series of attacks throughout the day. A Kamikaze crashed onto one of battleship *Maryland*'s gun turrets, putting it out of action and killing all those manning it. Another heading for carrier *Essex* was shot down just in time and crashed into the sea 100 yards to starboard. A destroyer and a destroyer escort were damaged by near misses.

Carrier *Hancock* was the unlucky one this time. At 1235, a Zero, ignoring heavy AA fire, dived on her. It first dropped a bomb which exploded in a hangar and among other damage buckled and jammed the forward elevator. Then the Zero itself hit the flight deck and careered along this, smashing through groups of *Hancock*'s aircraft, nineteen of which burst into flames, shedding blazing fuel that poured across the flight deck and into the sea. Fire-fighting equipment, of all things, was set alight and it seems probable that in an earlier period *Hancock* would have been lost. As it was, improved safety measures and better-trained damage control parties enabled the fires to be mastered after a tense forty minutes, but one determined suicide attacker had caused vastly more damage than the whole *Yamato* force, as well as killing seventy-two American sailors and wounding eighty-two others.

Vice Admiral Ugaki now began to build up his strength in preparation for a second Kikusui. This could not take place before 12 April but Ugaki sent out sizeable raids throughout the four days preceding it, if with little effect. Kamikazes hit carrier *Enterprise* twice and battleship *Missouri*, three destroyers and a destroyer escort once each, but even in the case of *Enterprise* the damage done was surprisingly slight. The attacks, however, did keep up the strain being felt by the Americans.

They naturally came under still greater strain on 12 April. The Kikusui was carried out by 185 Kamikazes, though again it seems this figure includes escorting fighters, accompanied by almost 200 orthodox bombers. The suiciders were manned by both navy and army personnel, as in the case of the first Kikusui, and as on that occasion also, Oka-carrying Bettys took part in the assault. The Japanese attempted to achieve surprise by dropping metal strips, called 'chaff' by the Americans and 'window' by the British, that sent out signals to confuse the American radar. Perhaps for that reason, only two of the nine Bettys involved were shot down before they could release their Okas, though six more of them were downed afterwards.

At last Captain Okamura's Oka Group made history. At about 1445 on 12 April, destroyer *Mannert L. Abele*, on radar-picket duty, was crashed by a Zero that exploded in her engine room, leaving her dead in the water. A minute later, an Oka, flown it is thought by Lieutenant (junior grade) Saburo Doi, arrived. It struck the destroyer's starboard side amidships and broke her in half. She sank in only five minutes with the loss of seventy-nine of her crew. Another destroyer, the *Stanly*, was also hit by an Oka, but survived to shoot down a second Oka at a safe distance. Even so, this was the Oka Group's most successful day ever.[4]

The standard Kamikazes also damaged US warships by either hits or near misses but, as with the first Kikusui, their tactical success disguised a strategic failure. They caused injury to three more destroyers, four destroyer escorts and three minesweepers, but again wasted most of their energies on the picket vessels and not on major targets. Battleships *Tennessee* and *Idaho* suffered moderate damage but the most valuable prizes, the aircraft carriers, were not harmed at all.

Another blow, however, fell on the United States navy on 12 April, though because of the time difference the men of Fifth Fleet did not learn of it until early on the following day, Friday the 13th. President Roosevelt's health had been causing concern for some time, he was clearly exhausted by his many great responsibilities and he had in fact retired to Warm Springs, Georgia to recuperate. Yet he was only 63 and his sudden death from a cerebral haemorrhage came as a tremendous and unexpected shock.

This was especially hard for the men of the United States navy to bear because of their service's previous relationship with the president. A capable amateur sailor who boasted he was never seasick and a diligent student of naval history, Roosevelt had officially been Assistant Secretary of the Navy prior to and during the First World War. In practice he ran the department, for his titular superior, Joseph Daniels, a good-natured newspaper proprietor with little knowledge of maritime affairs, was happy to leave matters in the hands of his energetic deputy. Later, as president, one of Roosevelt's foremost concerns was to expand 'my Navy' as he called it, and to improve its ability to wage war. In return, its personnel gave him steadfast loyalty and support and for them his passing was a personal loss, a cause of sincere sorrow and a severe jolt to morale.

Radio Tokyo's report on Roosevelt's death was brief, restrained and dignified; it displayed no hatred, only a proper decent respect.

Notes

1. The Japanese also experimented with other variants of manned bombs. There were, for example, the Yokosuka 'Shinryu' or 'Divine Dragon', a bomb-carrying glider that took off with the aid of a battery of rockets, and the Kawanishi 'Baika' ('Plum Blossom'), really a piloted German V-1. Japan's Axis partner Germany gave her a good deal of technological information and this enabled her to build her first jet-propelled aircraft, the Nakajima 'Kikka' ('Orange Blossom') that bore a distinct resemblance to the Messerschmitt Me 262. None of these, however, got beyond the production of their prototypes.

2. For the sake of convenience and clarity, the exploits and ordeals of the British warships will be dealt with separately later.

3. Volume XIV, *Victory in the Pacific 1945*, from which all immediately following quotations are taken. For the benefit of those not fluent in American it should be said that a ship's 'stack' is a funnel and her 'fantail' is her stern.

4. Despite many exaggerated stories of the deadliness of the Oka/Baka, later American reports such as *The United States Strategic Bombing Survey (Pacific War)* that examined the question in great detail reveal that it was responsible for only one vessel sunk – *Mannert L. Abele* – and perhaps four others damaged, none of them warships larger than a destroyer.

Chapter 7

The Fall of Okinawa

President Roosevelt's death was mourned in Britain as well as the United States. Churchill would declare that the news made him feel 'as if I had been struck a physical blow'; he was seen to be fighting back tears when he left a memorial service in St Paul's Cathedral. As in the United States, the sailors had been particular admirers of the president, gratefully recalling his responsibility for American assistance in the crucial Battle of the Atlantic even before the attack on Pearl Harbor. It is possible, however, that the men of the British Pacific Fleet, while grieving over the loss of a true friend, regretted that he had overruled his naval advisers and met Churchill's wishes to let them participate in the Okinawa campaign and hence face the wrath of the Kamikazes.

Task Force 57, as the Americans called Britain's Pacific Fleet, was built around carriers *Illustrious*, *Victorious*, *Indomitable* and *Indefatigable*. They had previously been found in the Indian Ocean, their final operations there taking place on 24 and 29 January 1945 when they delivered strikes on a pair of large oil refineries at Palembang, Sumatra. These, although costly, were extremely effective, one refinery being so damaged that its output was halved, while the other ceased production altogether for a couple of months.

As the British warships retired after their final raid on the 29th, half a dozen Japanese bombers launched a counter-attack, coming in at such a low level that *Illustrious* was hit by AA fire, losing twelve men killed and twenty-one wounded. It has been suggested that the bombers were manned by suicide crews, but they did no damage and according to Captain Roskill's *Official History*, 'their attempt was so half-hearted that the fighters and anti-aircraft guns had no difficulty in dealing with them'; in fact, they shot down the whole lot.

'Half-hearted' was not normally the description given to a suicide attack and the suggestion that this was one would probably never have been made had one bomber not been downed only 'a few hundred feet' away from *Illustrious*. Onlookers on nearby warships declared that otherwise it would 'certainly have crashed into *Illustrious*', but even if this had been the pilot's intention it would have been an 'impulse' suicide, not an organized Kamikaze strike. The attackers were identified as Mitsubishi Sally bombers. These were Army Air Force machines and, as we have seen, the Japanese army only resorted to planned suicide attacks a month or so later.

Immediately after this incident, the British Pacific Fleet set out for Australia. It left its commander-in-chief, Admiral Sir Bruce Fraser, in Sydney. Following the example of Admiral Nimitz, he felt he could best serve his Fleet by remaining ashore to coordinate all its administrative requirements, especially the formation of a Fleet Train to keep it supplied; this had to be done in great haste from those ships that were available, without much regard for their suitability. Vice Admiral Sir Bernard Rawlings took over command of the Fleet at sea, while the carriers were entrusted to Rear Admiral Sir Philip Vian, an officer with a brilliant and colourful record, mainly in light forces, though he had commanded carriers during the invasion of Italy and the attacks on Palembang.

Rawlings and Vian brought their ships to the appropriately-named Admiralty Islands, thence to Ulithi and finally to the Okinawa area. Now having become Task Force 57, they took up station south-west of Fifth Fleet and south of the Sakishima Islands, of which the most important are Miyako and Ishigaki, and which lie between Okinawa and Formosa. Japan still had her First Air Fleet and a Kamikaze training school in Formosa and the task of the British warships was to prevent reinforcements being sent or attacks launched from Formosa by way of the numerous airfields in the Sakishima Group. This they carried out by constant strikes on these airfields and also on ones in northern Formosa.

It was a difficult and thankless responsibility, made no easier by the fact that Task Force 57 was not very well suited for it. The Americans had insisted and the British had accepted that this force should be self-supporting. Unfortunately the United States navy had become used to operating over the vast distances of the Pacific and had built up a chain of auxiliary vessels that could supply the fighting warships with everything they needed to remain at sea for long periods of time. The Royal Navy, by contrast, did not have the same experience and its supplies had to be brought all the way to its new base in Australia and then all the way to the fighting front.

This was an immense undertaking and the reason why a Fleet Train was so important. It would ultimately total some sixty ships but despite all the efforts of the Royal Navy and magnificent and generous assistance from the government and people of Australia[1] it was not possible to solve all the problems. There were, for instance, never enough fast tankers available and their absence would be a considerable handicap to Task Force 57.

Vian's carriers also laboured under several disadvantages. Their anti-aircraft armament was less than that of US carriers. Between them they controlled 216 warplanes (plus two Walrus amphibians for air-sea rescue missions), but this was a strength considerably less than that of any four American fleet carriers. It was also composed of five different types which meant that large amounts of different spare parts and indeed spare aircraft were required. It proved necessary to allocate two British escort carriers to deliver these and a third to provide them with fighter cover. All these difficulties resulted in Vian's ships having to leave the combat zone for about a fortnight at a crucial period of the campaign in order to be refuelled and replenished; it is rather humiliating to have to report that during their absence four of the little American escort carriers proved perfectly capable of performing their duties.

Nonetheless, Vian's 'flat-tops' did have one crucial advantage over their American and indeed Japanese counterparts. *Illustrious*-class carriers, to which all those in Task Force 57 belonged, possessed an armour-plated flight deck that formed the roof of the hangar and rested on 100-ton girders. The sides of the hangar were also armoured and it was isolated from all machinery and given its own ventilation system that ensured it would not be penetrated by petrol vapour should the carrier be hit.

Illustrious herself would prove the value of this concept as early as 10 January 1941 when attacked by German Junkers Ju 87 Stuka dive-bombers. These scored six hits, three of them with 1,000lb bombs, and three near misses. The carrier was set badly on fire and was left unable to operate her aircraft, yet despite one further hit in a later raid, her armoured flight deck and hangar saved her when any other 'flat-top' then in service would have been lost. She was able to limp into Grand Harbour, Malta, where the island's AA guns, a handful of RAF Hurricanes and her own Fulmar fighters prevented her suffering any further serious damage before she was patched up sufficiently to retire from the combat zone, ultimately to the United States for extensive repairs.

Another of Vian's carriers, *Indomitable*, had a similar experience on 12 August 1942 when escorting a convoy to Malta. She was also attacked by Stukas and although these made 'only' two direct hits and three very near-misses, they started fierce fires and so buckled the flight deck that those of her fighters that were then airborne had to land on *Victorious* instead. *Indomitable*, like *Illustrious*, was repaired in the United States and, again like *Illustrious*, she had demonstrated the supreme value of deck armour on an aircraft carrier.

It would prove equally valuable against suicide attacks and for this Vian's men would have reason to be grateful. Curiously enough, while no American carriers were attacked by suicide aircraft on 1 April, the day of the landings on Okinawa, the British 'flat-tops' faced a succession of Kamikaze raids throughout the day. Fighters shot down most of the enemy aircraft at a safe distance, but inevitably some eluded them. A Zero narrowly missed *Victorious*, skimmed over her flight deck and went into the sea where it exploded, drenching the ship with water but causing no damage. Another near-missed destroyer *Ulster*. It too exploded when it hit the sea, but this time the blast caused serious damage to *Ulster*'s boiler room, killed two stokers and necessitated her being towed to Leyte for repairs.

Carrier *Indefatigable* was singled out by three Zeros. Her fighters brought down two of them and damaged the third, but not enough to prevent it from diving straight at its chosen victim. It was hit again repeatedly by AA fire and its pilot may well have been killed, but still it kept going. For a moment it looked as though it would go right down the funnel, but instead it smashed into the flight deck at the base of the island superstructure, where it disintegrated in a spectacular blast that killed eight men and wounded twenty-two others, six of whom died later. If the Kamikaze had hit an American carrier, it would have burst through to the hangar and turned this into a raging inferno. *Indefatigable*'s steel deck received only a dent, 3in deep.

On 6 April, the day of the first and largest Kikusui, Task Force 57 again came under attack, though not from Vice Admiral Ugaki's men based in

Kyushu but from Zeros, Judys and Frances bombers of Japan's First Air Fleet in Formosa. The Task Force's CAP and anti-aircraft gunners brought down most of the attackers in time but one bomber, hit repeatedly by AA fire, struck the superstructure of *Illustrious* with its starboard wing before exploding in the water and showering the carrier with debris and the gruesome remains of its pilot.

Task Force 57, which had previously concentrated its efforts on the Sakishima Islands, now retaliated with strikes against Formosa on 11, 12 and 13 April, destroying a large number of enemy aircraft on the ground and in the air. On the 12th, a pair of *Indefatigable*'s Fireflies[2] made a particularly successful interception: encountering five Army Air Force Mitsubishi Sonia light bombers heading for Okinawa, they shot down four of these and damaged the remaining one. Attempts by the Kamikazes to counter-attack were intercepted by the CAP and caused no damage.

Illustrious, which was badly in need of a refit, now retired from the combat area. She was replaced by another vessel of the same class, the *Formidable*, which joined with Vian's other carriers in renewed attacks on the Sakishima Group that lasted until 20 April. By that date, though, Task Force 57 badly needed to replace aircraft losses and the ships of the Fleet Train could no longer keep it properly supplied. It therefore retired to Leyte for rest and replenishment and would take no further part in the Okinawa campaign until 4 May.

Its return would not be a happy one. Eager to inflict the maximum damage on the Sakishima Islands, Vice Admiral Rawlings, with the full agreement of Vian, decided to use his heavy gunnery units as well as his carrier aircraft. While the latter concentrated on Ishigaki, Task Force 57's two battleships and five cruisers sailed to Miyako where they bombarded its three airfields with great effect. The price paid for this, however, was that the Force's carriers were deprived of the protection afforded by the radar sets and anti-aircraft guns of the bombardment vessels, making them much more vulnerable in the event of an air attack.

As any cynic could have predicted, the Kamikazes in Formosa duly delivered such an attack. It appears that they threw in every aircraft that was available for the raid, which while consisting chiefly of Zeros, also included Vals, Myrts, Judys and Jills. Once again the defending fighters performed magnificently and only three aircraft, all Zeros, broke past them to the carriers. Of these, one was shot down by AA fire. A second hit *Indomitable* but bounced off her into the sea where its bomb exploded. Damage was slight but included the destruction of the carrier's radar, an improved US version that was the only one in Task Force 57. Sadly, it could not be repaired as there were no spare parts available.

The third Zero, by the common consent of all those who watched its attack, was flown by a very capable and presumably experienced pilot. His target was *Formidable* and he was almost on top of her when she turned sharply to starboard and apparently spoiled his aim. He pulled out of his dive, climbed away steeply, then came in again. At the last moment he dropped his bomb, then followed this into *Formidable*'s flight deck at the base of the island superstructure and among her parked aircraft. The result would be graphically described by those on board her:

> It was a grim sight. A fire was blazing among wreckage close under the bridge, flames reached up the side of the island and clouds of black smoke billowed far above the ship. Much of the smoke came from the fires on deck but as much seemed to be issuing from the funnel and this for the moment gave the impression of damage deep below decks. The bridge windows seemed to gape like eye-sockets and much of the superstructure was blackened. The deck was littered with debris, much of it on fire and there was not a soul to be seen.[3]

Formidable's crew had naturally taken what cover they could, but now the attack was over they quickly emerged and set about saving their ship. Almost everywhere seemed to be on fire, including the fire-fighting headquarters, but the flames were mastered and eventually extinguished. *Formidable* had had 2 officers and 6 men killed and 6 officers and 41 men wounded, many very seriously, and she had lost 11 aircraft as well as all the tractors used for moving them. Yet the armoured deck had again proved its worth. A hole in this some 2ft square was filled up with rapid-hardening cement and covered with wood and steel plates. To the amazement of the Americans, six hours after sustaining a hit that would have knocked out a

US carrier, *Formidable* was back in action and could launch and land her warplanes.

On 5 May, Vian's carriers, including *Formidable*, resumed their strikes on the Sakishima Group, this time without retaliation. On the 9th, however, while Task Force 57 was again attacking airfields on Ishigaki and Miyako, the Kamikazes did hit back. A group of five Zeros was intercepted by the Combat Air Patrol, but after one enemy machine had been damaged, the British pilots made the mistake of concentrating on finishing this off, allowing the remaining four to get past them and come in fast and low upon their chosen targets.

Vice Admiral Rawlings had ensured that on this occasion his heavy gunnery vessels had remained with the carriers to provide increased anti-aircraft fire, but it did not daunt the Kamikazes. Battleship *Howe* found herself the object of one Zero's attention but her AA gunners were able to set this on fire; it hurtled over her and crashed alongside. *Victorious* and *Formidable* also scored hits on the Zeros attacking them but the suicide pilots could not be halted and both carriers were struck.

Victorious, in fact, was struck twice. One Kamikaze rammed her flight deck, damaging her forward lift, starting a fire and killing four of her crew. Moments later, another skidded over the flight deck, smashed through and wrecked four Corsair fighters and finally went into the sea. The Kamikaze that found *Formidable*'s flight deck landed squarely on a group of Corsairs and Avengers and disintegrated in a mass of flames that utterly destroyed seven of these and damaged fourteen more, eleven beyond repair. Amazingly, the only fatal casualty was the petty officer in charge of a pom-pom gun who was decapitated by a wheel blasted off an exploding aircraft. Moreover, both *Victorious* and *Formidable* were ready to resume operations less than an hour later.

Once more the armoured decks of the British carriers had prevented crippling injuries. The Americans had not previously favoured these. It is arguable that they affected their carriers' stability by their extra weight and they certainly made them extremely uncomfortable in hot climates and prevented their operating as many aircraft as their US and Japanese counterparts were able to do. Yet now the Americans freely admitted that they provided the best of all defences against Kamikaze attacks and when three 45,000-ton American carriers of a new class – *Midway*, *Coral Sea* and *Franklin D. Roosevelt* – appeared after the war, all had fully armoured flight decks.[4]

If the armoured decks could prevent the Kamikazes from achieving maximum damage, however, the ferocious determination that the Japanese displayed undoubtedly had a considerable and adverse effect on the men of Task Force 57. The officers of *Formidable* would later sum this up in the following terms: 'As a terror weapon, these Kamikazes have a quality of their own. There is something unearthly about an approaching aeroplane whose pilot is hell bent on diving himself right into the ship. Wherever you are he seems to be aiming straight for you personally.'

After 9 May, Task Force 57 continued to harry the Sakishima Islands without coming under further suicide attacks, but the threat of their resumption hung continuously over the British warships. Probably the strain thus imposed played a big part in a number of unfortunate incidents that were a cause of some anxiety to Rawlings and Vian. Of particular concern was the amount of landing accidents on the carriers: these were responsible for losses twice as high as those suffered in combat.

These mishaps inevitably led to a decline in morale that later incidents did nothing to check. On 18 May, a Corsair in *Formidable*'s hangar accidentally fired its guns, hitting an Avenger parked nearby in its fuel tank. This promptly exploded, starting a raging fire that consumed thirty aircraft – more than those destroyed in both the carrier's Kamikaze strikes put together – and put *Formidable* in considerable danger before, mercifully, it was brought under control. On the 20th, as a final shock, there was a collision in thick fog between *Indomitable* and destroyer *Quilliam* which resulted in the latter being left dead in the water.

It was perhaps time for Task Force 57 to have a break from its labours. *Quilliam*, her bow buckled out of recognition, had to be towed away from the combat area stern-first, but she was brought safely to Leyte. *Formidable*, now with only eleven Corsairs and two Avengers on strength, retired to Sydney. After a last blow at the Sakishima Islands on the 25th, the rest of Task Force 57 also withdrew to Sydney. Rawlings was heartened by a signal from Admiral Spruance expressing his 'appreciation' of the 'fine work' the Task Force had done and its 'splendid spirit of co-operation'. The tribute was deserved but the chief emotion of the Force's seamen was probably relief that they were no longer involved in the struggle for Okinawa.

Admiral Spruance would certainly not have criticized such an attitude, for by now he personally was also feeling the strain. If the British were harried by Kamikazes from Formosa, Spruance's Fifth Fleet was assaulted by the main strength of the Kamikaze Corps in Kyushu. Mitscher's fast carriers, Task Force 58, made several strikes on Kyushu and did undoubtedly deprive Vice Admiral Ugaki of some of his intended reinforcements, but the Kyushu aerodromes were too many, too widely scattered and too well covered by fighters and anti-aircraft guns for the American raids to have more than a marginal effect.

Moreover the British, as we have seen, faced suicide attacks only at intervals, whereas Fifth Fleet sometimes had to endure them for five or six consecutive days, and by the end of May, they had included six more Kikusui of more than 100 aircraft each. By now almost every form of suicide tactic has been described, as has almost every type of horrific damage and hideous death and injury that they could cause. A blow-by-blow description of every raid therefore, could only be repetitive and quickly become meaningless. It would seem more sensible to give the details only of outstanding or unusual attacks and emphasize instead the sheer number of vessels harmed which soon became sufficient to dishearten the most courageous.

Equally depressing was the knowledge that Fifth Fleet could not hope to elude the Kamikazes because it was compelled to remain in the vicinity of Okinawa in support of the US ground forces. The fast carriers and escort carriers alike flew constant missions, and naval gunfire was used more often and in greater strength than at any other period of the Pacific War. Night brought no respite, for it was then that Lieutenant General Ushijima's defenders preferred to deliver their counter-attacks. Fifth Fleet aircraft dropping flares and Fifth Fleet warships firing star-shells illuminated and helped to thwart their efforts, but they ensured that there would be little sleep for the US sailors and lack of this became another factor sapping physical and mental vitality.

Most disheartening of all for Spruance's men was the thought that they had no way of knowing how long their torture must be endured. Clearly it would last until the struggle for Okinawa had ended and there seemed no prospect of this in the foreseeable future. By 21 April, the Americans had effectively secured the northern three-quarters of the island, but this had been comparatively lightly defended. It was perhaps more important that they had also secured Ie Shima, an islet west of northern Okinawa, because this gave them another aerodrome on which land-based US fighters were ideally placed for intercepting Kamikaze formations from Kyushu.

No one could have been in doubt as to how valuable this capture would be, for from the time of Roosevelt's death until 21 April, the Kamikaze Corps had sunk destroyer *Pringle* with a casualty list of 65 dead and 110 injured, and damaged 7 other destroyers, 2 destroyer escorts, 3 minesweepers and a tanker. One of the damaged destroyers was the *Laffey* which was assaulted time and again over a period of about an hour and twenty minutes. The Combat Air Patrol prevented many suiciders from reaching her and her AA gunners shot down at a safe distance eight of those that did, but nothing could save her from all her attackers. These adopted the tactic of dropping bombs before attempting to ram, and four bomb hits and one very near miss added to the devastation caused by six aircraft smashing into her and one more that missed by a few feet.

At an earlier period of the war, it seems almost certain that *Laffey* would have been lost, but her damage control personnel and her fire-fighting parties were determined she would not be; though her upper works were reduced to smouldering ruins and she was left dead in the water, they were able to keep her afloat. She was towed out of harm's way and, after receiving temporary repairs, she was even able to leave the area unassisted and fully under control. She had, however, lost thirty-two seamen killed and seventy-one were in the sick bay, of whom, ominously, some fifty were suffering from what in a military campaign would have been called 'shell-shock'.

Both *Pringle* and *Laffey* had been on radar-picket duty and the presence of the picket destroyers had again proved of immense value, not only because of the warnings they had given but because of the number of raiders that had attacked them rather than pressing on to more crucial targets. Battleships *New York* and *Missouri* suffered unimportant injuries and the only major warship severely hurt by the Kamikazes was that unlucky carrier *Intrepid*. She was crashed twice, set badly on fire, suffered ninety-seven casualties, ten of them fatal, and had to retire from the area to effect repairs.

The capture of northern Okinawa and particularly that of Ie Shima now provided some good news for the embattled Fifth Fleet, but the prospects of defeating the main Japanese strength on Okinawa still seemed as remote as ever. By 9 April, the Americans had come up against Lieutenant General Ushijima's main defences, known as the Shuri Line. Progress ground to a halt and Lieutenant General Buckner paused, built up his strength and on 19 April, directed three army divisions against the Shuri Line, backed by massive naval gunfire and strikes by carrier-based aircraft. Ushijima's men threw them back with heavy casualties. Buckner added first one, then another Marine division to the weight of the attack, but for the rest of April, in the expressive words of Major Frank Hough in *The Island War*, 'advances were measured in yards, even feet'.

During these frustrating days, Fifth Fleet did everything possible to assist the US ground troops, while simultaneously fighting off suicide pilots. These again vented much of their fury on the smaller picket vessels, hitting or near-missing eleven destroyers, a destroyer escort, a destroyer transport and five minesweepers, one of which, the *Swallow*, was so badly damaged that she had to be scuttled. Though again unable to get at the major American warships, they did engage supply vessels, sinking an ammunition ship and, in a night attack, hitting the well-named hospital ship *Comfort*. She was fully lighted and clearly marked with a red cross in accordance with the rules of war, but some unpleasant individual crashed into her anyway, killing 36 people, among them 6 nurses, wounding 52 others including 4 more nurses, and arousing much justified anger and contempt.

May would begin with further unpleasantness and strengthen the grim feeling in Fifth Fleet that the Okinawa campaign looked like lasting indefinitely. Ushijima had been persuaded by his chief of staff, Major General Cho, to follow up the Japanese defensive successes by launching a full-scale counter-offensive, planned to commence on the 4th. To do further damage to American morale and prevent Fifth Fleet from aiding its ground troops, Vice Admiral Ugaki was asked to deliver Kamikaze attacks on both 3 and 4 May.

Ugaki was eager to oblige and had taken steps to do so with maximum effect. The placing of army fliers under his command and the practice of allocating whole units for 'special attack' duties without waiting for volunteers had ensured that he was not troubled by the usual Kamikaze problem, a shortage of pilots, but he had still found himself faced with a shortage of aircraft. He had therefore sent out an appeal for practically anything that could fly and by now he had gathered a sizeable collection of various types. Japanese records report that the aircraft taking part in suicide attacks in the Okinawa campaign in order of numbers used were first the Zero (clear favourite), then the Judy, Frances and Val. These names will cause no surprise, but fifth in the list comes the Nakajima Jean, a biplane used for training purposes.

Over the two days of 3 and 4 May, Ugaki hurled a total of 125 Kamikazes at Fifth Fleet, 75 of them flown by navy pilots and the rest by airmen of the Imperial Army. They flew aircraft of every variety from biplanes to Bettys carrying Oka manned bombs. The biplanes had more success than the Okas. One Oka did score a hit but destroyer-minelayer *Shea*, though badly damaged and having thirty-five killed and ninety-one wounded, still survived, whereas a pair of biplanes played a part in sinking a US warship. Destroyer *Morrison* was first rammed by two Zeros and then the two biplanes hit her immediately afterwards. They were too flimsy to do much damage but the bombs they carried were not and *Morrison* went to the bottom with the loss of 159 of her crew; 87 others were wounded.

Morrison had been on radar-picket duty and once again the devoted sentinels performing this vital task were subjected to the majority of the suicide assaults. Destroyer *Little* was hit four times and not surprisingly sank, with a loss of thirty seamen dead and seventy-nine wounded. Destroyer *Luce* was only hit twice but this was enough and she also went down, taking with her 150 of her crew, including Commander Waterhouse.

Kamikaze attacks also sank a pair of Landing Craft Medium converted to carry rockets, and damaged light cruiser *Birmingham*, four more destroyers and several auxiliary vessels. Of these, the hardest hit was destroyer-minelayer *Aaron Ward*. She was reportedly struck five times, set on fire, badly flooded, temporarily disabled and had her steering controls jammed. Of her crew, forty-five died and forty-nine were injured. Yet she shot down three other attackers, remained afloat and was later towed to safety. Rather sadly, though, she was never repaired and was scrapped soon after the end of the war.

One determined Kamikaze managed to get past the defenders and smashed into escort carrier *Sangamon*. Bursting through her flight deck, this aircraft exploded in the hangar, killing thirty-six men, wounding twenty-one more and starting the usual raging fires that were only mastered with great difficulty. So much damage was done that *Sangamon* had to leave the battle area to seek repairs and in fact saw no further service during the war.

Sporadic attacks over the next few days added half a dozen more warships or auxiliaries to Fifth Fleet's list of damaged vessels. Among these, special mention should be made of destroyer escort *England*. She had the proud title of the most successful 'submarine-killer' of the entire war, having sunk six Japanese ones – all confirmed in enemy records – north of the Solomons and north-east of the Admiralty Islands in the period 19 to 31 May 1944. Sadly, she was less able to cope with the Kamikazes and withdrew from the combat zone with thirty-seven men dead; like *Sangamon*, she took no further part in the war. Neither did destroyer escort *Oberrender*, which similarly retired with serious damage and twenty-four men dead.

Fortunately perhaps for American morale, the Japanese proved far less effective in their attacks on land. All Ushijima's assaults were thrown back by the US soldiers and Marines with terrible losses. It was now Buckner's turn to build up his forces for another general offensive. This was delivered on 11 May, but again failed to break through the enemy defences. Buckner was forced to resume his slow but relentless push forward, gaining precious ground at a high cost, 100 yards at a time.

Also on 11 May, Ugaki unleashed another Kikusui attack, repeating it over the next two days with such machines as were still available. The assault first fell, as usual, on the picket stations and in particular on one manned by destroyers *Evans* and *Hugh W. Hadley*. This dauntless pair faced a series of attacks that came in at intervals for over an hour and a half. Their AA gunners resisted with spirit and skill, shooting down thirty-five aircraft between them: fifteen by *Evans*, sixteen by *Hadley* and four shared. Inevitably, though, some Kamikazes were damaged but continued their dives: four struck *Evans* and three *Hadley* which was also hit by an Oka manned bomb. Both suffered heavy casualties, including *Hadley*'s skipper, Commander Mullaney, who died later of his injuries. Both were left dead in the water and though they were towed to the safety of Kerama Retto, they were never fully repaired and were scrapped after the war.

Despite gallant efforts by the Combat Air Patrol, some Kamikazes were able to reach Task Force 58, and two of them rammed Vice Admiral Mitscher's flagship, the great fleet carrier *Bunker Hill*. One, a Zero, dropped a bomb and then followed it onto her flight deck, ploughing through the warplanes parked there. It then went over the side, but it left the deck a mass of blazing aircraft.

The other suicide attacker, a Judy bomber, had moved directly above the carrier into its radar's 'blind spot'. As *Bunker Hill*'s crew watched in horrified fascination, this aircraft turned over and came down in a vertical dive. It struck the flight deck at the base of the island superstructure and smashed clean through it to explode in the heart of the ship. Literally in a flash she was reduced to a blazing, listing hulk. Her fires burned for five hours, but once again the ability of her fire-fighters and the effectiveness of their equipment saved a vessel that would have been lost earlier in the war. Nonetheless, she too had to withdraw from the battle area and she lost 392 officers and men killed and 264 wounded, of whom a dozen died later.

Over the next few days, other major US warships would fall victim to Ugaki's suicide pilots. Spruance's flagship, battleship *New Mexico*, was rammed, heavily damaged and set on fire; she lost 61 men killed and 119 wounded. Then it was the turn of the most famous of all US warships to suffer. It had been aircraft from the *Enterprise* that had destroyed three Japanese 'flat-tops' at Midway Island. Later this veteran carrier had fought with distinction at the Battles of the Eastern Solomons, Santa Cruz, the Philippine Sea and Leyte Gulf, and defied the worst that her enemies could do.

Now, though, a single Zero fighter-bomber flown by Lieutenant (junior grade) Shunsuke Tomiyasu would end *Enterprise*'s career in the Second World War. He crashed onto her forward elevator and burst through it into the elevator pit, where his bomb exploded. The carrier's flight deck was buckled by the blast, aircraft in her hangar caught fire, the main bulk of the elevator was blown a spectacular 400ft into the air, appearing to be balanced on the top of a towering column of smoke, and she sustained eighty-two casualties. Amazingly, only fourteen of these were fatal, but *Enterprise* became one more vessel to leave the area to effect repairs. They were completed in September 1945, but by that time the war was over.

Vice Admiral Mitscher had transferred his flag to *Enterprise* after *Bunker Hill* had been hit. He now moved it again to carrier *Randolph*, but the departure of *Enterprise* and *Bunker Hill*, added to that of *Intrepid* earlier, meant that Task Force 58 had to be reorganized in three Task Groups instead of its previous four. Mitscher had also lost members of his staff in the attacks on his former flagships and both he and Spruance were by this time starting to feel the effects of the continual burdens placed upon them. As Nimitz would sympathetically acknowledge, Fifth Fleet's sailors and airmen enjoyed some relief from the tension as their vessels withdrew to refuel, replenish, be overhauled or even be repaired, but Spruance and Mitscher 'remained at the scene of operations until the strain they were under became almost unbearable.'

They would have no relief for some time. During the next few days, suicide raids damaged nine warships or transports and on 24 May, Ugaki launched another Kikusui, massive strikes continuing throughout the day, to reach a culmination early on the 25th. The Combat Air Patrol made several effective interceptions but could not hope to stop all the suicide pilots, with the usual unpleasant consequences.

The destroyer transports supporting the US ground forces suffered especially severely. *Bates* was sunk outright. *Roper* was compelled to return to the United States for repairs, but was scrapped at the end of the war. *Barry* was so seriously damaged that it was considered there was no point in repairing her. She was therefore emptied and later used as a 'decoy' to divert the attention of the Kamikazes away from more valuable targets; in this she succeeded only too well, for on 21 June she would be hit again by a suicider and sunk.

Other warships were damaged as well and since we have recently recorded several hits on veterans, the experience of a newcomer might be worthy of notice. Destroyer *Stormes* had only joined Fifth Fleet on 23 May, but perhaps it was tempting fate for a vessel of that name to oppose pilots attempting to recreate the effects of a massive typhoon. Soon after 0900 on the 25th, one of these at the controls of a Zero and graciously described by Commander Wylie as 'an excellent flyer' who 'took full advantage of his tremendous speed without ever losing control of his plane', put first his bomb, then his Zero into the destroyer's superstructure. He caused considerable damage, started fires, killed twenty-one of her crew and wounded fifteen more. Just two days after reaching Okinawan waters, *Stormes* left them again to seek repairs.

If anyone had hoped that Ugaki might have exhausted his stock of available aircraft, they were quickly disappointed. On 27 May, the anniversary of Japan's great naval victory at the Battle of Tsushima in her war with Russia, another Kikusui was delivered. The attacks continued throughout the day and resumed on the 28th. In all and for the last time, more than 100 enemy aircraft took part and the Americans probably considered themselves fortunate that these sank only one warship and inflicted lesser harm on a few others.

Once again the picket stations endured the worst of the Kamikazes' fury. Destroyer *Drexler*, attacked by Army Air Force Nick fighters, was hit twice. The first blow left her dead in the water and the second one immediately afterwards caused her to roll over and sink in less than a minute, taking 158 of her crew with her; she also had 54 men wounded, 2 of whom died later. Destroyer *Braine* was attacked by four Vals. With the help of destroyer *Anthony*, she shot down two of these but the other two struck her and although she survived, 67 of her crew did not and 102 were wounded. *Anthony* was also damaged, as were a couple of minesweepers and some auxiliaries. Total American casualties were 290 dead and 207 wounded.

Admiral Nimitz, as he tells us, now 'took the unprecedented step of changing the command in the midst of a campaign.' At last there would be some rest for Spruance who was replaced by Admiral Halsey and for Mitscher who was replaced by Vice Admiral John McCain. Fifth Fleet became Third Fleet, Task Force 58 became Task Force 38, and when the British carriers returned to the combat zone in early July they ceased to be Task Force 57 and became Task Force 37. *Indomitable* and *Indefatigable* were refitting but *Victorious* and *Formidable* would soon be joined by another *Illustrious*-class carrier, the *Implacable*, and together would in effect be treated as if they were a fourth task group in Third Fleet's Fast Carrier Force.[5]

Halsey was not happy at being given what he saw as the 'purely defensive role' of assisting the US troops on Okinawa and protecting the vessels supporting them. In reality, though, by the time he took over, the end of the campaign was at last in sight. Buckner's superiority in men, equipment and aerial support enabled him to rest his front-line soldiers and Marines from time to time, but Ushijima had no such options and his men were rapidly becoming exhausted. On the same 27 May that Fifth Fleet became Third Fleet, the Americans finally broke through the Shuri Line to capture Okinawa's capital, Naha, and two days later, they took its key position, the old Shuri Castle, while the Japanese slowly fell back to the extreme south of the island.

The Kamikaze threat was also fading. The series of heavy attacks up to and including the 28th had cost Ugaki almost his whole reserve of aircraft and airmen. For a week, Third Fleet was harried only by occasional small formations that damaged just a single destroyer-transport and a single cargo ship. Encouraged by this slackening of the tension, Vice Admiral McCain, on 4 June, sent two of his task groups to hit the Kyushu airfields. They did so successfully, but as they retired early next morning, they encountered a different sort of divine wind.

It may be recalled that in the previous December, Third Fleet had been mauled by a typhoon that, among other damage, had sunk three destroyers with a terrible loss of life. The typhoon that hit Third Fleet on 5 June 1945 mercifully harmed ships and aircraft more than human beings, but the ordeal they endured was as savage as any caused by Ugaki's samurai. Some 150 aircraft were totally destroyed and many others damaged. No vessel was lost but thirty-six received structural injuries, the most spectacular of which befell heavy cruiser *Pittsburgh*, the bow of which was completely torn off.

As if the Americans had not been tried sufficiently, Vice Admiral Ugaki took advantage of the departure of the fast carriers from Okinawa to begin, on 5 June, a new series of attacks that continued over the next two days. This was officially considered to be a Kikusui assault but whereas Fifth Fleet had faced eight Kikusuis, in all of which more than 100 Kamikazes had taken part, in this one only 50 suicide aircraft were committed. These came in with their usual determination but with little luck. They hit six vessels including escort carrier *Natoma Bay*, battleship *Mississippi* and heavy cruiser *Louisville*, but only destroyer-minelayer *J. William Ditter* suffered severe damage. She had to return to the United States for repairs and, like so many others, was scrapped soon after the war ended.

Thereafter, Kamikaze missions ceased for almost a fortnight with two unpleasant exceptions, both of which, as so often, turned their attention to the picket destroyers and both of which demonstrated new ways in which the suicide pilots could sink American warships. On 10 June, destroyer *William D. Porter* shot down a Val but it crashed close to her side and as it sank beneath her its bomb exploded. This so damaged her hull that the resultant flooding could not be contained and she went to the bottom.

On 16 June, a more remarkable and more horrible incident took place. Destroyer *Twiggs* was attacked by a torpedo-plane. It was set on fire by her AA gunners but kept coming. In the past, Japanese aircraft had launched torpedoes at US warships and then tried to ram them or had rammed them with their torpedo still aboard. This one tried a new variation. It dropped its torpedo on top of *Twiggs* and then rammed her. There were two huge explosions and *Twiggs* quickly went down together with 152 of her seamen, including Commander Phipps.

Meanwhile, the comparative lull in Kamikaze raids had permitted McCain's fast carriers to return to Leyte Gulf for a well-earned rest. Third Fleet's escort carriers and supporting gunfire vessels, however, continued to help complete Okinawa's conquest, which was at last being achieved as the Americans pushed on south of the Shuri Line, aided by an amphibious landing at the tip of the Oroku Peninsula that runs south-west of Naha. By the 13th, the peninsula had been secured, and on the 16th, Lieutenant General Buckner ordered a full-scale assault on the final Japanese positions in the south of the island. On the 17th, Ushijima's exhausted forces began to collapse and next day he made a signal to his superiors, admitting defeat and sending his 'deepest apologies to the Emperor and the people of the homeland.'

It was also on the 18th that Okinawa's defenders struck a final defiant blow. Lieutenant General Buckner was making a tour of inspection of the front line, which by now was only some 2 miles from the southern end of Okinawa. In the early afternoon, he arrived at a section where the

8th Marine Division was preparing to engage the enemy. Major Frank Hough in *The Island War* describes what followed:

> The general had not come to the front especially to watch them, but by chance he found himself near their command post, on a hill which afforded an excellent view of what was going on up forward, and paused to watch the attack for a few minutes. By this time the Japanese artillery had been reduced close to the vanishing point. No shells had fallen in this area all morning. Now, however, by some devious quirk of destiny, a lone gun somewhere in the shrinking enemy territory let go a few random rounds. The first one felled the general, though none of the several others near him was so much as scratched. He died before they could evacuate him.

Buckner was succeeded by Marine Major General Roy Geiger who, for all practical purposes, quickly completed the conquest of Okinawa. By the evening of 21 June, the Americans had reached the sea and Japanese soldiers were no longer resisting but shooting themselves or blowing themselves to pieces with hand grenades. For the first time in the Pacific War, very large numbers were actually surrendering, though it seems likely that many, perhaps most, of the 10,755 prisoners were Korean or Okinawan labourers and conscripts of whom there had been some 30,000 altogether. Estimates of the number of Ushijima's men who died one way or another range from 110,000 to over 135,000; those of the Okinawan civilians killed vary from 10,000 to 25,000, with perhaps twice as many injured.

Lieutenant General Ushijima was not among the prisoners taken. In the early hours of 22 June, he enjoyed a last meal, then knelt on a white cloth and ripped open his abdomen with a ceremonial dagger called a 'wakizashi'. Immediately afterwards, an aide decapitated him with a sword. The chief of staff, Major General Cho, followed his leader's example and perished in the same way. Some young nurses who had no intention of surrendering either, committed suicide in an equally dramatic but less ghastly way by throwing themselves off a cliff into the sea.

Several members of the Kamikaze Corps also died on 21 or 22 June. Ugaki, for reasons difficult to fathom, chose these as the dates of a final Kikusui. It was a pitiful shadow of the ones that had mauled Fifth Fleet. A total of forty-five aircraft took part over the two days, including six Oka-carrying Bettys. The Okas again made no hits and only two Bettys got back to their base, as did fifteen other aircraft, presumably the escorting fighters. At a cost of six manned bombs and twenty-eight aircraft – if we include the missing Bettys – the Kamikazes damaged four minor warships. Among these was seaplane tender *Curtiss* which had once been the first vessel to be crashed, perhaps deliberately, by a Japanese warplane. She was now crashed again, this time quite certainly deliberately and had thirty-five men killed, but she survived and, unlike several other vessels, was fully repaired.

This was not the last time that attacks were directed at US vessels in the vicinity of Okinawa. For the rest of June, the Americans still had to kill or capture many thousands of Japanese troops holding out in caves and underground fortifications, and thereafter the island was turned into a massive advance base for the planned final advance on the Japanese homeland. Units of the United States navy remained on hand to assist and the Kamikaze Corps had not forgotten them. Ugaki could do little, however, for once again the supply of aircraft and pilots for the Corps had wasted away and in any case he wished to preserve his remaining strength to resist the anticipated invasion of Japan.

Nevertheless, there were sporadic suicide missions in June and July, apparently to remind the Americans of the price they would have to pay in that invasion. These were completely unsuccessful until 19 July, when destroyer *Thatcher* was badly damaged and had to return to the United States, becoming yet another vessel to be scrapped when the war ended. The transport *Marathon* was damaged two days later.

There was then a pause until the end of July, which saw a final flurry of assaults, carried out, as seems oddly symbolic, by the Kamikazes' elderly biplanes. In the early hours of 29 July, a flight of these attacked three radar-picket destroyers. Some were shot down but one struck USS *Callaghan* squarely on her main deck, its bomb going through this into the after engine room, which was wrecked. The usual fierce fires sprang up and *Callaghan* began to sink by the stern. Then the flames reached her magazines and the destroyer was shaken by a series of explosions as her 5in shells began to detonate. It was quickly realized that she was beyond help and she was abandoned, sinking soon afterwards.

Another biplane attacked destroyer *Pritchett*. It was shot down just before it could strike her, but its bomb was flung forward into her side where it exploded, causing considerable damage. The third destroyer, *Cassin Young*, was unhurt by this raid but her immunity lasted only until the early hours of 30 July, when she too was hit by a biplane, losing seventeen men killed and seventy-five wounded, of whom five died later. Shortly afterwards, a biplane near-missed destroyer transport *Horace A. Bass*. Its bomb went off as it hit the sea, and splinters killed one man and wounded fifteen others. It was the last Kamikaze attack of the Okinawa campaign.

The Americans had paid a fearful price for the capture of Okinawa. In the course of the fighting on land they had had more than 7,600 killed or missing and nearly 32,000 wounded. At sea, more than 4,900 sailors had died or were missing and in excess of 4,800 others had been injured. In the air, more than 650 American warplanes had been destroyed, as had almost 100 British ones. These were not reassuring statistics for the planners trying to assess the probable price of landings in Japan's home islands.

Since the only sortie by the Imperial Navy's surface vessels – the *Yamato* mission – had not approached close enough to engage American warships, virtually all the American naval casualties had been caused by air attacks. In addition, while American and indeed British aircraft had been lost in combat or on operations, most of those destroyed had been victims of air attacks on their carriers. The Japanese had sent out conventional bombers and fighters as well as Kamikazes but they had suffered losses of at least 2,200, while only a small fraction of their raids had proved successful; another illustration of the much greater effectiveness of the suicide attacks.

As for the Kamikazes, Japanese records are apparently and understandably incomplete, but it has been calculated that in the Okinawa campaign from late March until 22 June when the island was officially declared secure, there were some 1,900 Kamikaze sorties. These, as we have seen, were made by pilots of both Japan's navy and her army. From them fewer than 900 aircraft made it back to their base and these were either the escorting fighters which the Japanese never intended to sacrifice or occasionally those which had been unable to locate a target.

In return for its losses of more than 1,000 warplanes, the Kamikaze Corps had sunk 26 ships, though none of them were bigger than destroyers. It had damaged 176 others, many more than once, including carriers, battleships and cruisers. It should be noted that about fifty of the damaged vessels were put out of action for the rest of the war and many were scrapped when it ended. No wonder *The United States Strategic Bombing Survey (Pacific War)* concludes that had the suicide attacks been delivered 'in greater power and concentration they might have been able to cause us to withdraw or revise our strategic plans.'

Yet the fact remains that the suicide attacks did not cause the Americans to withdraw or revise their strategic plans; they did not prevent the fall of Okinawa. There were many factors that brought about this result. The sheer size and strength of Fifth Fleet, at which all but a few attacks had been directed, prevented it from being crippled when this would have been the fate of any other naval force. The wasting nature of suicide missions meant that the organizers of the Kamikaze Corps had to rely increasingly on elderly aircraft and ill-trained pilots. The Americans' equipment such as that for fire-fighting and damage control and their tactics such as their picket destroyers had alike improved. Most of all, however, the result was attained by the steadfast resolution of the men of the United States navy.

It is worth remembering that the very nature of a suicide dive with its effect of suggesting to every man on the target vessel that the enemy pilot was aiming at him personally was far more threatening than any conventional air attack, no matter how efficient and determined. This was seldom mentioned officially, but there are glimpses in action reports. Captain Armstrong of the much-battered HMAS *Australia*, for instance, states that the injuries suffered by his crew were 'mostly shock'. Commander Robinson, skipper of US destroyer *Caldwell* that had suffered during the Leyte campaign, agrees that 'Everyone was pretty much shaken up.' During the Okinawa campaign, there are frequent references to 'combat fatigue casualties' and 'shattered nervous systems'. Individual accounts long afterwards would honestly admit: 'I was terrified.'

If the attack itself was unusually frightening, the consequences of a hit could be unusually frightful. In *The Battle of Leyte Gulf*, Stan Smith, quoting Chief Yeoman Killen of *Franklin*, presents a stomach-churning description of what happened when that carrier was struck, not during the great battle but by a Kamikaze on 30 October 1944:

> The dead were littered over the deck (flight deck) and the wounded were moaning for help. Fires had broken out around the shattered, charred remains of the elevator, and smoke was pouring from the hole caused by the suicider. 'Don't try to get in there!' someone yelled. I looked around. An enlisted man was trying to support an officer – I think it was an officer – and both were burned, blackened and bloody. Behind them, screaming for help, was my division commander with his arm blown off and blood pouring into his pants. He was walking around talking to someone who wasn't there. He dropped dead when several men attempted his rescue, just looked at them and dropped dead. Another man had the pieces of a fighter wing's aluminum sticking out of his chest. When we attempted to get him out he just said 'Leave me, fellows' and collapsed. Pieces of human flesh stuck to the deck, and the blood lay bubbling from the excessive heat. I grabbed a man who was groaning and staggered out.

Fires, in fact, were the almost inevitable consequence of a successful suicide attack because the attacker's fuel tank was nearly always ignited. They were therefore more likely to be started by a crashing aircraft than by any shell, bomb or torpedo. As a result, many American sailors died a dreadful death and many others were hideously burned. American accounts of seamen who were consumed by the flames, trapped in compartments the hatches of which had been jammed, or who suffered unspeakable agonies, or who survived swathed in bandages and having to be fed intravenously, make grim reading.

Sights and experiences of this nature must have imposed further strain on the Americans, and their spirit and their resolve must have been weakened but were never broken. We can read just as many accounts of brave and brilliant rescues; of the devoted care given by medical personnel; of AA gunners staying at their posts until they were swallowed up by roaring fires; of inspiring examples like that of Commander George Davis, who when his destroyer, the *Walke*, was rammed during the fighting at Lingayen Gulf, 'burned like a torch' but remained in control of his ship until the attack was over and only then left his bridge to die of his injuries some hours later.

There were many reasons for the Americans' resolution. One simple one was that they were brave and well-trained. They were certainly better trained than most of the Kamikaze pilots and in some respects they were even braver. Unlike the Japanese, they had no long tradition of self-sacrifice and contempt for death. For them, death was far more terrible and they had no desire to die if this could be avoided. Yet they were fully prepared to risk death and would face it without flinching if this became necessary.

Their courage was undoubtedly bolstered by other factors. They were confident that they were winning. Had the Japanese fulfilled their aim at the Battle of Leyte Gulf and wrecked the Americans' beachhead and supply system, and had the American ground troops then been annihilated by Leyte's defenders, the new Kamikaze tactic must have come as a terrible and demoralizing threat. As it was, the Americans could see it was just a last desperate attempt to turn the tide. They were also less rigid than their enemies and their sense of humour did much to ease the tension. One cherishes the story of a hard-pressed picket destroyer, the crew of which painted an arrow on the deck, pointing over the side, accompanied by a message to the Kamikazes: 'Carriers That Way'.

Yet the most important motivation of the American sailors was their sense of duty. They were loyal to their ship, their shipmates and their country, and they fought and if necessary died for these. In this respect they were no different from the Japanese and perhaps it was the reason why almost all of them might regard the Kamikaze tactic with incomprehension and the Kamikaze organizers with abhorrence, but could respect and even admire the unselfish courage of its young pilots.

The Japanese, at the time anyway, do not seem to have paid a similar compliment to their enemies. This was surely unwise because it led them to underestimate American stamina and resilience. It was quite certainly unfair. The samurai of the Kamikaze Corps and the seamen of the United States navy were opponents worthy of each other.

Notes

1. In the first six months of 1945, Australia provided the Royal Navy with food, clothes, medical supplies, spare parts and other equipment amounting in all to over £21 million.

2. The Firefly was a two-seater naval fighter, designed to replace the Fulmar.

3. Quoted from *A 'Formidable' Commission*, the authors of which are stated to be 'Wardroom Officers of HM Aircraft Carrier *Formidable*'.

4. The US Navy's original *Midway* had been an escort carrier, but when it was felt that this would be a more suitable name for one of the planned new fleet carriers, she was rechristened. Experienced sailors consider this to be unlucky and it appears that they were right, for her new name was *St Lo* and it will be remembered that she was the first vessel sunk by the Kamikaze Corps.

5. Halsey would be far less gracious towards the British than Spruance had been, however. When in late July, Third Fleet's carriers struck the final blows at the Japanese navy, then helpless in harbour for lack of fuel, Halsey refused to allow the British 'flat-tops' to participate, not wishing anyone to share his credit. It is worth recording, though, that on 9 August, Lieutenant Robert Hampton Gray, a Canadian Corsair pilot from HMS *Formidable*, was awarded a posthumous Victoria Cross for sinking escort vessel *Amakusa* at the cost of his own life.

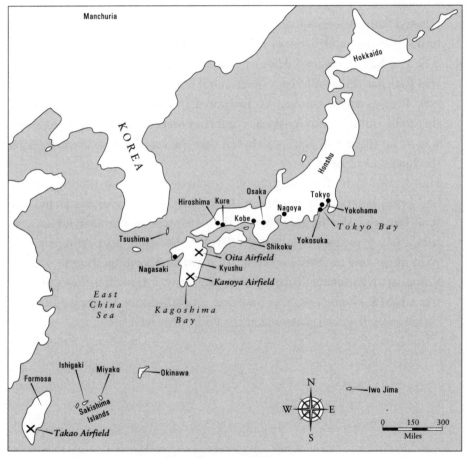

Map IV – The Approaches to Japan.

Chapter 8

'To Bear the Unbearable'

Ahead of the Americans there loomed the prospect of an invasion of the main Japanese islands. On 3 April 1945, General MacArthur was placed in overall command of the ground troops needed, whether soldiers or Marines, while Admiral Nimitz was given control of all supporting naval forces. Even as the struggle for Okinawa was being fought out, these officers and their staffs began to draw up plans for the culmination of the Pacific War.

Since the plans were never put into practice and indeed many details had not been settled before the end of the war, they need only be discussed briefly. At the end of October 1945, several small islands south of Kyushu would be captured and radar stations set up there to help repulse the Kamikaze attacks that the Americans were sure would be forthcoming. It was an essential preliminary to Operation OLYMPIC on 1 November: the invasion of Kyushu itself.

This would be the responsibility of General Walter Krueger's Sixth US Army, units of which would make landings on both sides of southern Kyushu and thereafter move northward to occupy about one-sixth of the island. The Americans had no intention of taking the rest of it. They would already have secured important airfields, including the Kamikazes' main base at Kanoya, and the 50-mile-long Kagoshima Bay that would provide an ideal refuge for the US navy. From these, their seamen and airmen would be able to support the second and more important part of the American plan.

Operation CORONET, provisionally estimated for 1 March 1946, would be carried out by both First and Eighth US armies. They would land on each side of Tokyo Bay and then deliver a pincer movement on the Japanese capital. MacArthur and his advisers considered, perhaps optimistically, that its fall would end Japanese organized resistance and bring a speedy conclusion to hostilities.

Since Japanese Intelligence continued to function with admirable efficiency, the country's leaders were kept well-informed of their opponents' plans and could make preparations to meet them. As was mentioned earlier, the most determined of the military diehards was the War Minister, General Korechika Anami, who could muster some 2.5 million soldiers plus naval personnel. They were short of food, weapons, ammunition, transport and equipment of all kinds, but Anami called on them to 'defend Imperial soil to the last'; to 'fight doggedly to the end in this holy war for the defence of our divine land', even if they were reduced to eating grass and sleeping in the open. They were urged to be ready to die and given the grimly realistic motto that 'each man will take an enemy to death with him.'

To support his soldiers, Anami demanded the raising of a volunteer militia, declaring that 'the total national manpower will be united into a fighting force that can furnish the necessary manpower for the co-ordinated war plans of the army and navy.' Men too old or medically unfit for military service, female factory workers, boys of 15, girls of 17, assessed, officially at least, at a total of 28 million, did volunteer, were given military drill and, in lieu of modern weapons, provided with bamboo spears or converted farm implements. Like the soldiers, they were warned that 'all war preparations will be carried out in the spirit of suicide attacks', taught the slogan 'a hundred million die together' and told that it was their duty to kill 'at least one enemy soldier'.

Anami intended to direct maximum effort against the Kyushu landings, hoping that this might so emphasize the difficulties the Americans would have in subduing the Japanese islands that it would persuade them to agree to a favourable peace. At the very least, he thought it would delay the later landings threatening Tokyo. Yet for all his exhortations to his troops and his belief that civilian volunteers would reinforce them, he trusted the Kamikazes to cause the most havoc among the Kyushu invasion forces.[1]

Since Vice Admiral Takijirō Ōnishi was vice chief of the naval general staff, Vice Admiral Matome Ugaki was still in tactical command of the Kamikaze Corps, and both held views similar to those of General Anami, there was no question of the Corps not co-operating fully. As seen earlier, Ugaki made occasional attacks on US warships in the vicinity of Okinawa during July 1945, and on the 26th of that month, bombers of Japan's Army

Air Force made a single, somewhat pointless strike against British vessels in the Indian Ocean. Of the seven Kamikazes involved, three were shot down by fighters and two by AA fire, but one near-missed aircraft carrier *Ameer*, causing some damage, and one hit minesweeper *Vestal*, injuring her so badly that she had to be sunk; the only Royal Navy vessel to be destroyed by suicide attack.

August 1945 saw no Kamikaze missions flown until the 9th, by which date a lot of other events had taken place. That afternoon, an attempt was made to attack Task Force 38. Most of the suiciders were intercepted and brought down by US fighters, but a Val hit and damaged destroyer *Borie* which, it hardly needs saying, was on radar-picket duty, killing forty-eight men and wounding sixty-six; the last warship to be struck by a Kamikaze.

For the most part, though, the Kamikazes' organizers concentrated on building up the number of their machines and training the pilots to fly them, ready for the anticipated invasion of Kyushu. By early August, they could boast a strength of 5,350 aircraft prepared for suicide attacks and perhaps another 4,000 that could be converted to such use if required. To avoid American air-raids, these were largely removed from major air bases and dispersed among some 325 small grass strips scattered throughout northern Kyushu, the nearby large island of Shikoku and the main island of Honshu. They were hidden when possible in natural caves or carefully constructed underground hangars and, when not so protected, were concealed under clever and effective camouflage.

During earlier campaigns, both Ōnishi and Ugaki had told their men to make aircraft carriers their primary objectives, with the vessels carrying or supporting the landing forces only the second-best targets. Now, though, in response to promptings by Anami and other army officers, it was decided that the invasion transports would be singled out for the Kamikazes' attention. Considering the number of aircraft at his disposal, Ugaki would have been able to deliver several Kikusui attacks and had these been as successful as the ones at Okinawa, the Americans estimated that they would have sunk 90 ships and damaged more than 800 others. It was a terrifying prospect.

Quite apart from the losses inflicted by the Kamikazes, the examples of Iwo Jima and Okinawa gave warning that even after the American troops had got ashore, they would have to fight long arduous battles and suffer extremely high casualties. Moreover, an invasion of the home islands would almost certainly prompt a slaughter of all Allied prisoners of war, since the Japanese would be unlikely to waste manpower guarding enemies who, in their eyes, should never have survived in the first place.

It was inevitable, therefore, that the Americans should recoil in horror from the thought of invasion and look for another way of achieving victory. One alternative would be to increase the existing naval blockade of Japan. This had already reduced the country to a pitiful state. By August 1945, she had lost 90 per cent of her merchant shipping and with it the ability to import the raw materials that she had gone to war to obtain. Oil, coal, iron-ore and bauxite (the main commercial source of aluminium) were all in desperately short supply. To the shortages were added the bombings of factories and as a result Japan's production of munitions had been reduced to only 30 per cent of its pre-war capability.

Nor was it only raw materials that Japan had to import. A mountainous country, her acreage of arable land was small and she relied on her merchantmen to bring in food. The rice harvest for 1945 was the worst for more than thirty-five years, while 90 per cent of her rice imports were lost en route, and even in a good year over one-fifth of Japan's rice had to be imported. Her fishing boats had also suffered terrible losses and in 1945 were supplying only about 40 per cent of their usual catch. Again the bombings made a bad situation worse. By driving large numbers of homeless out of the cities and disrupting the transport system, it prevented food being brought quickly to where this was most needed. A shortage of fuel and warm clothing added to the miseries of malnutrition and the rapid spread of disease. Economic planners feared that as many as 10 million citizens would soon be facing starvation.

So great was the chaos that the military extremists who still thought that an invasion could be defeated admitted that if the Americans did not invade but attempted to bomb and starve Japan into surrender, this would be 'the most troublesome possible course which could be adopted against us.' Many in Britain and America, Churchill for one, were certain that such a course was bound to bring about a surrender. It would, however, take time, during which Allied lives would continue to be lost, and it seems that everyone recognized the undoubted discipline and fortitude of the Japanese people but had not fully realized the desperate plight to which they had been reduced. Also in mid-July a new weapon had become available that promised to avoid any need for lengthy delay.

Yet there was a way in which the war could be brought to an end without an invasion or the use of the new weapon. It had been Japan's tragedy that she had fallen under the power of a brutal, aggressive and fanatical military clique, but this had always been opposed by some of the most important men in the country and their opposition was now coming to a head.

Even at the time of Japan's entry into the Second World War there had been opposition. In July 1937, the military extremists had led their country into a savage war with China. As a result, the United States, where China's ruler, Chiang Kai-shek, enjoyed considerable support, had put increasing pressure on Japan by way of economic sanctions. In July 1941, this had culminated in the freezing of all Japanese assets in America, amounting to £33 million in value, and meant that, for want of funds, Japan was unable to obtain essential raw materials, especially oil. With her oil reserves disappearing at the rate of 12,000 tons a day, she was, declared the Chief of Naval Staff, Admiral Nagano, on 31 July, 'like a fish in a pond from which the water is gradually being drained away.'

Japan had to act quickly before her resources dried up completely and she had only two courses open to her, neither of them pleasant ones. She could seize the raw materials she needed by force, but that would mean war with America, Britain and the Netherlands. Or she could persuade the Americans to lift the embargoes but the price for that, it soon became clear, would be a total withdrawal of all her forces from China.

Japan's politicians and business interests would gladly have terminated the hideously costly war with China. The Japanese Prime Minister, Prince Fumimaro Konoe, a member of the ancient and illustrious house of Fujiwara, who viewed war with America as a nightmare, therefore sought a summit conference with President Roosevelt that might settle their differences and also give him the prestige he needed to be able to control the army. Sadly, however, his suggestion was rejected by the Americans.

Konoe accordingly lost, not gained, prestige and on 16 October, he resigned. His successor was the leader of the military extremists, General Hideki Tōjō who, like Anami later, was Minister of War and was not known as 'The Razor' for nothing. He regarded a withdrawal from China as a massive 'loss of face' that would destroy Japan's morale, honour and 'very existence'. In practice, therefore, war had become inevitable.

Tōjō's attitude was particularly deplorable because he had been told that a still higher authority wished to avoid war at an Imperial Conference of 6 September. As the name suggests, such meetings were held with the Emperor present, but he had always remained silent. In fact the provisions of Japan's constitution and the counsel of his advisers united to keep the Emperor 'above the clouds', detached from all decision-making or controversy and hence from all criticism.[2]

It was therefore a tremendous shock to the assembled ministers when Hirohito unexpectedly rose to address them. When he had succeeded to the throne in 1926, he had, as was the custom, selected a title for the period of time during which he would reign: his choice was 'Showa', meaning 'Enlightened Peace'. It was with this in mind that he now recited a poem composed by his grandfather, Emperor Meiji, which may be translated as follows:

> The four seas are brothers to one another.
> Why then do the waves seethe and the winds rage?

This poem, he added, expressed his grandfather's great love of peace and was one that he personally had always admired.

Though a somewhat cryptic utterance, all present realized it indicated that their sovereign desired peace. Tōjō constantly stated that he would never do anything contrary to the Emperor's wishes. Had he been true to his word, he would have abandoned his refusal to withdraw from China forthwith. He did nothing of the kind, and on 7 December 1941, the Pacific War began.

The series of swift successes that followed the raid on Pearl Harbor naturally delighted the Japanese public. Some leading figures like Konoe and Marquis Koichi Kido, Lord Keeper of the Privy Seal and the Emperor's chief adviser, continued to oppose both the war and the military faction that controlled it, but understandably enjoyed little support. By early 1944, however, as the Americans' strategy of 'island-leapfrogging' brought them steadily closer to Japan, the opposition became more vocal and was directed particularly against Tōjō who had retained his post of War Minister when he became premier and in February 1944 had also become Chief of the Army General Staff. The loss of Saipan completed his ruin. On 18 July, his government fell and he resigned from all his offices.

Tōjō was followed as prime minister by retired General Kuniaki Koiso, to whom the Emperor made it clear that he must try to 'put an end to the war in Asia' as soon as possible. Unhappily Koiso, despite his ringing nickname of 'The Tiger of Korea', was less forceful and less capable than Tōjō. He did make tentative moves to start peace negotiations through the good offices of the Swedish Minister to Japan, the Soviet Ambassador in Tokyo and the Japanese Ambassador in Moscow, but nothing came of these. Meanwhile, for all the efforts of the Kamikazes, Japan's position became ever more desperate and on 5 April 1945 Koiso in turn submitted his resignation.

Unlike Tōjō, Koiso had not tried to take all control into his own hands. Instead he had created a six-man Supreme War Council. This would manage affairs for the remainder of the conflict, but its effectiveness was considerably diminished by the varying characters and outlooks of the men who comprised it.

First of these was the new prime minister, the elderly Admiral Baron Kantarō Suzuki who, although not receiving definite instructions, perhaps to avoid a direct confrontation with the militarists, was 'given to understand' that his Emperor wanted an early end to the war. This indeed was common knowledge and had been learned by US Intelligence. Supporting Suzuki were two other moderates, the Navy Minister, Admiral Mitsumasa Yonai, and the newly-appointed Foreign Minister, Shigenori Tōgō, to whom Suzuki promised 'a free hand'. Tōgō tried to open direct negotiations for peace through contacts in neutral Switzerland and when these failed, reluctantly – for he rightly distrusted the Soviet dictator Joseph Stalin – he resumed Koiso's attempts to seek peace through the mediation of Russia.

Opposing Suzuki's Peace Party were the other three members of the Supreme War Council: the War Minister General Anami, the Army Chief of Staff General Yoshijirō Umezu and the Navy Chief of Staff Admiral Toyoda. Anami was also strongly supported by the navy's vice chief, a certain Vice Admiral Ōnishi. These diehards made matters very difficult for Suzuki and his colleagues, but it should be recorded that they were not as totally unrealistic as is usually made out.

As has already been mentioned, the Cairo Declaration of November 1943 had demanded that the Japanese withdraw from all the territories they had captured, and it was appreciated that the Russians would also insist on this as a price for acting as mediators. Yet Anami and his followers approved the attempts by Koiso and Tōgō to obtain Russian mediation, so clearly they accepted the Cairo Declaration. Churchill confirms that by the time the Allies met at the Potsdam Conference in July 1945: 'We knew of course that the Japanese were ready to give up all conquests made in the war.'

The extremists, then, were willing to accept hard terms. They were, however, not prepared to surrender on any terms the Allies wished. If this was insisted upon, they would fight to the death. Suzuki and his followers were prepared to accept more terms more readily and thought it infinitely preferable to settle any remaining differences by negotiation, not further conflict, but they also hesitated to stop fighting on no terms at all. In short, what really blocked the road to peace was the Allied requirement that Japan's surrender be unconditional.

It is easy to understand Japanese fears. Mercy to the defeated had rarely been shown in Japan's endless civil wars or to prisoners taken by the Japanese in the present war. That American air-raids were burning to death tens of thousands of Japanese and their naval blockade was slowly but steadily starving to death still greater numbers also suggested that Japan would not receive gentle treatment from her conquerors.

Suzuki and his followers were in fact in a more difficult position than the diehards. They dared not appear too eager for peace because this might strengthen the American determination for a total surrender. It would also bring the risk of their assassination by military fanatics. It has been argued that most potential assassins were now serving abroad, but the days to come would see extremists quite prepared for rebellion and murder. Suzuki, who in 1926 had been shot three times, spent several days on the critical list and still carried a bullet too close to his heart for it to be removed safely, must have been particularly conscious of this danger.

Accordingly, on taking office, Suzuki declared: 'We have no alternative but to fight.' However, he also made it clear why there was no alternative:

'unconditional surrender' was 'out of the question' because 'peace under such terms would mean the destruction of Japan and the Imperial system.' This latter point was of vital importance to all Japanese since the Imperial family 'unbroken through ages eternal' was the distinguishing mark of their uniqueness as a nation, while the Emperor personally was the symbol of their unity in a manner far exceeding that of other heads of state. The thought that Japan's 'national essence' might be broken by the removal of the Imperial family or the Emperor be listed as a war criminal by the victors and lose his throne, his freedom or even his life, was anathema to both Anami and Suzuki.

Suzuki's comments were made in early April. In May, Stalin revealed to President Harry Truman's personal envoy, Harry Hopkins, that the Japanese were putting out 'peace feelers' and he personally believed that they would accept almost any terms the Allies cared to offer but would never surrender unconditionally. In July, at the Potsdam Conference, Stalin repeated these views to Churchill, who passed them on to Truman. In fact the president was better informed than either Churchill or Stalin, since American Intelligence, having broken the Japanese diplomatic code, could read the messages passing between Foreign Minister Tōgō and Japan's ambassador in Moscow, Naotake Satō.

As a result, the Americans knew beyond any doubt that their enemies would surrender on harsh terms but not unconditionally or without reassurances as to the safety of the Emperor and the survival of the Imperial family. After studying the evidence, the US Secretary for War, Henry Stimson, sent a memorandum to Truman suggesting the terms that should be offered and urging that it would 'substantially add' to the chances of their being accepted if Japan was advised that they did not 'exclude a constitutional monarchy under her present dynasty'. His ideas were strongly supported by Truman's Chief of Staff, Admiral William Leahy, and the former US ambassador to Japan, Joseph Grew.

It appears that Stimson's memorandum received less attention than it deserved because Truman had just had other news of tremendous importance. On 16 July, the first atomic explosion was detonated at the Alamogordo bombing range in New Mexico. A few hours later, the components of the first atomic bomb were put on board Admiral Spruance's old flagship, heavy cruiser *Indianapolis*, which had been at San Francisco repairing the damage caused by her Kamikaze hit. After delivering these to Tinian in the Marianas, she set out for Leyte but during the night of 29/30 July was sunk by a Japanese submarine with the loss of 883 of her crew, many more than those killed by any Kamikaze attack. It was a fitting prelude to the horrors that were to follow.

The atomic bomb was now ready, but there were many who thought it should not be used. One group of atomic scientists led by Professor James Franck warned that it would cause 'a wave of horror and repulsion' against the United States. Admiral Leahy protested against attempting to win a war 'by destroying women and children'. General Eisenhower objected, not only because he believed America 'should avoid shocking world opinion', but because 'Japan was already defeated' so 'dropping the bomb was completely unnecessary.' General MacArthur was not even consulted.

Regrettably, many of Truman's political advisers favoured dropping the bomb on the grounds that this would strengthen America's position in the Far East and send a grim warning to Russia or any other possible future enemy. Those scientists who had previously lobbied for the bomb's production were enthusiastic for its use. Their shameful reason is set out by Admiral Leahy: to justify 'the vast sums that had been spent on the project', $2 billion thus far.

One politician did argue for moderation. Churchill was willing to accept a nuclear attack on Japan, but wanted to be sure that it was necessary. He also appreciated that the Japanese could not accept unconditional surrender. He therefore tactfully suggested to Truman that perhaps this could 'be expressed in some other way' so that the Allies would obtain 'all the essentials for peace and security' but the Japanese be left with 'some show of saving their military honour and some assurance of their national existence.' When Truman retorted that the Pearl Harbor attack had shown that the Japanese had no military honour, Churchill quietly observed that 'at any rate they had something for which they were ready to face certain death in very large numbers.'

Churchill would have no further opportunity to be a moderating influence since on 26 July, he learned that he had lost a General Election and left the conference, but his urgings had had their effect and on that same day America, Britain and China – with Russia later concurring – issued the Potsdam Declaration. This at last set out the terms for peace and removed many of Japan's deepest fears. It promised that the Japanese would not be 'enslaved as a race nor destroyed as a nation'; that they could maintain industries needed to sustain their economy and would be given access to raw materials; and that Japanese servicemen, once disarmed, could return home 'to lead peaceful and productive lives'.

As was to be expected, there were many less welcome conditions. The terms of the Cairo Declaration had to be observed and Japan's sovereignty limited to her home islands. Her power to make war must be destroyed and those responsible for her aggressive policies deprived 'for all time' of any 'authority and influence'. 'Stern justice' would be 'meted out to all war criminals' and it was expressly stated that this term would include those who had ill-treated prisoners of war: judgement would be given on the basis of Western, not Japanese ethics. Finally, Japan would be occupied by the Allied powers so that they could be sure their requirements were carried out.

Considering the ferocity with which the war had been fought, these terms were by no means unreasonable so far as they went. Even Anami's extremists could accept most of them. They wanted war criminals to be tried by Japanese courts but it is unlikely that this alone would have prevented agreement, for when an international tribunal did bring major Japanese figures to trial, this aroused little interest. They objected to occupation, but in view of the reassurances given and a promise that occupation would only be temporary, some face-saving formula could surely have been negotiated: for instance, the Japanese could have 'invited' an American occupation to confirm they were 'sincere' in meeting their obligations.

Tragically, though, the Declaration forbade further negotiation. It stated flatly that the terms given were final and must be accepted promptly and without alteration; 'the alternative for Japan' would be 'complete and utter destruction'. This threat naturally stiffened the backs of the hard-liners and increased their feelings that some of the terms were unacceptable. Worse still, although the Declaration was based on Stimson's memorandum, Truman and his political advisers had not followed Stimson's advice and it contained nothing that would have reassured the Japanese that the Emperor and the Imperial system would not be harmed by the surrender.

This was something that could not be tolerated by Suzuki's followers, let alone those of Anami.

Tragedy followed tragedy. Because the Potsdam Declaration made no mention of the Emperor, Prime Minister Suzuki announced that it added nothing to the Cairo Declaration, so was of no importance. It seems that he intended to hint that Japan had no major objections to the conditions already presented, but there were further matters on which she would like clarification. In the circumstances, though, the Americans could hardly be expected to realize this and it was surely unforgivable of Suzuki not to have 'come clean' and laid down the real reason why the Potsdam Declaration was unacceptable.

For the Allied warnings of destruction were not idle ones and there were politicians and scientists only too eager to see them fulfilled. On 6 August, an atomic bomb obliterated the Japanese city of Hiroshima. On the 8th, Stalin declared war on Japan, sent his armies into Manchuria and claimed a share of the spoils. On the 9th, a second atomic bomb fell on the city of Nagasaki.

While Japan burned, the Supreme War Council argued incessantly but remained deadlocked. Mercifully, on the evening of 9 August, the Peace Party realized, somewhat belatedly, that they had a vital ally whose desires were the same as theirs. Suzuki and Tōgō hurriedly asked the Emperor for permission to call an Imperial Conference and it seems that they also at least strongly indicated the action they intended to take, for when Hirohito came to the conference he brought prepared notes with him. The President of the Privy Council, Baron Kiichirō Hiranuma, also attended and supported the Peace Party, but General Anami and his followers remained adamant in their rejection of the Potsdam Declaration.

The conference began just before midnight and continued for some two hours. Finally, Suzuki, after lamenting the lack of progress, proposed 'with the greatest reverence' that the Emperor be asked for his opinion. General Anami, who was well aware of his sovereign's wishes, though he had constantly ignored them, protested that this was unconstitutional. He was quite right, but he received no support from Umezu or Toyoda; they may well have been grateful for an excuse to change their attitude. The Emperor stated clearly that he could not 'bear to see my innocent people suffer any longer.' The Potsdam Declaration, he agreed, was a hard one, but to avoid 'a prolongation of bloodshed and cruelty' he and they must be prepared 'to bear the unbearable'[3] and accept it.

Notification of this decision was promptly sent to the Allies, including Russia, through neutral Sweden or Switzerland, but there was a proviso which all members of the Supreme War Council had required: acceptance was given on the understanding that the Declaration did not imply 'any demand which prejudices the prerogatives of His Majesty as a Sovereign Ruler.' After lengthy debates, Stimson, Leahy and Grew persuaded Truman to agree to the proviso, but to appease those who disliked any form of monarchy, two further conditions were stated. The 'ultimate form of government of Japan' should be decided by 'the freely expressed will of the Japanese people.' 'From the moment of the surrender the authority of the Emperor and the Japanese government to rule the state shall be subject to the Supreme Commander of the Allied Powers', a post to which Truman had appointed General Douglas MacArthur.

Needless to say, the extremists, particularly General Anami, took the opportunity to argue that these qualifications were unacceptable, but the Emperor rightly trusted the loyalty of his people and it was perhaps easier for the Japanese to approve the transfer of power to someone other than the sovereign after the many centuries when it had been exercised by the Shōguns. Indeed, MacArthur would be nicknamed 'the American Shōgun' by the Japanese and his own countrymen alike. At another Imperial Conference on 14 August, Hirohito declared that he considered the Allied reply satisfactory and ordered that his ministers 'forthwith accept it'.

To ensure that the Emperor's wishes were obeyed by Japan's inhabitants and by the huge Japanese army contingents overseas, it was decided that he would announce them over the radio: the first time most of his people would have heard his voice. That night a recording was made of his speech and it was duly broadcast at noon on 15 August. Since his advisers would not allow the Emperor to utter horrid words like 'defeat' or 'surrender', it contained stupidities such as 'the war situation has developed not necessarily to Japan's advantage', but this scarcely mattered. It was enough that the Emperor declared that the war was over, Japan had agreed to the requirements of the Allies, and his 'good and loyal subjects' must avoid any 'outbursts of emotion' or 'fraternal contention and strife'.

In fact, these had happened already. On the previous night, a group of fanatical army officers who had learned of the Emperor's intentions broke into the palace to get hold of the recording before it could be broadcast; they also planned to assassinate the 'traitors' who had advised Hirohito to make it. The Commander of the Imperial Guards Division, General Takeshi Mori, who refused to join the conspirators, was shot dead but Premier Suzuki escaped his would-be murderers just in time and the precious recording, which had been hidden in a wall safe, could not be found. The rebels were still looking for it when General Ryūkichi Tanaka, Commander of the Eastern Army, the headquarters of which was in Tokyo, confronted them and accused them of humiliating the Emperor by doubting his decision. His words and his personality were so powerful that they apologized and withdrew.

Another who doubted the Emperor's decision was Vice Admiral Takijirō Ōnishi, though in fairness he never contemplated or approved of armed insurrection. He had been a convinced supporter of General Anami and a very vocal one. He had tried fervently to persuade his colleagues to continue the struggle: arguing, pleading and threatening. He had constantly harried the unfortunate Admiral Yonai, begging with tears in his eyes that Yonai leave the Peace Party and reject any thought of surrender.

Indeed, Ōnishi seems to have been the most extreme of the extremists and the one with the least grasp of reality. Anami and his other followers were prepared to accept some hard terms in any case and other hard terms if the Emperor insisted. Ōnishi, apparently, was not prepared to accept any hard terms, whatever anybody said. He publicly announced at an operations conference that he personally would 'fight to the bitter end, no matter what happened.'

Ōnishi's attitude was the more peculiar since it contradicted his earlier intentions. When he had first formed the Kamikaze Corps, he had hoped it would turn the tide of the war. After the Corps had been driven out of Luzon, however, he had hoped only that it would at least obtain some reasonable terms for Japan. Any terms must be better than a surrender under no terms at all and, as we have seen, those granted by the Potsdam Declaration were not unreasonable and included reassurances for the future.

Considering that the losses and casualties the Kamikaze Corps had inflicted at Okinawa and the threat of its inflicting still greater ones should Japan herself be invaded had undoubtedly been factors prompting the release of the Declaration, it could be argued that Onishi and his suicide pilots had achieved their aim. Admittedly the thought of those losses and casualties had influenced the dropping of the atomic bombs as well, but that had been a separate issue and could have been averted but for the errors of politicians, both Allied and Japanese.

Yet Ōnishi seems to have felt no satisfaction from the Declaration and, unlike the other diehards, his outlook was unaltered by either the Emperor's wishes, which he intended to ignore, or the Emperor's commands, which he intended to thwart if he possibly could. Captain Inoguchi, who had been transferred to Tokyo early in August, suggested to his chief that he ought to 'abide by whatever the Emperor said'. Ōnishi retorted: 'Am I supposed to go on carrying out orders even while our nation perishes?'

Bearing in mind that the Potsdam Declaration had expressly promised that the Japanese nation would not perish, Ōnishi's reaction was quite disgraceful. It seems that he had lost his grip on reason. He is reported to have become 'desperate'. 'On the verge of a nervous breakdown' would appear a more appropriate description.

Ōnishi's aim now was to find some way of delaying the Imperial Conference of 14 August which he correctly anticipated would finally end hostilities; this might give him time to persuade others to 'fight to the bitter end'. Frantically he rushed around Tokyo trying to enlist support, but in vain. All those he approached rejected his pleas, among them Hirohito's brother Prince Takamatsu, whom Ōnishi had hoped would influence the Emperor, and even General Umezu who had been one of Anami's staunchest allies.

So on 15 August 1945, Japan, on the basis of the conditions set out in the Potsdam Declaration and the conditions subsequently agreed regarding the status of the Emperor, made an 'unconditional' surrender – which may perhaps stand as the final comment on the political and strategic folly of that idiotic slogan. The date, incidentally, was the anniversary of the original Divine Wind that had saved Japan from the Mongols.

Notes

1. The Japanese also intended to send literally thousands of 'special attack' vessels – suicide boats and human torpedoes – against the landings. In view of their previous failures, however, not to mention the fact that the Americans planned heavy raids on their bases prior to the invasion, it seems unlikely that they would have been very effective. It seems quite possible, indeed, that the Japanese themselves had little real faith in them.

2. It is astonishing that so many British critics of the Emperor fail to understand his position. It was very similar to that of the British monarch, who has to approve Acts of Parliament before they can become law, but could never imagine withholding consent, whatever his or her personal opinion.

3. This was another reference to Hirohito's grandfather, Emperor Meiji, who in 1895 had used this expression when commanding his subjects to accept the 'Triple Intervention' of Russia, Germany and France, requiring Japan to return Port Arthur and the Liaodong Peninsula to China after they had been ceded to her by the Treaty of Shimonoseki. When she complied, the Russians had calmly seized these territories for themselves, thereby initiating the lasting ill-feeling between Russia and Japan.

Chapter 9

'The Moon Rose Radiant'

Hostilities had ended, and the suicides began. The rebels who had invaded the palace to prevent the surrender broadcast took their own lives as an apology to the Emperor. General Anami sent his apology to the Emperor in writing. This was not in connection with the plot – though he had known of it and tried neither to encourage nor prevent it – but because Japan's army had failed to win the war. He then committed ritual 'seppuku'. Prince Konoe took poison, his pride unable to bear the thought of being put on trial as a war criminal. General Tōjō shot himself. He bungled even that, was nursed back to health, tried, condemned and executed, though he did regain some respect by admitting full responsibility for his actions and endeavouring to shield his subordinates.

Actions far more deserving of respect were taken by Hirohito and those of his ministers who sincerely desired peace. To ensure that no fanatics attempted to continue the fight, members of the Imperial family or high-ranking officers were sent to army and navy commands throughout Japan and her occupied territories, reminding their personnel that it was their duty to obey the Emperor's commands regardless of their own beliefs and wishes. Mercifully, all these orders were obeyed, if only after some anxious moments.

Ironically, one of these peace missions brought about the death of a notable hard-liner. Captain Shigenori Kami, the aggressive staff officer chiefly responsible for the sortie of the *Yamato* squadron, was sent to Hokkaido, the most northern of the main Japanese islands, to ensure obedience from the naval forces stationed there. To his credit, he performed this duty satisfactorily, but on the return flight his aircraft was compelled to 'ditch'. Its crew survived but Kami, who was widely renowned as a strong swimmer, was never seen again. It is believed that he deliberately allowed himself to drown. Perhaps he was glad of an excuse not to survive defeat.

There were still plenty of other militants left, and the Japanese authorities were particularly concerned about the reactions of the Kamikaze Corps. Its members, far from being pleased or relieved that the coming of peace meant that they would not have to die, were making drunken boasts that they would continue to sink scores of Allied vessels, kill General MacArthur and so on. It was difficult to take this wild talk seriously but it did cause concern, particularly as during 15 August, Allied carriers had been threatened and a Judy had dropped two bombs very close to HMS *Indefatigable* before being shot down by Corsairs from USS *Shangri-La*. The pilot seems to have made no attempt to ram his target and he may not have been a Kamikaze, but if a 'normal' airman could act in this way, it was easy to imagine what the suicide pilots might attempt.

Fortunately by the end of 15 August, the Kamikaze Corps was in practice no longer a danger. The pilots most determined to die had already done so, about forty of them by deliberately flying their aircraft into the sea, while those who remained were left without orders because their leaders had perished as well. It should be recorded of the organizers of this 'suicide club' that they did not just send ardent young men to their deaths. As true samurai, they were perfectly willing to meet death themselves and did so.

Vice Admiral Matome Ugaki had promised his men throughout the Okinawa campaign that he would follow them in death, and such was his obvious honesty that they believed him completely. They were right to do so. On 15 August, Ugaki was at his Fifth Air Fleet Headquarters which had been transferred from Kanoya to Oita in north-eastern Kyushu. Early that morning, he gave orders for a suicide attack on Okinawa by three Judys of 701st Air Group and announced that he was going to accompany them.

By now all senior officers were aware that it was almost certain that surrender was imminent. Many of Ugaki's subordinates accordingly felt that his action was 'not now practical'. Rear Admiral Yokoi, still Ugaki's chief of staff, Captain Miyazaki, senior staff officer of Fifth Air Fleet, and Rear Admiral Jojima, a close personal friend of Ugaki, united in pleading with him to abandon his intention 'for the good of everyone concerned'. 'This is my chance to die like a warrior,' Ugaki replied quietly, 'I must be permitted this chance.'

Preparations for the raid were therefore put in hand by Lieutenant Tatsuo Nakatsuro, commanding 701st Air Group, and while this was being done, the Emperor's announcement of surrender was heard over the radio. Ugaki now knew that his proposed sortie was contrary not only to the Emperor's wishes but to the Emperor's express instructions. Nonetheless, he remained unmoved and after a brief farewell party, he strode onto the airfield. Like Rear Admiral Arima, so long ago it seemed, he had removed all badges of rank but carried with him a sword presented to him by Admiral Yamamoto when he had been that officer's chief of staff.

To everyone's surprise, Lieutenant Nakatsuro had got not three but eleven Judys ready for take-off, explaining that his whole squadron wished to accompany their admiral on his last flight. After Ugaki had expressed his gratitude, he climbed into Nakatsuro's machine, telling the observer/wireless operator, Warrant Officer Endo, that he was now relieved. Endo, however, would have none of this. He insisted on taking his usual seat, forcing Ugaki to move over and make room for him. Then the dive-bombers took off. In a last signal Ugaki declared that he intended to 'make an attack at Okinawa where my men have fallen like cherry blossoms'.

In that final message, Ugaki expressed the hope that 'all units under my command will understand my motives.' It is easy to accept that after his previous promises he felt obliged to join his fallen pilots in death, but his chosen method of dying appears frankly incomprehensible. That he should have disregarded his Emperor's direct commands need cause little astonishment: as we have seen, leading Japanese military or naval commanders never paid any attention to the Emperor if they did not want to, for all their protestations of loyalty. How, though, could he not have foreseen the ghastly results of a successful attack causing heavy Allied losses? It could have looked like the grossest treachery and the possible consequences to Ugaki's wretched countrymen hardly bear thinking about.

It is just possible that some of Ugaki's companions had been reflecting on these matters since four of the attacking aircraft quickly returned to base, claiming engine trouble. Certainly by this date the Japanese were experiencing many problems in keeping their machines serviceable. Even so, four instances of engine malfunction was a large number, especially in a bomber as reliable as the Judy.

Be that as it may, the Allies had wisely allowed for the possibility that some fanatics might ignore the Emperor's commands. A strong Combat Air Patrol had been retained, its pilots amusingly instructed that 'any ex-enemy aircraft' encountered should be 'shot down in a friendly manner'. Ugaki's squadron was intercepted and all seven aircraft were downed by Allied fighters. The last Kamikaze mission had, mercifully, been a failure.

Vice Admiral Takijirō Ōnishi did not long survive his commander-in-the-field. After the Emperor's broadcast he must have realized there was nothing more that he could do and he seemed to regain his poise and balance. On the evening of 15 August, he invited several staff officers to his home where they had drinks and Ōnishi talked with them calmly and reasonably. At about midnight, the guests left, apparently totally unsuspecting of what was to follow.

In the early hours of 16 August, Ōnishi's aide discovered the admiral in his study, still conscious but horribly injured: he had disembowelled himself with a Japanese short sword. 'Do not try to help me,' he ordered the aide. Thereafter, resolutely refusing either medical aid or a quick finish, he lingered all day in unspeakable agony before finally expiring. In a letter he had written before the fatal act, he praised his 'special attackers' and declared his death to be an atonement for his failure to ensure that their sacrifice achieved the victory he had promised them.

The rest of the story may be told quickly. General MacArthur fully appreciated the difficulties the Japanese authorities might face in enforcing obedience to the Emperor's instructions. Wisely he gave them time to sort out their affairs. On 19 August, Japanese delegates flew to Manila to discuss with MacArthur arrangements for the American occupation, but not until the 28th did a small party of American troops under Colonel Charles Tench arrive at Atsugi airfield, and not until the morning of the 30th were they joined by reinforcements from the US 11th Airborne Division. MacArthur flew to Atsugi that afternoon.

Atsugi, situated west of Yokohama and south-west of Tokyo, had been a major Kamikaze base and a very belligerent one. The response of its pilots to the Emperor's surrender broadcast had been to drop leaflets over Tokyo protesting that Hirohito had been 'tricked' by his advisers and that the fighting should continue. They had been particularly loud in those stupid but disturbing threats to which reference has already been made and although they had done nothing to suit their actions to their words, they had remained openly disobedient until as late as 26 August.

Happily, on that date, Hirohito and his ministers acted decisively. Prince Takamatsu was sent to Atsugi and in the Emperor's name ordered the malcontents back to their allegiance. Presumably with some satisfaction, since he had never approved of 'special attack' operations and personally disliked Vice Admiral Ōnishi, he formally grounded the Kamikazes, had the propellers of all their aircraft removed to ensure that they stayed grounded, and directed a picked security squad to the airfield to prevent any further misconduct and see that Atsugi was made ready to receive the Americans. On 2 September, the formal instrument of surrender was signed by Japanese dignitaries and representatives of the Allied powers on board the US battleship *Missouri* in Tokyo Bay. The Kamikazes made no protest and caused no trouble.

From the first day of the Pacific War, Japanese pilots had rammed targets of opportunity on the impulse of the moment, but organized Kamikaze attacks where the airmen set out with no intention of returning had begun with Rear Admiral Arima on 15 October 1944 and ended with Vice Admiral Ugaki on 15 August 1945. Those ten months had been ennobled by immense courage, astonishing unselfishness, loyalty to country and cause, fortitude, tenacity and determination, but marred by brutal fanaticism, unreasoning obstinacy and the inherent negativity of the Kamikaze creed of kill and be killed, derived from the attitudes of their predecessors, the samurai.

After the war, certain Japanese academics would go further and claim that the Kamikaze spirit was actively harmful to the Japanese war effort. They argued that a knowledge of the unselfish heroism of their men had led Japan's military and naval leaders to neglect the best means of fighting: they had relied on valour, while ignoring technological and scientific advances. It is a contention that may have some force with regard to the Imperial Army, but not to the Imperial Navy from which most and for a long time all the suicide attackers came.

Of course America's industrial might was so great that she could produce ships and aircraft at a rate impossible to be matched by Japan, or any other country for that matter. Also the Americans often used the weapons at their disposal more effectively than the Japanese. For instance, Japanese submarines, true to their warrior heritage, much preferred to engage enemy warships, while those of the Americans, though not neglecting Japanese warships, were equally ready to wage remorseless war on Japanese merchant vessels, with the results already described.

In quality, though, the Imperial Navy had little need to be concerned about its equipment. Indeed, its officers had reason to boast of its *Yamato*-class battleships, its original carrier division, its magnificent destroyers, its fine aircraft like the Zero, Val, Kate, George, Judy and Jill, and its superlative 24in 'Long Lance' torpedoes, fuelled by liquid oxygen, far superior to any Allied equivalent, and the capabilities of which remained long unknown to Japan's enemies, making this probably the most effective 'secret weapon' of the war. All the above, however, were of course methods of destruction like the Kamikaze Corps.

Weapons become obsolete but virtues do not. The pitiful state of Japan at the end of the war has been examined earlier. Almost the first act of General MacArthur as the new Shōgun was to pour in reserves of food, dragging thousands of Japanese back from the brink of starvation. Other early acts of the American occupation authorities, however, made Japan's situation even worse. At a time when she desperately needed capable experienced administrators, most of these were forcibly driven from office. At a time when she desperately needed to revive her industries as soon as possible, these were broken up in the erroneous belief that they had eagerly aided the militants. MacArthur, incidentally, regarded all these actions as 'basically unfair and vindictive'.

Yet within the short space of fifteen years, Japan had made an amazing economic, political and industrial recovery, and what enabled this was her people's possession of the Kamikaze virtues, now used in a constructive not destructive, a positive not negative role. Courage and fortitude allowed the Japanese to survive the years of despair and degradation. Determination and tenacity drove them to restore their country's fortunes. Loyalty and unselfishness brought an extraordinary co-operation and 'team spirit' to this task. Moreover, because these attributes were used positively, they were not soured by either the Kamikaze faults or any sacrifice of quality.

Thus instead of sending out soldiers on acts of brutal aggression against neighbouring countries, the Japanese sent out businessmen to establish a trading empire that was far wider and far more profitable. They revived their shattered merchant marine and instead of giant battleships, built huge tankers and cargo vessels. They restored their industries and instead of devoting most of their efforts and their budget to military concerns, manufactured an amazing variety of admirable products: cars, motorcycles, cameras, watches, contact lenses. Their cities rose literally from the ashes with new modern buildings and architectural wonders like the incredible Tokyo Skytree. Their transport system, once badly neglected, spread rapidly, linking the country together with new tunnels and bridges, and a railway network envied throughout the world for its unfailing punctuality and its gleaming symbol of the 'bullet train'.

Just before his death, the creator and chief of the Kamikaze Corps, Vice Admiral Takijirō Ōnishi, composed a traditional Japanese poem of seventeen syllables known as a 'haiku'. It was intended to stand as a tribute to his pilots, but in retrospect it appears more a prophecy of Japan's revival:

> Refreshingly
> After the violent storm
> The moon rose radiant.

Bibliography

Arnold-Foster, Mark, *The World at War* (Collins, 1973)

Axel, Albert and Kase, Hideaki, *Kamikaze: Japan's Suicide Gods* (Longman, 2002)

Baldwin, Hanson W., 'The Battle for Leyte Gulf', in *Combat Pacific Theater* (ed. Don Congdon) (Dell Publishing, 1958). Includes comments by Admirals Kinkaid and Halsey.

Bennett, Geoffrey, *Naval Battles of World War II* (Batsford, 1975)

Brown, David, *Carrier Fighters* (Macdonald & Jane's, 1975)

Brown, David, *Carrier Operations in World War II*, 2 Volumes (Ian Allen, 1968)

Busch, Noel F., *A Concise History of Japan* (Cassell, 1973)

Butow, R.J.C., *Japan's Decision to Surrender* (Stanford University Press, 1954)

Butow, R.J.C., *Tōjō and the Coming of the War* (Princeton University Press, 1961)

Churchill, Sir Winston, *The Second World War*, 6 Volumes (Cassell, 1948–53). In particular Volume VI: *Triumph and Tragedy*.

Costello, John, *The Pacific War* (Collins, 1981)

D'Albas, Captain Andrieu, *Death of a Navy* (Robert Hale, 1957)

Dull, Paul S., *A Battle History of the Imperial Japanese Navy (1941–1945)* (Patrick Stephens, 1978)

Fuller, Major General J.F.C., *The Decisive Battles of the Western World*, Volume 3 (Eyre & Spottiswoode, 1957)

Fuller, Major General J.F.C., *The Second World War 1939–1945* (Eyre & Spottiswoode, 1948. Revised edition, 1954)

Gill, G. Hermon, *Royal Australian Navy 1942–1945* (Australian War Memorial, Canberra, 1968)

Griffith, Brigadier General Samuel B., *USMC: The Battle for Guadalcanal* (The Nautical & Aviation Publishing Company of America, 1979)

Hough, Major Frank, *The Island War* (J.B. Lippincott & Co., Philadelphia, 1947)

Howarth, Stephen, *Morning Glory: A History of the Imperial Japanese Navy* (Hamish Hamilton, 1983)

Hubbard, Ben, *The Golden Age of the Samurai* (Amber Books, 2017)

Inoguchi, Captain Rikihei and Nakajima, Commander Tadashi with Pineau, Roger, *The Divine Wind* (Hutchinson, 1959)

Iredale, Will, *The Kamikaze Hunters: Fighting for the Pacific 1945* (Macmillan, 2015)

Jackson, Robert, *Strike from the Sea* (Arthur Barker, 1970)

Johnson, Brian, *Fly Navy* (David & Charles, 1981)

Kahn, David, *The Codebreakers* (Weidenfeld & Nicolson, 1973. Revised edition, 1996)

Kemp, Lieutenant Commander P.K., *Victory at Sea 1939–1945* (Frederick Muller, 1957)

Killen, John, *A History of Marine Aviation 1911–68* (Frederick Muller, 1969)

Lewin, Ronald, *The Other Ultra: Codes, Ciphers and the Defeat of Japan* (Hutchinson, 1982)

Liddell Hart, Captain B.H., *History of the Second World War* (Cassell, 1970)

Lord, Walter, *Day of Infamy: Pearl Harbour, December 7th 1941* (Longmans, Green & Co., 1957)

MacArthur, General Douglas, *Reminiscences* (William Heinemann, 1964)

Macintyre, Captain Donald, *Aircraft Carriers: The Majestic Weapon* (Macdonalds, 1968)

Macintyre, Captain Donald, *The Battle for the Pacific* (Batsford, 1966)

Macintyre, Captain Donald, *The Thunder of the Guns* (Frederick Muller, 1959)

Macintyre, Captain Donald, *Wings of Neptune: The Story of Naval Aviation* (Peter Davies, 1963)

Mattiske, David, *Fire Across the Pacific* (Privately published, 2000)

Millot, Bernard A., *Divine Thunder: The Life and Death of the Kamikazes* (Macdonalds, 1971)

Morison, Professor Samuel Eliot, *History of United States Naval Operations in World War II*, 15 Volumes (Little, Brown & Co., 1947–62). In particular Volume V: *The Struggle for Guadalcanal: August 1942–February 1943*; Volume XII: *Leyte: June 1944–January 1945*; Volume XIII: *The Liberation of the Philippines: Luzon, Mindanao, The Visayas 1944–August 1945*; Volume XIV: *Victory in the Pacific 1945.*

Morison, Professor Samuel Eliot, *The Two Ocean War: A Short History of the United States Navy in the Second World War* (Little, Brown & Co., 1965). This is not only a summary but an updating of his earlier history.

Morris, Ivan, *The Nobility of Failure* (Holt, Reinhart & Winston, 1975)

Morris, Jan, *Battleship Yamato* (Pallas Athene, 2018)

Mosley, Leonard, *Hirohito: Emperor of Japan* (Weidenfeld & Nicolson, 1966)

Naval Analysis Division, *The United States Strategic Bombing Survey (Pacific War)* (US Government Publication, 1946)

Okumiya, Masatake and Hirikoshi, Jiro with Caidin, Martin, *Zero!: The Story of the Japanese Naval Air Force 1937–1945* (Cassell, 1957)

Poolman, Kenneth, *'Illustrious'* (Kimber, 1955)

Potter, E.B. and Nimitz, Fleet Admiral Chester W., *The Great Sea War* (George W. Harrap & Co., 1961)

Roskill, Captain S.W., *The Navy at War 1939–1945* (Collins, 1960)

Roskill, Captain S.W., *The War at Sea*, 3 Volumes (HMSO, 1954–1961)

Ruge, Vice Admiral Friedrich, *Sea Warfare 1939–1945: A German Viewpoint* (Cassell, 1957). Includes actions in the Pacific from a Japanese viewpoint.

Sakai, Saburo, *Samurai* (Kimber, 1959)

Shores, Christopher, *Air Aces* (Bison Books, 1983)

Smith, Michael, *The Emperor's Codes* (Bantam Press, 2000)

Smith, Peter C., *Kamikaze: To Die for the Emperor* (Pen & Sword, 2014)

Smith, Stan, *The Battle of Leyte Gulf* (Belmont Books, 1961)

Spurr, Russell, *A Glorious Way to Die* (Sidgwick & Jackson, 1982)

Stewart, Adrian, *The Battle of Leyte Gulf* (Robert Hale, 1979)

Stewart, Adrian, *Carriers at War 1939–1945* (Pen & Sword, 2013)

Stewart, Adrian, *Guadalcanal: World War II's Fiercest Naval Campaign* (Kimber, 1985)

Storry, Professor Richard, *A History of Modern Japan* (Penguin Books, 1960)

Taylor, A.J.P., *The War Lords* (Hamish Hamilton, 1978)

Turnbull, Stephen, *The Samurai: A Military History* (Osprey Publishing, 1977)

Turnbull, Stephen, *The Samurai Sourcebook* (Arms & Armour, 1998)

Van Der Rhoer, Edward, *Deadly Magic* (Charles Scribner's Sons, 1978)

Wardroom Officers of HM Aircraft Carrier 'Formidable', *A 'Formidable' Commission* (Seeley Services, 1947)

Watts, A.J., *Japanese Warships of World War II* (Ian Allan, 1966)

Winton, John, *The Forgotten Fleet* (Michael Joseph, 1969)

Woodward, C. Vann, *The Battle for Leyte Gulf* (Macmillan, 1947)

Wragg, David, *Wings over the Sea: A History of Naval Aviation* (David & Charles, 1979)

Index

Index of Ships